60 Hikes Within 60 Miles: San Diego

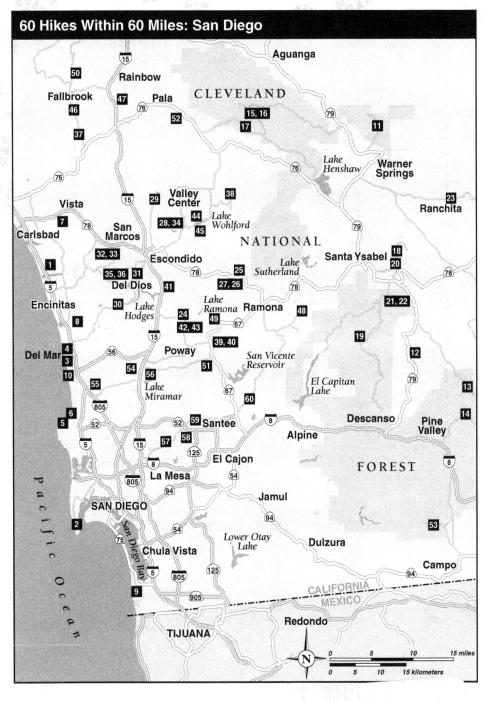

Aguanga

CLEVELAND

50

15

Rainbow

Fallbrook

47

Pala

52

15, 16

17

79

11

46

37

76

76

Lake
Henshaw

Warner
Springs

15

29

Valley
Center

38

23

Vista

7

78

San
Marcos

28, 34

44

Lake
Wohlford

45

Ranchita

Carlsbad

32, 33

Escondido

NATIONAL

Santa Ysabel

18

20

1

78

25

Lake
Sutherland

35, 36

31

Del Dios

41

27, 26

78

21, 22

Encinitas

30

Lake
Hodges

Lake
Ramona

Ramona

48

8

24

42, 43

49

67

19

12

15

Poway

39, 40

San Vicente
Reservoir

Del Mar

4

56

3

54

51

El Capitan
Lake

79

10

55

56

Lake
Miramar

67

60

13

805

Descanso

14

5

6

52

59

Santee

8

**Pine
Valley**

5

52

15

57

58

125

Alpine

FOREST

8

8

La Mesa

125

El Cajon

54

805

94

SAN DIEGO

2

54

Jamul

53

75

94

Chula Vista

Lower Otay
Lake

Dulzura

5

805

125

Campo

94

9

905

CALIFORNIA
MEXICO

Redondo

TIJUANA

N

0   5   10   15 miles

0   5   10   15 kilometers

Pacific Ocean

San Diego Bay

←→ ➡ Directional arrows	▬▬▬ Featured trail	·············· Alternate trail
═════ Freeway	═══ Highway with bridge	──── Minor road
▥▥▥▥▥ Boardwalk	·········· Stairs	══════ Unpaved road
Cliffs	╫╫╫╫╫ Railroad	●──●──● Power line
Park/forest	Water body	River/creek/ intermittent stream

✝ Air field	✳ Garden	▲ Peak/hill
✈ Airport	●–● Gate	(Phone access
♨ Amphitheater	● General point of interest	🌲 Picnic area
⌐ Bench	🏌 Golf course	🏠 Picnic shelter
🚤 Boat launch	🛡 Group campsite	🚽 Pit toilets
▲ Campground	🏇 Horseshoes	🛝 Playground
🛶 Canoe access	⑦ Information kiosk	🗼 Radio tower
⚱ Cemetery	🗼 Lighthouse	🚻 Restrooms
✦ Dam	⚶ Marsh	🚐 RV campground
🥤 Drinking water	▲ Monument	🎬 Scenic view
苴 Electrical tower	🏍 Motorbike trail	🕴 Trailhead
$ Fee station	▲ Overlook	🏔 Viewing platform
🎣 Fishing access	Ⓐ Pacific Crest Trail	Ⓢ Volleyball court
🍴 Food service	🏠 Park office	// Waterfall/cascades
✕ Footbridge	🅿 Parking	

Overview Map Key

Other cities in the 60 Hikes Within 60 Miles series:

Albuquerque

Atlanta

Baltimore

Boston

Chicago

Cincinnati

Cleveland

Dallas and Fort Worth

Denver and Boulder

Harrisburg

Houston

Madison

Minneapolis and St. Paul

Nashville

New York City

Philadelphia

Phoenix

Pittsburgh

Richmond

Sacramento

Salt Lake City

San Antonio and Austin

San Francisco

Seattle

St. Louis

Washington, D.C.

60 HIKES WITHIN 60 MILES

SAN DIEGO

Including North, South, and East Counties

THIRD EDITION

Sheri McGregor

MENASHA RIDGE PRESS
Birmingham, Alabama

**FOR THOSE WHO LOVE TO COMMUNE WITH NATURE.
MAY YOU DO SO WITH UTTER RESPECT, DEEP APPRECIATION,
AND A SENSE OF JOY . . . ALWAYS JOY.**

—Sheri McGregor

60 Hikes Within 60 Miles: San Diego

Copyright © 2016 by Sheri McGregor
All rights reserved
Printed in the United States of America
Published by Menasha Ridge Press
Distributed by Publishers Group West
Third edition, second printing

Managing editor: Ritchey Halphen
Cartography and cover design: Scott McGrew
Text design: Annie Long
Cover and interior photos by Sheri McGregor, except where noted
Indexer: Ann Weik Cassar / Cassar Technical Services

Library of Congress Cataloging-in-Publication Data
Names: McGregor, Sheri, 1961– author.
Title: 60 hikes within 60 miles of San Diego : including north, south, and east counties /
Sheri McGregor.
Other titles: Sixty hikes within sixty miles, San Diego
Description: Third edition. | Birmingham, AL : Menasha Ridge Press, 2016.
Includes index.
Identifiers: LCCN 2015044628 | ISBN 978-1-63404-024-2 (pbk.) | eISBN 978-1-63404-025-9
ISBN 978-1-63404-175-1 (hardcover)
Subjects: LCSH: Hiking—California—San Diego County—Guidebooks. | San Diego
(Calif.)—Guidebooks.
Classification: LCC GV199.42.C22 S2647 2016 | DDC 796.510979498—dc23
LC record available at **lccn.loc.gov/2015044628**

 **MENASHA RIDGE PRESS**
An imprint of AdventureKEEN
2204 1st Ave. S., Suite 102
Birmingham, AL 35233

Visit **menasharidge.com** for a complete listing of our books and for ordering information. Contact us at
our website, at **facebook.com/menasharidge,** or at **twitter.com/menasharidge** with questions or
comments. To find out more about who we are and what we're doing, visit our blog, **trekalong.com.**

DISCLAIMER

This book is meant only as a guide to select trails in the San Diego area and does not guarantee hiker
safety—you hike at your own risk. Neither Menasha Ridge Press nor Sheri McGregor is liable for property
loss or damage, personal injury, or death that may result from accessing or hiking the trails described in
this guide. Be especially cautious when walking in potentially hazardous terrains with, for example, steep
inclines or drop-offs. Do not attempt to explore terrain that may be beyond your abilities. Please read
carefully the introduction to this book, as well as safety information from other sources. Familiarize yourself with current weather reports and maps of the area you plan to visit (in addition to the maps provided
in this guidebook). Be cognizant of park regulations, and always follow them. While every effort has been
made to ensure the accuracy of the information in this guidebook, land and road conditions, phone numbers and websites, and other information can change from year to year.

Table of Contents

Inland South 222

Appendixes 254

Acknowledgments

FIRST, I'M GRATEFUL FOR MY PARENTS; may they rest in peace. My father's ability to live in the moment or my mother's simple delight over a hoppy little bird or a bushy-tailed squirrel often comes back to me when out on the trail. Much thanks to my family for their continued support. Hiking San Diego's trails with my husband, my now-adult children, and even my grandchildren is always fun. I cherish that quality time that helps keep our relationships strong—and helps these books stay up-to-date!

Thanks also to my writer friends, Lori and Julie, who provided encouragement and looked over my new hike write-ups before I passed them along to Tim Jackson, acquisitions editor at Menasha Ridge Press. Thanks to Menasha Ridge managing editor Ritchey Halphen for his positive attitude, sharp eye for detail, and occasional joke (always arriving at just the right moment). I'd also like to thank cartographer Scott McGrew for his mapping magic, chief operating officer Molly Merkle for her professional behind-the-scenes presence, and all the other people involved in pulling this volume together. Thanks also to Brady Pesola of the San Diego School of Survival for endorsing this newest edition of the book.

Finally, thank you to my readers—fellow hikers I greet along the trail. You know the bond that nature provides among us. I enjoy hearing from you, too, so don't hesitate to send me an e-mail, or join the San Diego Hikes Facebook page (**tinyurl.com/sandiego hikesfacebook.**)and tell me about your latest hike.

—*Sheri McGregor*

Foreword

WELCOME TO MENASHA RIDGE PRESS'S *60 Hikes Within 60 Miles,* a series designed to provide hikers with the information they need to find and hike the very best trails surrounding large metropolitan areas.

Our strategy is simple: First, find a hiker who knows the area and loves to hike. Second, ask that person to spend a year researching the most popular and very best trails around. And third, have that person describe each trail in terms of difficulty, scenery, condition, elevation change, and other categories of information that are important to hikers. "Pretend you've just completed a hike and met up with other hikers at the trailhead," we told each author. "Imagine their questions, and be clear in your answers."

An experienced hiker and writer, Sheri McGregor has selected 60 of the best hikes in and around San Diego. From relaxing beach walks to flora- and fauna-rich outings in the mountains to a trek in the desert, Sheri provides hikers (and walkers) with a great variety of hikes—and all within roughly 60 miles of San Diego.

You'll get the most from this book if you take a moment to read the Introduction, which explains how to read the trail listings.

As much to free the spirit as to free the body, let these hikes elevate you above the urban fray.

All the best,
The Editors at Menasha Ridge Press

About the Author

AS A CHILD GROWING UP IN SAN DIEGO, **Sheri McGregor** remembers lying in the grass watching tiny bug-worlds crawl by. Today, with five children of her own, she still watches bugs—and sometimes feels just as tiny among the towering trees, majestic mountains, and free-flowing waters of San Diego County. Writing this hiking guide allowed Sheri to enjoy the local wilderness with a purpose: to share her love of nature with readers. Out on the trails, even the shadows fall into intricate patterns that display the poetry of the natural world.

PHOTO: WILLIAM KORDELA

Sheri's other books for Menasha Ridge Press are *Day & Overnight Hikes: Anza-Borrego Desert State Park,* which explores the local desert wilderness, and *Easy Hikes Close To Home: San Diego.* Those books, like this one, were a labor of love. Sheri also contributed to the seventh edition of *The Unofficial Guide to California with Kids,* published by Menasha Ridge's parent company, AdventureKEEN.

In addition to writing about nature and the outdoors, Sheri holds a bachelor's degree in psychology and a master's degree in human behavior, and she is a certified life coach. At **rejectedparents.net,** she writes and conducts research for her book to help parents of estranged adult children.

Sheri has also published two novels and a novella, and she writes about a variety of subjects. From psychology and fitness to travel and home decor, her articles, essays, and short fiction have appeared in themed anthologies; a supplemental textbook; and national and international publications including *The Washington Post,* Salon.com, *Chickens* magazine, *InfoWeek, LA Parent,* Reader's Digest Publications, and Sunset Publishing. She also assists organizations with their communication needs. On local television and around town, Sheri enjoys speaking about hiking and nature and their positive influence on physical and mental health.

Visit the companion websites to this book at **sandiegohikes.com** and **tinyurl.com /sandiegohikesfacebook.**

Preface

IN SAN DIEGO COUNTY, a variety of exquisite outdoor escapes awaits you. Stand at the ocean's edge and let the cool breeze ruffle your hair as the surf foams around your ankles. An hour's drive takes you to the mountains, where the pine air always smells like Christmas. Yet from an eastern bluff, you can look out over the gaping mauve-brown expanse of the Anza-Borrego Desert. This diverse topography is a paradise for hikers looking for quick getaways from urban bustle and for healthy variety in their wilderness treks.

County hiking experiences range from an easy stroll over well-defined paths to strenuous peak treks gaining 1,000 feet within a few short miles of rocky trail. With more than two dozen lakes in San Diego County and several land-preservation groups working to keep open spaces safe from urban development, hiking opportunities abound. Marshland and lagoon areas provide homes to rare or endangered types of birds, and scrub areas provide nesting sites for others, such as the endangered least Bell's vireo.

Enjoying the Great Outdoors

Amid the routine struggles of life, just driving out of the city toward a favorite destination brings a sense of release. Once you're on the trail, whatever irritations remain to cloud the mind are swept away by the music of wind rushing through the trees, or carried off on the dark-tipped tail of a mule deer bounding off into the woods. Even a honeybee seems to carry away burdens—collected in the fat, yellow pollen pockets on hind legs he drags heavily behind as he buzzes off to a distant flower. Make a conscious effort to put aside your concerns and troubles, and let yourself lighten up and take a break while on the trail. With a relaxed mind and an easy spirit, you may be surprised at the tiny wonders you'll see.

60 Hikes by Category

Hike Categories

✓ 0.5–3 Miles	✓ 6+ Miles	✓ Bird-Watching
✓ 3–6 Miles	✓ Family Hikes	✓ High Traffic

REGION Hike Number/Hike Name	page	0.5–3 Miles	3–6 Miles	6+ Miles	Family Hikes	Bird-Watching	High Traffic
THE COAST							
1 Batiquitos Lagoon Trail	18	✓			✓	✓	
2 Bayside Trail	21	✓			✓		
3 Beach Walk and Torrey Pines State Reserve Loop	25		✓		✓	✓	✓
4 Crest Canyon Open Space Preserve Loop	30	✓					✓
5 La Jolla: Coast Walk Trail	33	✓				✓	✓
6 La Jolla Shores: Tide Pools Walk	36	✓			✓		✓
7 Lake Calavera Preserve Loops	39		✓		✓	✓	
8 San Elijo Lagoon: La Orilla to Rios Avenue	43		✓			✓	✓
9 Tijuana Estuary Trail	46		✓		✓	✓	
10 Torrey Pines State Reserve: Guy Fleming Trail	50		✓		✓	✓	✓
THE MOUNTAINS							
11 Agua Caliente Creek Trail	56			✓			
12 Cuyamaca Rancho State Park: Stonewall Peak Trail	60		✓				✓
13 Laguna Mountains: Penny Pines Trail	64			✓			
14 Laguna Mountains: Sunset Trail	68		✓				✓
15 Palomar Mountain: Fry Creek Campground Trail	72	✓			✓		
16 Palomar Mountain: Observatory Trail	76		✓		✓		
17 Palomar Mountain: Overview Loop	80		✓		✓		
18 Santa Ysabel Open Space Preserve East: Kanaka Loop Trail	84			✓			
19 Three Sisters Waterfalls Trail	87		✓				✓

REGION Hike Number/Hike Name	page	0.5–3 Miles	3–6 Miles	6+ Miles	Family Hikes	Bird-Watching	High Traffic
THE MOUNTAINS (*continued*)							
20 Volcan Mountain Preserve Trail	91		✓				
21 William Heise County Park: Combined Trails Loop	94		✓		✓		
22 William Heise County Park: Kelly Ditch Trail	98		✓				
THE DESERT							
23 Anza-Borrego Desert State Park: California Riding and Hiking Trail	104		✓				
INLAND NORTH							
24 Blue Sky Trail to Lake Ramona	110		✓				
25 Clevenger Canyon North: East Trail	114			✓			
26 Clevenger Canyon South: East Trail	118		✓				
27 Clevenger Canyon South: West Trail	122	✓					
28 Daley Ranch: Combined Trails Loop	126			✓	✓		
29 Daley Ranch: Engelmann Oak Loop	131		✓		✓		
30 Del Dios Gorge, Dam, and Lake Hodges Trek	135			✓			✓
31 Del Dios Highlands Preserve Trail	140	✓					
32 Discovery Lake and Double Peak Trails	143		✓		✓		
33 Discovery Lake and Hills Loop	147	✓			✓		
34 Dixon Lake: Shore View Trail	151		✓			✓	✓
35 Elfin Forest Recreational Reserve: Botanical Loop	155	✓			✓		
36 Elfin Forest Recreational Reserve: Way Up and Equine Incline Trail	158		✓				
37 Heller's Bend Preserve Trail	162	✓					
38 Hellhole Canyon Open Space Preserve Trail	165		✓				
39 Iron Mountain Peak Trail	169			✓			✓
40 Iron Mountain to Lake Ramona Overlook and Pond	172			✓			
41 Lake Hodges: North Shore Trail	175		✓			✓	✓
42 Lake Poway Loop	179		✓				✓
43 Lake Poway to Mount Woodson Peak Trail	183			✓			✓
44 Lake Wohlford North: Kumeyaay Trail	187	✓				✓	✓
45 Lake Wohlford: South Trails	190	✓				✓	
46 Los Jilgueros Preserve Trail	193	✓			✓		
47 Monserate Mountain Trail	197	✓					✓

REGION Hike Number/Hike Name	page	0.5–3 Miles	3–6 Miles	6+ Miles	Family Hikes	Bird-Watching	High Traffic
48 Mount Gower Open Space Preserve Trail	201			✓			
49 Mount Woodson: East Trail	205		✓				✓
50 Santa Margarita River Trail	209		✓				
51 Sycamore Canyon: Goodan Ranch Open Space Preserve Loop	213			✓	✓		
52 Wilderness Gardens Preserve: Combined Trails Loop	217		✓		✓		✓
INLAND SOUTH							
53 Lake Morena Trail	224		✓		✓		
54 Los Peñasquitos Canyon Preserve: East End to Waterfall Loop	228		✓		✓		✓
55 Los Peñasquitos Canyon Preserve: West End to Waterfall Loop	233			✓			✓
56 Miramar Reservoir Loop	237		✓				✓
57 Mission Trails Regional Park: Combined Trails Loop	240		✓				
58 Mission Trails Regional Park: Cowles Mountain Loop	244		✓				
59 Santee Lakes Loop	247	✓			✓	✓	
60 Stelzer Park Loop	251	✓			✓		

More Hike Categories

✓ Wildlife   ✓ Spring Wildflowers   ✓ Fall Colors   ✓ Young Children
✓ Strenuous Climbs   ✓ Diverse Hikes   ✓ Dogs Allowed

REGION Hike Number/Hike Name	page	Wildlife	Strenuous Climbs	Spring Wildflowers	Fall Colors	Diverse Hikes	Young Children	Dogs Allowed
THE COAST								
1 Batiquitos Lagoon Trail	18						✓	✓
2 Bayside Trail	21							
3 Beach Walk and Torrey Pines State Reserve Loop	25	✓	✓	✓			✓	
4 Crest Canyon Open Space Preserve Loop	30							✓

REGION Hike Number/Hike Name	page	Wildlife	Strenuous Climbs	Spring Wildflowers	Fall Colors	Diverse Hikes	Young Children	Dogs Allowed
THE COAST (*continued*)								
5 La Jolla: Coast Walk Trail	33	✓						
6 La Jolla Shores: Tide Pools Walk	36	✓						
7 Lake Calavera Preserve Loops	39					✓	✓	✓
8 San Elijo Lagoon: La Orilla to Rios Avenue	43							✓
9 Tijuana Estuary Trail	46						✓	
10 Torrey Pines State Reserve: Guy Fleming Trail	50	✓	✓	✓		✓		
THE MOUNTAINS								
11 Agua Caliente Creek Trail	56	✓				✓		
12 Cuyamaca Rancho State Park: Stonewall Peak Trail	60							
13 Laguna Mountains: Penny Pines Trail	64					✓		
14 Laguna Mountains: Sunset Trail	68			✓				
15 Palomar Mountain: Fry Creek Campground Trail	72				✓			
16 Palomar Mountain: Observatory Trail	76	✓		✓				
17 Palomar Mountain: Overview Loop	80	✓		✓	✓			
18 Santa Ysabel Open Space Preserve East: Kanaka Loop Trail	84	✓						✓
19 Three Sisters Waterfalls Trail	87							
20 Volcan Mountain Preserve Trail	91	✓			✓			
21 William Heise County Park: Combined Trails Loop	94		✓		✓	✓		✓
22 William Heise County Park: Kelly Ditch Trail	98		✓		✓	✓		
THE DESERT								
23 Anza-Borrego Desert State Park: California Riding and Hiking Trail	104	✓		✓				
INLAND NORTH								
24 Blue Sky Trail to Lake Ramona	110			✓				✓
25 Clevenger Canyon North: East Trail	114		✓					
26 Clevenger Canyon South: East Trail	118			✓				✓
27 Clevenger Canyon South: West Trail	122			✓				✓
28 Daley Ranch: Combined Trails Loop	126			✓				✓
29 Daley Ranch: Engelmann Oak Loop	131							✓

REGION Hike Number/Hike Name	page	Wildlife	Strenuous Climbs	Spring Wildflowers	Fall Colors	Diverse Hikes	Young Children	Dogs Allowed
30 Del Dios Gorge, Dam, and Lake Hodges Trek	135					✓		✓
31 Del Dios Highlands Preserve Trail	140		✓					✓
32 Discovery Lake and Double Peak Trails	143		✓	✓				✓
33 Discovery Lake and Hills Loop	147				✓		✓	✓
34 Dixon Lake: Shore View Trail	151							
35 Elfin Forest Recreational Reserve: Botanical Loop	155							✓
36 Elfin Forest Recreational Reserve: Way Up and Equine Incline Trail	158							✓
37 Heller's Bend Preserve Trail	162						✓	✓
38 Hellhole Canyon Open Space Preserve Trail	166		✓		✓			✓
39 Iron Mountain Peak Trail	169		✓					✓
40 Iron Mountain to Lake Ramona Overlook and Pond	172	✓						✓
41 Lake Hodges: North Shore Trail	175				✓			✓
42 Lake Poway Loop	179			✓				✓
43 Lake Poway to Mount Woodson Peak Trail	183		✓			✓		✓
44 Lake Wohlford North: Kumeyaay Trail	187				✓			
45 Lake Wohlford: South Trails	190				✓			
46 Los Jilgueros Preserve Trail	193						✓	✓
47 Monserate Mountain Trail	197		✓					✓
48 Mount Gower Open Space Preserve Trail	201		✓					
49 Mount Woodson: East Trail	205		✓					
50 Santa Margarita River Trail	209							✓
51 Sycamore Canyon: Goodan Ranch Open Space Preserve Loop	213							✓
52 Wilderness Gardens Preserve: Combined Trails Loop	217			✓				
INLAND SOUTH								
53 Lake Morena Trail	224			✓	✓	✓		✓
54 Los Peñasquitos Canyon Preserve: East End to Waterfall Loop	228	✓						✓
55 Los Peñasquitos Canyon Preserve: West End to Waterfall Loop	233							✓
56 Miramar Reservoir Loop	237							✓
57 Mission Trails Regional Park: Combined Trails Loop	240		✓				✓	✓

REGION Hike Number/Hike Name	page	Wildlife	Strenuous Climbs	Spring Wildflowers	Fall Colors	Diverse Hikes	Young Children	Dogs Allowed
INLAND SOUTH (*continued*)								
58 Mission Trails Regional Park: Cowles Mountain Loop	244		✓					✓
59 Santee Lakes Loop	247						✓	
60 Stelzer Park Loop	251			✓				✓

More Hike Categories

✓ Flat Hikes	✓ Hikes Along Water	✓ Multiuse	✓ Hikes with Views
✓ Hikes for Solitude	✓ Trails for Runners	✓ Historical Interest	

REGION Hike Number/Hike Name	page	Flat Hikes	Hikes for Solitude	Hikes Along Water	Trails for Runners	Multiuse	Historical Interest	Hikes with Views
THE COAST								
1 Batiquitos Lagoon Trail	18	✓		✓				
2 Bayside Trail	21						✓	✓
3 Beach Walk and Torrey Pines State Reserve Loop	25			✓				✓
4 Crest Canyon Open Space Preserve Loop	30							
5 La Jolla: Coast Walk Trail	33							✓
6 La Jolla Shores: Tide Pools Walk	36	✓		✓				
7 Lake Calavera Preserve Loops	39			✓	✓	✓		
8 San Elijo Lagoon: La Orilla to Rios Avenue	43	✓			✓			
9 Tijuana Estuary Trail	46	✓		✓				
10 Torrey Pines State Reserve: Guy Fleming Trail	50							✓
THE MOUNTAINS								
11 Agua Caliente Creek Trail	56			✓				
12 Cuyamaca Rancho State Park: Stonewall Peak Trail	60							✓

REGION Hike Number/Hike Name	page	Flat Hikes	Hikes for Solitude	Hikes Along Water	Trails for Runners	Multiuse	Historical Interest	Hikes with Views
13 Laguna Mountains: Penny Pines Trail	64							✓
14 Laguna Mountains: Sunset Trail	68							✓
15 Palomar Mountain: Fry Creek Campground Trail	72							
16 Palomar Mountain: Observatory Trail	76							
17 Palomar Mountain: Overview Loop	80							
18 Santa Ysabel Open Space Preserve East: Kanaka Loop Trail	84				✓	✓		
19 Three Sisters Waterfalls Trail	87							
20 Volcan Mountain Preserve Trail	91		✓					
21 William Heise County Park: Combined Trails Loop	94		✓					
22 William Heise County Park: Kelly Ditch Trail	98		✓					
THE DESERT								
23 Anza-Borrego Desert State Park: California Riding and Hiking Trail	104		✓					
INLAND NORTH								
24 Blue Sky Trail to Lake Ramona	110							
25 Clevenger Canyon North: East Trail	114		✓					
26 Clevenger Canyon South: East Trail	118							
27 Clevenger Canyon South: West Trail	122							
28 Daley Ranch: Combined Trails Loop	126				✓	✓		
29 Daley Ranch: Engelmann Oak Loop	131					✓		
30 Del Dios Gorge, Dam, and Lake Hodges Trek	135			✓	✓	✓	✓	
31 Del Dios Highlands Preserve Trail	140					✓		
32 Discovery Lake and Double Peak Trails	143							✓
33 Discovery Lake and Hills Loop	147			✓	✓			
34 Dixon Lake: Shore View Trail	151			✓				
35 Elfin Forest Recreational Reserve: Botanical Loop	155							
36 Elfin Forest Recreational Reserve: Way Up and Equine Incline Trail	158				✓	✓		
37 Heller's Bend Preserve Trail	162							
38 Hellhole Canyon Open Space Preserve Trail	165		✓				✓	

REGION Hike Number/Hike Name	page	Flat Hikes	Hikes for Solitude	Hikes Along Water	Trails for Runners	Multiuse	Historical Interest	Hikes with Views
INLAND NORTH (*continued*)								
39 Iron Mountain Peak Trail	169					✓		✓
40 Iron Mountain to Lake Ramona Overlook and Pond	172					✓		✓
41 Lake Hodges: North Shore Trail	175					✓		
42 Lake Poway Loop	179			✓		✓		
43 Lake Poway to Mount Woodson Peak Trail	183					✓		✓
44 Lake Wohlford North: Kumeyaay Trail	187							
45 Lake Wohlford: South Trails	190	✓						
46 Los Jilgueros Preserve Trail	193	✓			✓			
47 Monserate Mountain Trail	197				✓		✓	✓
48 Mount Gower Open Space Preserve Trail	201		✓					✓
49 Mount Woodson: East Trail	205							✓
50 Santa Margarita River Trail	209			✓		✓		
51 Sycamore Canyon: Goodan Ranch Open Space Preserve Loop	213					✓	✓	
52 Wilderness Gardens Preserve: Combined Trails Loop	217							
INLAND SOUTH								
53 Lake Morena Trail	224					✓		
54 Los Peñasquitos Canyon Preserve: East End to Waterfall Loop	228	✓		✓	✓	✓		
55 Los Peñasquitos Canyon Preserve: West End to Waterfall Loop	233			✓		✓		
56 Miramar Reservoir Loop	237				✓	✓		
57 Mission Trails Regional Park: Combined Trails Loop	240							✓
58 Mission Trails Regional Park: Cowles Mountain Loop	244							✓
59 Santee Lakes Loop	247	✓		✓				
60 Stelzer Park Loop	251							

Introduction

WELCOME TO *60 Hikes Within 60 Miles: San Diego.* If you're new to hiking, or even if you're a seasoned trailsmith, take a few minutes to read the following introduction. We'll explain how this book is organized and how to get the best use of it.

How to Use This Guidebook

OVERVIEW MAP, MAP KEY, AND MAP LEGEND

The overview map on the inside front cover shows the primary trailheads for all 60 hikes. The numbers on the overview map pair with the key on the facing page. A legend explaining the map symbols used throughout the book appears on the inside back cover.

REGIONAL MAPS

The book is divided into regions, and prefacing each regional section is an overview map. The regional overview maps provide more detail than the main overview map, bringing you closer to the hikes.

TRAIL MAPS

In addition to the overview map on the inside cover, a detailed map of each hike's route appears with its profile. On each of these maps, symbols indicate the trailhead, the complete route, significant features, facilities, and topographic landmarks such as creeks, overlooks, and peaks.

To produce the highly accurate maps in this book, I used a handheld GPS unit to gather data while hiking each route, then sent that data to Menasha Ridge Press's expert cartographers. Be aware, though, that your GPS device is no substitute for sound, sensible navigation that takes into account the conditions that you observe while hiking.

Further, despite the high quality of the maps in this guidebook, I strongly recommend that you always carry an additional map, such as the ones noted in "Maps" in each hike's Key At-a-Glance Information.

ELEVATION PROFILES

Most hikes contain a detailed elevation profile that corresponds directly to the trail map. This graphical element provides a quick look at the trail from the side, enabling you to visualize how the trail rises and falls. On the diagram's vertical axis, or height scale, the number of feet indicated between each tick mark lets you visualize the climb. To keep flat hikes from looking steep and vice versa, varying height scales provide an accurate image of each hike's climbing challenge. Elevation profiles for loop hikes show total distance; those for out-and-back hikes show only one-way distance. Note that hikes with an elevation gain or loss of fewer than 100 feet do not include an elevation profile.

GPS TRAILHEAD COORDINATES

As noted in "Trail Maps," on the previous page, I used a handheld GPS unit to obtain geographic data and sent the information to the cartographers at Menasha Ridge. Provided for each hike profile, the GPS coordinates—the intersection of latitude (north) and longitude (west)—will orient you from the trailhead. In some cases, you can park within viewing distance of a trailhead. Other hikes require a short walk to the trailhead from a parking area.

The latitude–longitude grid system is likely quite familiar to you, but here's a refresher, pertinent to visualizing the coordinates:

Imaginary lines of latitude—called *parallels* and approximately 69 miles apart from each other—run horizontally around the globe. The equator is established to be 0°, and each parallel is indicated by degrees from the equator: up to 90°N at the North Pole, and down to 90°S at the South Pole.

Imaginary lines of longitude—called *meridians*—run perpendicular to lines of latitude and are likewise indicated by degrees. Starting from 0° at the Prime Meridian in Greenwich, England, they continue to the east and west until they meet 180° later at the International Date Line in the Pacific Ocean. At the equator, longitude lines also are approximately 69 miles apart, but that distance narrows as the meridians converge toward the North and South Poles.

In this book, latitude and longitude are expressed in degree–decimal minute format. For example, the coordinates for Hike 1, Batiquitos Lagoon (page 18), are as follows:

N33° 5.618' W117° 18.080'

To convert GPS coordinates given in degrees, minutes, and seconds to degrees and decimal minutes, divide the seconds by 60. For more on GPS technology, visit **usgs.gov.**

Hike Profiles

Each hike contains seven key items: an In Brief description of the trail, a Key At-a-Glance Information box, directions to the trail, GPS coordinates, a trail map, an elevation profile (in most cases), and a trail description. Many hikes also include notes on things to see and do nearby.

IN BRIEF

A "taste of the trail." Think of this section as a snapshot focused on the historical landmarks, beautiful vistas, and other sights you may encounter on the hike.

KEY AT-A-GLANCE INFORMATION

This gives you a quick idea of the statistics and specifics of each hike:

LENGTH How long the trail is from start to finish. There may be options to shorten or extend the hikes, but the mileage corresponds to the described hike. Use the Description (see next page) as a guide to customizing the hike for your ability or time constraints.

CONFIGURATION Defines the type of route—for example, an out-and-back (which takes you in and out the same way), a point-to-point (or one-way route), a figure-eight, or a balloon-and-string (a loop with an entrance or exit trail).

DIFFICULTY The degree of effort an average hiker should expect on a given hike. For simplicity, the trails are rated as *easy, moderate,* or *strenuous.* Moderate or strenuous hikes may have earned those ratings due to a particularly steep segment of sustained duration within a generally easy whole, while hikes longer than 5 miles may have been rated difficult due to length alone. Altitude also affects the rating—thinner air makes hiking more difficult. If you're not in the best shape, stick to hikes described as easy, building up your endurance and agility before you try moderate or strenuous hikes.

SCENERY Rates the overall environs of the hike and what to expect in terms of plant life, wildlife, natural wonders, and historical features.

EXPOSURE A quick check of how much sun you can expect on your shoulders while you're out on the trail. Descriptors are self-explanatory and include terms such as *shady, exposed,* and *sunny.*

TRAFFIC Indicates how busy the trail might be on an average day and if you might be able to find solitude out there. Trail traffic, of course, varies from day to day and season to season.

TRAIL SURFACE Indicates whether the path is paved, rocky, smooth, or composed of a mixture of elements.

HIKING TIME How long it takes to hike the trail. For these hikes, I (Sheri) averaged about 2 mph, more for strenuous terrain. If you hike slowly because you stop to take a lot of photos, rest, or enjoy the scenery, adjust the hiking time provided to suit your own needs.

ACCESS Notes any fees or permits needed to access the trail, whether the trail has specific hours, and/or whether pets and other forms of trail use are permitted.

Parking/entry fees for these hikes generally range from $2 to $8. For hikes that lie within some national forests, you'll need to purchase a **USDA Adventure Pass** ($5 per day or $30 per year); visit **tinyurl.com/usfsadventurepass** or t**inyurl.com/adventurepass vendors** for more information. In most cases, no fees or permits are required.

WHEELCHAIR-ACCESSIBLE? Notes whether the trail described (or trails nearby) can be used by persons with disabilities.

MAPS Which supplementary map is the best for a particular hike. See Appendix B (page 256) for map resources.

FACILITIES Restrooms, phones, water, and other niceties available at the trailhead or nearby.

INFO Listed here are phone numbers and/or websites for checking trail conditions and gleaning other basic information.

SPECIAL COMMENTS Provides you with those little extra details that don't fit into any of the previous categories. These may include insider information or special considerations about the trail, access, or warnings, along with ideas for enhancing your hiking experience.

GPS COORDINATES

Trailhead latitude and longitude can be used to locate the trail in addition to the Directions (see below) if you enter the data into your GPS unit before you set out. See page 2 for more information.

DIRECTIONS

These will help you locate each trailhead. Where pertinent, highway exit numbers are included.

DESCRIPTION

The heart of each hike, summarizing the trail's essence and highlighting any special traits the hike has to offer. The route is clearly outlined, including any landmarks, side trips, and possible alternate routes along the way. Ultimately, the Description will help you choose which hikes are best for you.

NEARBY ACTIVITIES

Due to space constraints, not every hike has this listing, but for hikes that do, look here for information about places of interest in the vicinity of the trail.

Weather

The climate in San Diego is generally mild. The following chart offers a snapshot of averages for the city.

Around San Diego County, you'll find some extreme weather, such as snow at higher elevations and thunderstorms and flash floods in other areas. When hiking in the mountains and/or desert regions, be sure to consult weather reports and be prepared for abrupt changes.

MONTH	HIGH	LOW	HUMIDITY	RAINFALL	SUNSHINE
JAN	65°F	48°F	63%	2.11"	72%
FEB	66°F	50°F	66%	1.43"	72%
MAR	66°F	42°F	67%	1.60"	72%
APR	68°F	55°F	67%	0.70"	72%
MAY	69°F	58°F	70%	0.74"	59%
JUN	71°F	61°F	74%	0.06"	58%
JUL	76°F	65°F	74%	0.01"	68%
AUG	78°F	67°F	74%	0.11"	70%
SEP	77°F	65°F	72%	0.19"	69%
OCT	75°F	60°F	70%	0.33"	68%
NOV	70°F	54°F	66%	1.10"	75%
DEC	66°F	49°F	64%	1.36"	73%

Source: **sandiego.org**

Temperatures in inland regions and mountainous areas can change drastically from day to night. Mild or even hot daytime temps, say, in the 70s or 80s, may dip below freezing at night. If hiking in these areas, you'll want to make sure you have layers of clothing you can peel away during the day and pile on as the air cools.

Water

How much is enough? Well, one simple physiological fact should convince you to err on the side of excess when deciding how much water to pack: A hiker walking steadily in 90-degree heat needs about 10 quarts of fluid per day—that's 2.5 gallons. A good rule of thumb is to hydrate before your hike, carry (and drink) 6 ounces of water for every mile you plan to hike, and hydrate again after the hike. For most people, the pleasures of hiking make carrying water a relatively minor price to pay to remain safe and healthy, so pack more water than you anticipate needing, even for short hikes.

If you find yourself tempted to drink "found water," proceed with extreme caution. Many ponds and lakes you'll encounter are fairly stagnant, and the water tastes terrible. Drinking such water presents inherent risks for thirsty trekkers. Giardia parasites contaminate many water sources and cause the intestinal ailment giardiasis, which can last for weeks after onset. For more information, visit **cdc.gov/parasites/giardia.**

Effective treatment is essential before you use any found water. Boiling water for 2–3 minutes is always a safe measure for camping, but dayhikers can consider iodine tablets, approved chemical mixes, filtration units rated for giardia, and ultraviolet filtration. Some of these methods (for example, filtration with an added carbon filter) remove bad tastes typical in stagnant water, while others add their own taste. Even if you've brought your own water, consider bringing along a means of water purification in case of an emergency or you forgot to bring enough.

CLOTHING

Weather, unexpected trail conditions, fatigue, extended hiking duration, and wrong turns can individually or collectively turn a great outing into a very uncomfortable one at best. Some helpful guidelines:

➤ *Choose silk, wool, or moisture-wicking synthetics for maximum comfort in all of your hiking attire*—from hats to socks and in between. Cotton is fine if the weather remains dry and stable, but you won't be happy if that fabric gets wet.

➤ *Always wear a hat, or at least tuck one into your daypack or hitch it to your belt.* Hats offer all-weather sun and wind protection as well as warmth if it turns cold.

➤ *Be ready to layer up or down as the day progresses and the mercury rises or falls.* Today's outdoor wear makes layering easy, with such designs as jackets that convert to vests and zip-off or button-up legs.

➤ *Biting bugs, poison oak, and thorny bushes found along many trails can generate short-term discomfort and long-term agony.* A lightweight pair of pants and a long-sleeved shirt can go a long way toward protecting you from these pests.

➤ *Wear hiking boots or sturdy hiking sandals with toe protection.* Flip-flopping along a paved urban greenway is one thing, but you should never hike a trail in open sandals or casual sneakers. Your bones and arches need support, and your skin needs protection.

➤ *Pair that footwear with good socks.* If you prefer not to sheathe your feet when wearing hiking sandals, tuck the socks into your daypack—you may need them if temperatures plummet or if you hit rocky turf and pebbles begin to irritate your feet.

➤ *Don't leave rainwear behind, even if the day dawns clear and sunny.* Tuck into your daypack, or tie around your waist, a jacket that's breathable and either water-resistant or waterproof. Investigate different choices at your local outdoors retailer. If you're a frequent hiker, ideally you'll have more than one rainwear weight, material, and style in your closet to protect you in all seasons in your regional climate and hiking microclimates.

THE TEN ESSENTIALS

One of the first rules of hiking is to be prepared for anything. Always consider worst-case scenarios such as getting lost, hiking back in the dark, broken gear (for example, a broken hip strap on your pack or a water filter that gets plugged), twisting an ankle, or a brutal thunderstorm. The simplest way to be prepared is to carry the "Ten Essentials." In addition to carrying the items that follow, you need to know how to use them, especially navigational aids. These items don't cost a lot of money, don't take up much room in a pack, and don't weigh much—but they might just save your life.

Extra food: trail mix, granola bars, or other high-energy snacks.

Extra clothes: raingear, a change of socks, and, depending on the season, a warm hat and gloves.

Flashlight or headlamp with extra bulb and batteries.

Insect repellent. For some areas and seasons, this is vital.

Maps and a high-quality compass. Don't leave home without them, even if you know the terrain well from previous hikes. As previously noted, you should bring maps in addition to those in this book and consult them before you hike. If you're GPS-savvy, bring that device, too, but don't rely on it as your sole navigational tool—battery life is limited, plus storms and rocky terrain can interfere with reception. Be sure to check your unit's accuracy against that of your maps and compass.

Pocketknife and/or multitool.

Sun protection: sunglasses, lip balm, sunscreen, and sun hat.

Water. Again, bring more than you think you'll drink. Depending on your destination, you may want to bring a container and iodine or a filter in case you run out.

Whistle. It could become your best friend in an emergency.

Windproof matches and/or a lighter, as well as a fire starter.

First-Aid Kit

In addition to the preceding items, the ones that follow may seem daunting to carry along for a dayhike. But any paramedic will tell you that the products listed here are just the basics. The reality of hiking is that you can be out for a week of backpacking and acquire only a mosquito bite . . . or you can hike for an hour, slip, and suffer a cut or broken bone. Fortunately, the items listed pack into a very small space. Convenient prepackaged kits are available at your pharmacy or online.

Ace bandages or Spenco joint wraps

Adhesive bandages

Antibiotic ointment (*such as Neosporin*)

Aspirin, acetaminophen (*Tylenol*), or ibuprofen (*Advil*)

Athletic tape

Blister kit (*such as Moleskin or Spenco 2nd Skin*)

Butterfly-closure bandages

Diphenhydramine (*Benadryl*), in case of allergic reactions

Epinephrine in a prefilled syringe (*EpiPen*), typically available by prescription only, for people known to have severe allergic reactions to bee stings and other mishaps

Gauze (*one roll and a half-dozen 4-by-4-inch pads*)

Hydrogen peroxide or iodine

Hiking with Children

Flat, short, and shaded trails are best with an infant. Toddlers who haven't quite mastered walking can still tag along, riding on an adult's back in a child carrier. Use common sense to judge a youngster's capacity to hike a particular trail, and be ready for the child to tire quickly and need to be carried. Also make sure that children are adequately clothed for the weather, have proper shoes, and are protected from the sun with sunscreen. Kids dehydrate quickly, too, so be sure to bring plenty of fluids for everyone. Hikes suitable for young children are noted on pages xiii–xvi of "60 Hikes by Category."

Hiking with Your Dog

One of the biggest changes to this edition is that almost all San Diego County parks allow leashed dogs on the trails now. You'll find specifics in "60 Hikes by Category," pages xiii–xvi, as well additional notes in the Special Comments section of each hike.

Make sure your dog is physically fit enough for your chosen trail; consult your veterinarian if you're not sure. Short jaunts might build fitness before longer treks. Carry a collapsible bowl, and pack food for energy and extra water to keep your pet hydrated. A canine pack might be appropriate for able pets to carry their own food and water.

Follow all leash rules, keep control of your pet at all times, and be courteous to other hikers with their dogs, bicyclists, and horseback riders. Stop and calm your pet if necessary. Let horseback riders know your dog has never seen a horse if that's true, and help them proceed cautiously as you hold your dog at the side of the trail. Finally, please don't take aggressive dogs out onto the trails.

General Safety

While many hikers hit the trail full of enthusiasm and energy, others may find themselves feeling apprehensive about possible outdoor hazards. Although potentially dangerous situations can occur anywhere, your hike can be as safe and enjoyable as you had hoped, as long as you use sound judgment and prepare yourself before hitting the trail. Here are a few tips to make your trip safer and easier:

> ➢ HIKE WITH A BUDDY. Not only is there safety in numbers, but a hiking companion can help you if you twist an ankle on the trail or if you get lost, can assist in carrying food and water, and can be a partner in discovery. A buddy is good to bring along not only to infrequently traveled or remote areas but also to urban areas.

> ➢ IF YOU DECIDE TO HIKE ALONE, leave your hiking itinerary with someone you trust, and let him or her know when you return.

> ➢ DON'T COUNT ON A MOBILE PHONE FOR YOUR SAFETY. Reception may be spotty or nonexistent on the trail, even on an urban walk—especially one embraced by towering trees.

- ➤ DON'T LEAVE VALUABLES UNATTENDED IN YOUR CAR. If you must leave something behind, don't invite trouble: Conceal items rather than placing them in plain view.

- ➤ ALWAYS CARRY FOOD AND WATER, EVEN ON SHORT HIKES. Food will give you energy and sustain you in an emergency until help arrives. Bring more water than you think you'll need—we can't emphasize this enough. Hydrate throughout your hike and at regular intervals; don't wait until you feel thirsty. Treat water from streams or other sources before drinking it.

- ➤ ASK QUESTIONS. Public-land employees can help. It's a lot easier to solicit advice before a problem occurs, and it will help you avoid a mishap away from civilization when it's too late to amend an error.

- ➤ STAY ON DESIGNATED TRAILS. Most hikers get lost when they leave the path. Even on the most clearly marked trails, you usually reach a point where you have to stop and consider the direction in which to head. If you become disoriented, don't panic. As soon as you think you may be off-track, stop, assess your current direction, and then retrace your steps back to the point where you went awry. Using a map, compass, and this book—and keeping in mind what you've passed thus far—reorient yourself and trust your judgment about which way to continue. If you become absolutely unsure of how to continue, return to your vehicle the way you came in. Should you become completely lost, remaining in place along the trail and waiting for help is most often the best option for adults and always the best option for children.

- ➤ ALWAYS CARRY A WHISTLE. It could become a lifesaver if you get lost or hurt.

- ➤ BE ESPECIALLY CAREFUL WHEN CROSSING STREAMS. Whether you're fording the stream or crossing on a log, make every step count. If you have any doubt about maintaining your balance on a foot log, go ahead and ford the stream instead. When fording a stream, use a trekking pole or stout stick for balance and *face upstream as you cross.* If a stream seems too deep to ford, turn back. Whatever is on the other side isn't worth risking your life for.

- ➤ BE CAREFUL AT OVERLOOKS. While these areas may provide spectacular views, they are potentially hazardous. Stay back from the edge of outcrops, and be absolutely sure of your footing.

- ➤ STANDING DEAD TREES AND STORM-DAMAGED LIVING TREES pose a hazard to hikers and tent campers. Loose or broken limbs could fall at any time. When choosing a spot to rest, camp, or snack, *look up.*

- ➤ KNOW THE SYMPTOMS OF HEAT EXHAUSTION, OR HYPERTHERMIA. Lightheadedness and loss of energy are the first two indicators. If you feel these symptoms coming on, find some shade, drink your water, remove as many layers of clothing as practical, and stay put until you cool down. Marching through heat exhaustion leads to heatstroke—which can be deadly. If you should be sweating and you're not, that's the signature warning sign. If you or a companion reaches this point, your hike is over: Do whatever you can to cool down, and seek medical help immediately.

➢ LIKEWISE, KNOW THE SYMPTOMS OF SUBNORMAL BODY TEMPERATURE, OR HYPOTHERMIA. Shivering and forgetfulness are the two most common indicators of this stealthy killer. Hypothermia can occur at any elevation, even in the summer—especially if you're wearing lightweight cotton clothing. If symptoms develop, get to shelter, hot liquids, and dry clothes ASAP.

➢ MOST IMPORTANTLY, TAKE ALONG YOUR BRAIN. A cool, calculating mind is the single most important asset on the trail. Think before you act. Watch your step. Plan ahead. Avoiding accidents before they happen is the best way to ensure a rewarding and relaxing hike.

Plant and Animal Hazards

Hikers should be aware of the following concerns regarding plant life and wildlife:

PLANTS Throughout the book, I describe individual flowers and native plants found on trails, along with nonnative plants that thrive in some areas; plant communities such as chaparral are also discussed on some hikes. Other beauties, such as wild roses and mule-fat bushes, which release white tufts to drift through the air in a cottony blizzard, are also noted. I hope my descriptions will help you identify some of the vegetation. You may want to consult a book on native plants for even more detail.

You'll also see potentially harmful plants while hiking. Be wary of **cactus,** with its prickly needles that can lodge in your skin. Once in, the needles have a tendency to break off if tugged upon, making removal difficult. A fall into a large stand of cactus near a hiking trail could prove to be very painful.

Poison oak can be another big threat to your comfort. This deciduous plant *(below)* grows as a sparse ground cover, vine, or shrub in moist areas all over San Diego County, in the shade of trees or near water sources; a close encounter can result in the plant's oil coming into contact with your skin.

Poison oak has three leaflets, with two leaves on opposite sides of the stem and one extending from the stem's center. The leaves can grow in attractive boughs twining up around trees. The plant is easiest to spot in summer and early autumn, when the leaves flush bright-red; it can also be rosy-red and/or yellow-gold, beautiful fall colors that may lure you to touch. Sometimes the plants grow artfully up over branches, forming lovely arches above the paths. Beware of unknown bare-branched shrubs and vines in winter: The entire plant can cause a rash, no matter what the season, so learn to recognize all of the parts of the plant.

Urushiol, the oil in the sap of the plant, is responsible for the rash. Reactions may start almost immediately or not appear until a week after exposure. Raised lines and/or blisters will appear, accompanied by a terrible itch. Try to refrain from scratching, though, because bacteria under your fingernails can cause an infection. Wash and dry the affected area thoroughly, applying calamine lotion to help dry out the rash. Seek medical attention if the itching or blistering is severe.

Most people come into contact with poison oak while bushwhacking or traveling off-trail, so stay on established trails whenever possible. The easiest way to avoid contact is by wearing long pants and sleeves. If you do knowingly touch the plant, you must remove the oil within 15–20 minutes to avoid a reaction. Rinsing off the oil with cool water—hot water spreads it—is impractical on the trail, but some commercial products such as Tecnu are effective in removing urushiol from your skin. To keep from spreading the misery to someone else, wash not only any exposed parts of your body but also any oil-contaminated clothes, hiking gear, and pets.

In the hike text, I've noted poison oak where I've encountered it on individual trails.

SNAKES Whether I've noted the possibility of snakes on an individual hike or not, you should always be wary of them. **Rattlesnakes** are common nearly year-round in the areas

covered in this book; they're especially active in spring. Although they don't seek out contact with humans, they will strike if cornered. The vibrations caused by a walking stick repeatedly tamped against the ground warns snakes you're headed in their direction; with that advance notice, they're likely to slide off into the brush, or rattle in warning, which puts you on alert. That said, some of my hiking friends and I have noticed that on some high-traffic trails, the snakes seem to have become less leery—so be cautious and alert.

The standard advice for hiking in rattlesnake territory is as follows:

➢ Don't put your hands or feet where you can't see them—say, at the top of a rock outcrop, or in tall grass or a log pile.

➢ Be extra-cautious in hot weather, when snakes are more active.

➢ Scan the trail continuously as you hike.

➢ Keep kids from running ahead on the trail. Bites to children are more severe than those to adults.

Should you encounter a rattlesnake, its body language will reveal its mood. A coiled rattler is primed for a strike, while a relaxed rattler is more sanguine (although snakes have been reported to lunge). If the snake is within striking distance, stand motionless and wait for it to calm down and move on. Taking small, slow steps backward is another smart strategy. If you're out of immediate range, you can either skirt the snake or wait for it to move. Some people believe tapping the ground with a stick—from a safe distance, rather than in the snake's face—will encourage the snake to move on.

In the case of a bite, the California Department of Fish and Game recommends removing jewelry near the bite site—for instance, a bracelet near a bite on the arm—to prevent constricted circulation as swelling occurs. Remain calm and get to a doctor as soon as possible. Consult a first-aid guide or check other reputable resources for specific information about what to do in the case of a bite. There is some controversy over the safe use of snake-bite kits.

INSECTS, ETC. Vivid butterflies add color along dusty trails. Nature's geometric perfection is highlighted on dewy mornings when spiders' webs glisten. Beetles scuttle along as if they own the path. With an attitude of wonder on your part, the tiniest of insects can inspire a sense of awe.

But there are bothersome insects, too. Pesky **flies** and **mosquitoes** have been noted in individual hike write-ups when they're a common occurrence.

Ticks can also be a problem throughout the spring, summer, and fall. These arachnids like to hang out in the brush that grows along trails and need a host for most of their life cycle in order to reproduce. The ticks that alight onto you while hiking will be very small, sometimes so tiny that you won't be able to spot them. All ticks need to attach for several hours before they can transmit disease.

A few precautions: Use insect repellent that contains DEET, preferably a product designed for use on clothing rather than on skin. Wear light-colored clothing, which will make it easy for you to spot ticks before they migrate to your skin. When your hike is done, inspect your hair, the back of your neck, your armpits, and your socks. During your posthike shower, take a moment to do a more complete body check. To remove a tick that is already embedded, use tweezers made especially for this purpose. Treat the bite with disinfectant solution. On hikes that allow dogs, you'll also want to check your canine buddies for these unwanted pests.

MOUNTAIN LIONS You'll usually find signs posted in areas where these majestic 150-pound animals live. Give them a healthy dose of respect as you tread through their habitat. Make noise to announce your presence—pound the ground with a stick or speak loudly—so the cats can move out of your way.

If you do encounter a mountain lion, here are a few helpful guidelines:

➢ Keep your children close to you, or hold your child. Observed in captivity, mountain lions seem especially drawn to small children.

➢ *Do not run* from a mountain lion. Running may stimulate the animal's instinct to chase.

➢ Don't approach a mountain lion. Instead, give it room to get away.

➢ Try to make yourself look larger by raising your arms and/or opening your jacket (if you're wearing one).

➢ Don't crouch, kneel down, or bend over. These movements could make you look smaller and more like the lion's prey.

➢ Try to convince the lion that you're dangerous. Without bending or crouching down, gather nearby stones or branches, and toss them at the animal. Slowly wave your arms above your head and speak in a firm voice.

➢ If all fails and you get attacked, *fight back.* Hikers have successfully fended off attacking lions with rocks and sticks. Try to remain facing the animal, and fend off attempts to bite at your head or neck—a lion's typical aim.

Topographic Maps

The maps in this book have been produced with great care and, used with the hike text, will direct you to the trail and help you stay on course. However, you'll find superior detail and valuable information in the US Geological Survey's 7.5-minute-series topographic maps. At **MyTopo.com,** for example, you can view and print USGS topos of the entire United States free of charge. Online services such as **Trails.com** charge annual fees for additional features such as shaded relief, which makes the topography stand out more. If you expect to print out many topo maps each year, it might be worth paying for such extras. The downside to USGS maps is that most are outdated, having been created 20–30 years ago; nevertheless, they provide excellent topographic detail.

Digital programs such as DeLorme's Topo North America enable you to review topo maps on your computer. Data gathered while hiking with a GPS unit can be downloaded into the software, letting you plot your own hikes. Of course, **Google Earth** (**earth.google .com**) does away with topo maps and their inaccuracies . . . replacing them with satellite imagery and its inaccuracies. Regardless, what one lacks, the other augments. Google Earth is an excellent tool whether you have difficulty with topos or not.

If you're new to hiking, you might be wondering, "What's a topo map?" In short, it indicates not only linear distance but elevation as well, using contour lines. These lines spread across the map like dozens of intricate spiderwebs. Each line represents a particular elevation, and at the base of each topo a contour's interval designation is given. If, for example, the contour interval is 20 feet, then the distance between each contour line is 20 feet. Follow five contour lines up on the same map, and the elevation has increased by 100 feet.

In addition to the sources listed previously and in Appendix B, you'll find topos at major universities, outdoors shops, and some public libraries, as well as online at **national map.gov** and **store.usgs.gov.**

Limitations

A few hikes from the second edition have been removed and replaced with other hikes. I chose some of the new ones because of their popularity, new features, or additions that make them novel or have connected them to others. You'll see updates about how trees have regenerated since the wildfires of 2003, 2007, and even 2014.

San Diego, with its diverse landscape, has much to be explored. I've outlined hiking trails ranging from mountain terrain to desert to coastal shores and open space areas close to the city. While even 60 hikes can't cover all the spirit-lifting nature opportunities in the county, I've nonetheless strived for a well-rounded mix here and added a few new favorites—more than enough hikes to allow for one per week.

Trail Etiquette

Whether you're hiking in a city, county, state, or national park, always remember that great care and resources (from nature as well as from your tax dollars) have gone into creating these spaces. Treat the trail, wildlife, and fellow hikers with respect.

Here are a few general principles to keep in mind while you're on the trail:

> ➢ *Hike on open trails only.* Respect trail and road closures (ask if you're not sure), avoid possible trespassing on private land, and obtain all permits and authorization as required. Also, leave gates as you found them or as marked.

> ➢ *Be sensitive to the ground beneath you.* This also means staying on the existing trail and not blazing any new trails. Pack out what you pack in. **Leave No Trace** ethics make hiking and camping more fun for others (see **lnt.org** for more information).

> *Never spook animals.* An unannounced approach, a sudden movement, or a loud noise can startle them. A surprised snake or skunk can be dangerous to you, others, and itself. Give animals extra room and time to adjust to your presence.

> *Plan ahead.* Know your equipment, your ability, and the area in which you are hiking—and prepare accordingly. Be self-sufficient at all times; carry necessary supplies for changes in weather or other conditions. A well-executed trip is a satisfaction to you and to others.

> *Be courteous to other hikers, bikers, and equestrians you encounter on the trails.* Hikers and bikers should yield to equestrians, bikers should yield to hikers, and, whenever safe, everyone should yield to uphill hikers, bikers, or equestrians.
>
> When you encounter equestrians, it's very helpful to move off-trail to the downhill side and greet the rider. This helps the horse understand that you aren't a threat.

Let Nature Transform You

As I was writing the original version of this guide, my family was enduring many troubles. Getting out among the trees, letting the tangy scents of sage and the sweet songs of native birds fill my senses, was a healing salve.

The fall 2003 fires required the first edition's postponement. Some of my work literally went up in smoke. But closed trails began to reopen, allowing treks onto charred paths to inform my edits for the book's accuracy. And in the spring of 2004, after my oldest son nearly died in a car crash caused by a drunk driver, seeing Mother Nature's regenerative powers helped me scrape past the gloom of uncertainty and stress and begin a cheerful new season. As charred oak trees formed leafy green wreaths of new growth at their bases, I was inspired to smile again, renewed, invigorated, and equipped to move past a time of trouble. And when wildfires yet again sent my work up in smoke in 2007, as I'd just about completed my revisions for the second edition, it was nature's regenerative powers that inspired me again.

Anytime I'm on the trail, I am reminded of those regenerative powers—day to day, season to season, and year to year. Just as prickly caterpillars steal away into darkness and emerge as brilliant butterflies to delight the eye, the earth too emerges brilliant after a season of darkness . . . or simply from winter to spring to summer to fall. And so can you.

In this book, I've tried to call attention to tiny, sometimes overlooked details in my eagerness to elicit in you a child's sense of marvel. It's my hope that this guide not only provides the necessary concrete logistics of directions and maps but also inspires you to begin—or continue—a joyful relationship with the natural world.

THE COAST

Abundant feathered wonders delight at Batiquitos Lagoon (Hike 1).

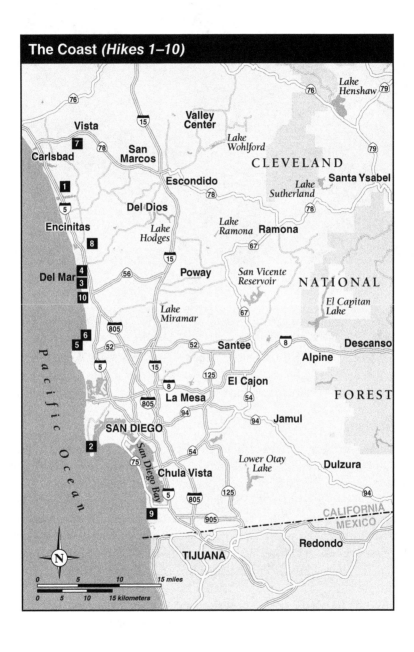

The Coast (Hikes 1–10)

1 Batiquitos Lagoon Trail

California goldenrod in bloom

In Brief

Cool ocean breezes and glassy water that laps soothingly at the shore make this a refreshing hike for hotter days, and the trail is easy. Bring your children for an educational experience, including a visit to the nature center, where friendly guides enjoy sharing information.

Description

Walk southeast on the paved section; you quickly come to the nature center. There, colorful seabird cutouts offer still-life clues as to what you're likely to see in full living color ahead: birds, birds, and more birds—grebes, herons, plovers, terns, and more.

Just past the nature center, the dirt trail begins. The lagoon waters gently lap the shore to the right of the path while, beyond it, the freeway incessantly hums. Concentrate on the birds floating along where the ripples take them or ducking their heads beneath the glassy water in search of food. Slow-winged gulls sail along on the air. Drawing your attention to the moment, the yellow-beaked gulls seem to carry the traffic noise away on their lazy flight.

Information panels offer facts about surrounding marsh vegetation, like the fleshy pickleweed, rustling cattail, heath, or salt grass. Look closely amid the greenery: a plover rests atop a stick in the mud, and an egret stands so still that he looks like part of the landscape.

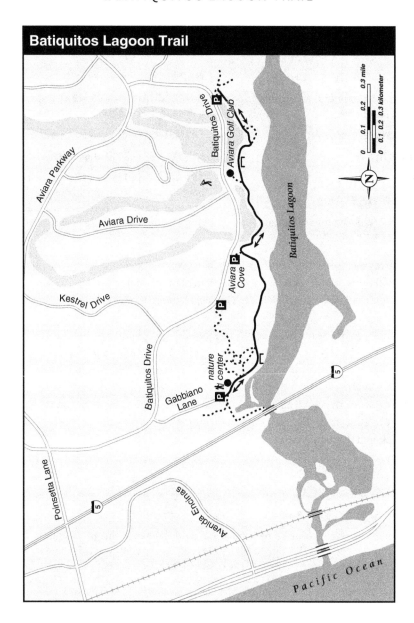

Batiquitos Lagoon Trail

Benches are placed about every third of a mile and overlook the lagoon the same way several houses on the left do, poised to enjoy the rippling water through south-facing windows shaded against the afternoon sun—or perhaps thrown open to allow in the musky scent of thriving coastal sage scrub.

The route bears left through eucalyptus trees with trunks that creak and squeak as the wind pushes them against each other. Note Aviara Cove on the left (another entrance to the lagoon) and continue east. A golf course appears, with its manicured grass looking

LENGTH & CONFIGURATION 3-mile out-and-back	Monday–Friday, 9 a.m.–12:30 p.m., and weekends 9 a.m.–3 p.m.
DIFFICULTY Easy	**MAPS** At the website below
SCENERY Native sage scrub; birds and their nesting sites	**WHEELCHAIR-ACCESSIBLE?** Generally; soft sand in spots could be a hassle.
EXPOSURE Sunny and shady	**FACILITIES** Restroom at the nature center
TRAFFIC Heavy	**INFO** 760-931-0800, **batiquitosfoundation.org**
TRAIL SURFACE Sandy soil	**SPECIAL COMMENTS** The nature center offers guided walks and lots of learning opportunities. Leashed dogs are welcome, but bikes and horses are prohibited.
HIKING TIME 1 hour	
ACCESS Free. The nature center is open	

almost artificial against this natural setting. Two worlds usually so far apart collide here, where golfers in collared shirts wave at hikers in boots or running shoes. Look up into the trees as you head through this section. Guides tell of great blue herons nesting overhead year after year.

Another quarter-mile or so brings you past the golf clubhouse and then to the eastern entrance, which is a good place to turn around. You'll notice a protected nesting area for the threatened snowy plover and endangered least tern. Their nesting season is generally May–August.

Enjoy the fresh coastal air and absorb the ever-changing palette of nature's canvas as you retrace your steps. The late-afternoon sun forms stripes on the lagoon waters as though filtered through blinds.

GPS INFORMATION AND DIRECTIONS

N33° 5.618' W117° 18.080'

Take Interstate 5 to the Poinsettia Lane exit and drive 0.3 mile east to Batiquitos Drive. Turn right and continue 0.4 mile to where the road curves southwest. Turn right on Gabbiano Lane and drive 0.3 mile to the parking lot at the trailhead.

2 Bayside Trail

In Brief

Cool coastal breezes and sweeping views of San Diego's bay make the Bayside Trail a top choice for warm spring and summer days. Taking in the nearby historic lighthouse and museum lend a historical perspective to this hike.

Description

Its close proximity to the historic Old Point Loma Lighthouse and the Juan Rodriguez Cabrillo Museum make the Bayside Trail a favorite among energetic tourists. Locals come for the pleasant hike with breathtaking bay views.

From the parking area, proceed south across the road—there's a crosswalk—and head up the sidewalk toward the lighthouse. A sign to the west of the lighthouse indicates the route to the Bayside Trail. Follow this asphalt route down to the southwest for about 0.3 mile to the marked trailhead, where there is a bench from which you can see the bay. Foghorns warn sailboats and military vessels to slow down at regular intervals.

The gravel trail, once used as a military patrol road, gradually descends to the southeast. The valley to your right is furred with thick coastal sage scrub. In the past, a cluster of silver dollar trees was prominent here, stretching up from the cleft base. However, on our last visit, we noticed the trees' diminished health—likely due to California's drought conditions, which have persisted for several years. On the left, the sandstone cliff rises as the trail descends. Numerous whiptail and Western fence lizards scuttle from open sunning spots into the scrub at the side of the trail. Some will dash across the trail, then pause to look up with curiosity, as if assessing your reaction to their presence.

On warm days in the late winter, one can see signs of spring. Like flaming match heads, bright, coral-red Indian paintbrush blooms peep from the ground. The daisylike flowers of the low-growing encelia shrub bloom in yellow profusion all along the trail, while California buckwheat grows in thick stands that are covered in drifts of creamy blooms alongside last year's dried brown leftovers.

This eastbound path stretches down about 0.3 mile, then bends to the right (north), where the trail levels out for a while. You may hear sea lions barking and catch a glimpse of them frolicking in the water or sunning themselves on the rocks far below. Meanwhile, the blue-green water endlessly undulates, and sailboats of varying sizes bob peacefully or tilt precariously in the wind. It's not unusual to see a Navy submarine, partially submerged, gliding south like a gray whale among the pleasure boats.

The trail follows a V-shaped inlet in the cliff westward for several hundred yards, past locked metal military bunkers from World War II. The trail swings farther left, taking you north for about 0.25 mile and affording views of rocky shore, the bright-blue curve of

Bayside Trail

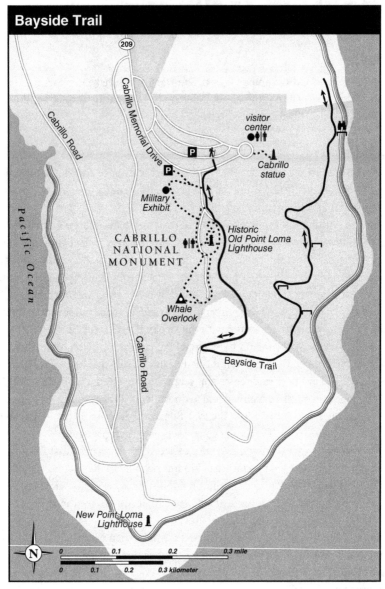

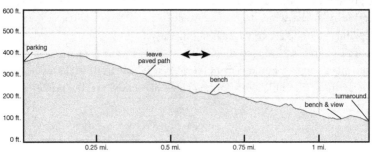

LENGTH & CONFIGURATION
3-mile out-and-back

DIFFICULTY Moderately easy

SCENERY View of San Diego Bay,
coastal sage scrub, wildflowers

EXPOSURE Mostly sunny

TRAFFIC Moderate

TRAIL SURFACE Gravel

HIKING TIME 1.5 hours

ACCESS $5/car parking fee, free with
a National Parks and Federal Recreational
Lands Annual Pass ($80; **store.usgs.gov**
/pass); open daily, 9 a.m.–5 p.m.

MAPS Distributed with parking fee at
ranger booth

WHEELCHAIR-ACCESSIBLE? Yes, for
the opening paved section. The rest of
the trail is graveled and difficult, although
in-shape wheelchair users may be able
to navigate the terrain. The trip down
is easier than the trip back up. As noted
below, there are steep drop-offs in some
sections, so please exercise caution.

FACILITIES None on the trail; restrooms
at nearby Cabrillo National Monument
Visitor Center and also near the lighthouse

INFO 619-557-5450, **nps.gov/cabr**
/index.htm

SPECIAL COMMENTS Stay close to
children on this trail, where cliffs drop
to rocky bay shores several hundred feet
below in some sections.

the Coronado Bay Bridge far to the east, and the buildings of downtown San Diego looking like a child's model in the foreground. Don't let kids run ahead or get too close to the
edge—the sandstone cliffs can be dangerous.

Another, slightly shorter, inlet takes you into a shaded V where toyon and lemonadeberry bushes thrive, growing in thick, man-tall groupings. Wild-cucumber vines with
delicate white blossoms creep over the smaller shrubs, and tiny hummingbirds hover,
twitching this way and that. Be careful as the trail heads east toward the bay—the inlet
valley isn't as guarded by shrubs on this side.

Along this last stretch of northbound trail, watch for the succulent tubes of the lady-
finger plant along the ground. Also notice the tall, spindly bladderpod and its narrow,
pale-green leaves and yellow flowers with protruding stamens. The sweet smell of black
sage fills the air. You may also note the tangy-sweet smell of wild licorice. Watch for its
pale, fernlike leaves growing on foot-high bushes with vanilla-white blooms.

A sign announces the trail's end, and a chainlink fence several yards past the sign
blocks farther passage. Follow the trail back the way you came, this time uphill. On hot
days, you'll enjoy the shady V inlets as you make the gradual 300-foot climb. Take your
time. Notice the subtle patterns on succulent agaves growing on the cliff. Spot the creamy
white of tiny milkmaids. These clustered flowers peek from beneath cascading ferns that
thrive in the cooler nooks of the inlet trail. Later, you can think about these tiny wonders,
the sweeping views of the ocean, and the feel of the coastal breeze on your skin—and
relive the serenity of this natural space.

Nearby Activities

Historic **Old Point Loma Lighthouse** has a spiral staircase and glassed-in rooms furnished with artifacts and notations that chronicle the lives of the keeper, Robert Israel, and his family. The visitor center offers a museum describing the expeditions of Juan Rodríguez Cabrillo (João Rodrigues Cabrilho in Portuguese), the first European explorer to set foot on the west coast of the United States. There is also a gift shop, plus vending machines and pay-per-view telescopes for viewing the bay. For more information, call 619-557-5450 or visit **nps.gov/cabr/planyourvisit.**

GPS INFORMATION AND DIRECTIONS

N32° 40.434' W117° 14.443'

From I-5 North or I-8 East, exit at Rosecrans Street and turn right on Canon Street, then left on Catalina Boulevard/CA 209. Follow Catalina Boulevard past Fort Rosecrans Cemetery and drive into the park. Turn left into the well-marked parking area.

3 Beach Walk and Torrey Pines State Reserve Loop

Snowy egret hunting at the shore

In Brief

Your eyes will thank you for the restful views on this 3.7-mile loop that starts from the North Beach Parking lot, heads south on the sand then leads up through the pitted cliffs into Torrey Pines State Reserve.

Description

There's a reason that so many tourists choose this hike when visiting San Diego. And as you head west from the North Beach parking lot, you begin to see why. Just beyond the overpass, sand, surf, and wide open sky stretch out before you—and the cares of the day melt away.

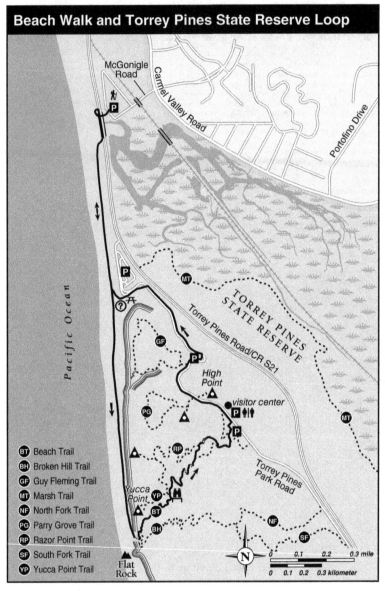

Beach Walk and Torrey Pines State Reserve Loop

McGonigle Road

Carmel Valley Road

Portofino Drive

Pacific Ocean

T O R R E Y P I N E S
S T A T E R E S E R V E

Torrey Pines Road/CR S21

High Point

visitor center

Torrey Pines Park Road

Yucca Point

BT Beach Trail
BH Broken Hill Trail
GF Guy Fleming Trail
MT Marsh Trail
NF North Fork Trail
PG Parry Grove Trail
RP Razor Point Trail
SF South Fork Trail
YP Yucca Point Trail

Flat Rock

N

0   0.1   0.2   0.3 mile

0   0.1   0.2   0.3 kilometer

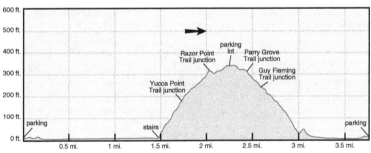

600 ft.
500 ft.
400 ft.
300 ft.
200 ft.
100 ft.
0 ft.

parking

stairs

Yucca Point
Trail junction

Razor Point
Trail junction

parking
lot

Parry Grove
Trail junction

Guy Fleming
Trail junction

parking

0.5 mi.   1 mi.   1.5 mi.   2 mi.   2.5 mi.   3 mi.   3.5 mi.

LENGTH & CONFIGURATION 3.7-mile balloon-and-string	at the end of Hike 10, Guy Fleming Trail (see page 53).
DIFFICULTY Moderate	**MAPS** Download from the website below or obtain at the park.
SCENERY Possible wildlife sightings, sweeping ocean views	
EXPOSURE Sunny	**WHEELCHAIR-ACCESSIBLE?** No, due to beach sand and stairs
TRAFFIC Heavy	**FACILITIES** Restrooms in the North Beach parking lot and at the upper park-ing lot inside the reserve
TRAIL SURFACE Packed sand, silty soil	
HIKING TIME 1.5–2 hours	**INFO** 858-755-2063, **torreypine.org**
ACCESS Day-use fee to park: $10–$12 Monday–Thursday, $12–$15 Friday–Sunday and holidays (low–high season); additional fees for buses and on major holidays. Open daily, 7:15 a.m.–sunset (visitor center opens at 9 a.m.). As crowds permit, you may opt to park in free stalls along the beach, as described in the note	**SPECIAL COMMENTS** Check tide reports on weather sites so you can enjoy a wide ribbon of sand without the danger of being pushed up alongside the cliffs in rising tides. If you want more solitude on this popular hike, come in fall and winter, when cool weather and gray skies don't attract the crowds.

There's usually too much water flowing in the channel to your left to immediately start your beach walk. So turn right, up the bridge path, and then right again at the top. You'll walk a few yards alongside the street to cross the bridge. At its end, step back down to the right again and head away from the road in a soft-sand path to the beach. From here, begin walking south. As you step forward, it's impossible not to let the ocean breeze lift your spirits.

In the ocean, you may see people standing on paddleboards, sweeping a single oar through the water. People also fish here, watching over the poles they've affixed into stands. In the sky above, pelicans float gracefully along. A gull or two may call out a greet-ing or simply watch you as you pass, stepping quickly away on spindly legs to stay at a safe distance. Although San Diego has many gull varieties, it's likely the Western gull with a wingspan of nearly 60 inches you'll see here. This large, dark-backed gull has a yellow bill that sports a red spot where its chicks peck to stimulate feeding.

An 8- to 10-minute beach walk (about 0.6 mile) puts you directly beneath the reserve's entrance kiosk, up at street level on your left. Here, you'll continue along on the beach. The cliffs rising on your left envelop you in the roaring sound of powerful ocean waves and the buffeting of wind. If you've come at low tide as recommended, the shore's packed, water-slickened sand reflects the sky. Lacy patterns on its surface intrigue the eyes; bird and human tracks, along with the marks left by seaweed that's swept into the shore and then out again, form an intricate and ever-changing weave. Notice also the trails made by sand crabs. Submerged in the shifting sands of the swash zone where they spend their time facing the sea to feed, these crabs are often the ones that get eaten! On our last visit here, a snowy egret feasted, nearly oblivious to gawking passersby.

Be sure to look up at the rutted golden cliffs, eroded into interesting shapes and patterns. Perhaps you'll glimpse an osprey standing guard. These raptors have slate-colored backs, a white underbelly and head, and a darker eye band that looks a little like a mask. If you're fortunate enough to see one fly out above the water to feed, you'll be impressed by their 5-foot wingspan. They hover above the water in keen-eyed concentration to home in on prey. Then they drop to the water, feet outstretched, and pluck up the unsuspecting fish.

You'll spot Flat Rock in the distance. In the warmth of late spring, people swarm on the rock, investigating the many tiny pools left by receding waters for crabs and sea anemones. At just shy of 1.5 miles, and not quite to Flat Rock, you'll see the stairs on your left that lead up into Torrey Pines State Reserve. You'll turn here and head up them, pausing to look back at the view—as will become a pattern on this uphill climb that moves inland, away from the vast ocean and its cooling breeze. At the top of the fairly short set of beach stairs, bear left, ignoring the offshoot to the right (explore it another day—the trails all eventually lead to the top).

Keep heading upward on the earthen path that's interspersed with boardwalks that cross gullies. Among the coast chaparral, you may see lizards scuttling away, as well as squirrels that make their home here. In spring, yellow mariposa flowers bloom on lanky stalks, their petals ruffling in the wind.

At 1.7 miles into the hike, you'll come to an ocean overlook, Yucca Point, on your left. Pause for a break and enjoy the view if you'd like. In the winter months, you may see

People look like ants swarming on Flat Rock as you look back from the trail in Torrey Pines State Reserve.

gray whales as they migrate down the coast. Dolphins are spotted year-round. Past Yucca Point, the trail nearly levels for a stretch, allowing a bit of a breather as you walk. A bench alongside the trail, at 1.8 miles, is positioned for glorious westerly views of the sea.

At 1.9 miles, a side trail comes in from the right. You'll bear left, around a plateau formation, and then right around its other side. At 2.2 miles, you'll find yourself in the parking lot, with restrooms to your right. Head left to begin your trek down the long road, back toward the sea. A path enclosed by curbs on the west side of the road affords glimpses of ocean between the pines the park is named for. The Torrey pine is the rarest pine in the United States, growing only in the small strip of San Diego's coast from Del Mar to La Jolla, and also on the island of Santa Rosa, 70 miles to the north.

You'll pass the visitor center, across the road on your right. It's worth a look if you have the time. There are whale bones that provide an up-close perspective of the mammals' size, as well as some lovely northeasterly viewing spots around the back. Heading past the visitor center, you'll see signs for High Point Overlook and Parry Grove Trail. Passing these by, the curbed area ends, so be careful as you walk down the narrow strip of earth alongside the park road. Because of the reserve's popularity, tourists entering in cars may not be aware that people will be walking on the paved road.

At 2.5 miles, the Guy Fleming Trail (see Hike 10, page 50) opens on your left. Instead of the ocean, views of scenic Del Mar spread before you, and you'll notice a small earthen parking lot. You'll pass the parking lot, head down some steps, and then cross the park road. There's a crosswalk, but watch for cars. Prickly pear cactus is interspersed with trees and brush near the road. A squirrel may gaze at you from the safety of a rock perch. In the spring, bees are active among the cactus blooms. As if the cup-shaped flowers are yellow pools, the bees dive in, their hind legs quickly packing with the sticky pollen.

At 2.9 miles, you'll cross the road again, then move down the earthen path toward the beach. Make a right and head back up the shore, retracing your route in. It's common to linger a little, walking more slowly on this last half-mile of the hike. The ocean waves, the gentle breezes . . . there's no hurry.

GPS INFORMATION AND DIRECTIONS

N32° 56.095' W117° 15.606'

From Interstate 5, exit at Carmel Valley Road and drive west about 1.5 miles. Turn left on McGonigle Road and drive beneath the coaster tracks into the North Beach parking lot. Or use the directions for the Guy Fleming Trail (see page 53) to access free parking or park in the south lot as described.

4 Crest Canyon Open Space Preserve Loop

In Brief

Scarcely more than a stone's throw from the beaches of Del Mar, Crest Canyon is a pleasant walk through coastal sage scrub that can seem a world away from the hustle and bustle of a busy life.

Description

The trail opens through scrub brush to the right of the sign, continues west for several yards, and then drops abruptly off a wide earthen step. If making a 2- to 3-foot drop seems ungainly, a narrow path to the right will lead you more gradually past this point.

Past the drop, continue west, descending rapidly on a semislippery dirt surface. At the bottom, about 0.1 mile from the start, turn right onto the well-defined flat canyon path. You'll hear the roar of traffic on busy Del Mar Heights Road and perhaps the sounds of people going about their day in and around the houses along the bluff on the right. An airplane may buzz by. Tune your ears to the life within this small canyon strip instead, letting the sounds of civilization drift away as you attend the gentle sound of chaparral rippling in the breeze.

A few large pines dot the area, mingling with some much smaller trees. You'll see lots of lemonadeberry with its leathery green leaves, along with bushy coyote brush—covered in tiny white flowers in the fall. California buckwheat is also prevalent, bursting with snowy bloom-tufts that turn pink and rust as summer ends and fall settles.

The canyon is a haven for birdlife. Mockingbirds run through their mimicking repertoire, sounding colorful compared with the repetitive, bouncing call of the wrentit and the heckling of common ravens that soar overhead, their black bodies stark against the sky.

At about 0.5 mile, the trail creeps along near homes on the left, their back fences made of chain link and other open-weave materials for a view of the canyon. Dogs in these yards sound the alarm, the barking message traveling along the canine alert team. Late in the day, you're likely to encounter nearby residents who exercise their dogs here. Big and little, bushy and smooth, the dogs' looks vary as much as those of the owners who walk them.

It's about 0.75 mile to the north end of the canyon, which runs up against Racetrack View Drive. You can see San Dieguito Wetlands just across the narrow road. If you have the time and inclination, cross the pavement for an even better look at the water, stretching like a curvy snake over the land. Fishing is allowed from the shoreline, but the most prevalent fishers are huge groups of waterfowl near the shore. If startled by visitors, the birds pad from the muddy banks down into the water in a flapping, splashing riot to the relative safety beyond the water's edge. There, they float effortlessly along in the shallows, with reflected clouds and the blue of sky brushing the surface like a Monet painting.

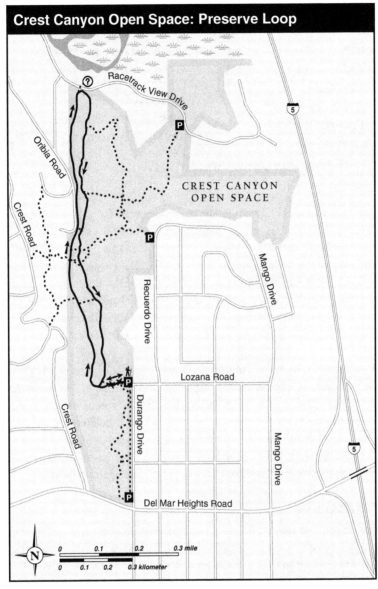

Crest Canyon Open Space: Preserve Loop

Racetrack View Drive

Oribia Road

Crest Road

CREST CANYON
OPEN SPACE

Mango Drive

Recuerdo Drive

Lozana Road

Durango Drive

Crest Road

Mango Drive

Del Mar Heights Road

N

0   0.1   0.2   0.3 mile

0   0.1   0.2   0.3 kilometer

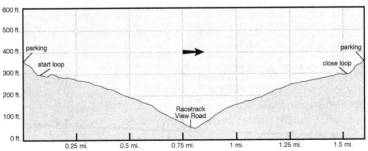

LENGTH & CONFIGURATION 1.5-mile loop	**MAPS** Download from **sdrp.org/word press/trails.**
DIFFICULTY Easy	**WHEELCHAIR-ACCESSIBLE?** No, due
SCENERY Trees, wetlands	to steep drop at outset, rocky areas, and narrow sections of trail
EXPOSURE Mostly sunny	**FACILITIES** None
TRAFFIC Moderately heavy	**INFO** 858-674-2275, **sdrp.org**
TRAIL SURFACE Sandy soil	**SPECIAL COMMENTS** Leashed dogs are welcome.
HIKING TIME 1 hour	
ACCESS Free; open daily, sunrise–sunset	

An information panel tells more about the wetlands and area restoration efforts. From here, either return the way you came or turn right past the sign. You'll find the narrower path that heads south and closes the canyon loop. This narrow trail briefly heads uphill, adding a little more exertion to this easy hike. The chaparral grows closer along this singletrack route, lending a more desolate feel despite the closeness of the city.

Return to the sloping entry path and make your way back up to the road. Or, if you want to walk another half-mile, continue south on the main path all the way to Del Mar Heights Road. Turn east on the dirt path, then make a left at Durango Drive and head back to your car.

On your return hike, be sure to stop periodically and look to the north. Views of the sky above the canyon bluffs can be awe-inspiring. Often, hot-air balloons launched from nearby Encinitas will drift lazily by. The scenery is especially pretty in fall or early spring, when the sun shines but the air is crisp, with puffy clouds holding moisture. Consider coming here at the end of the day, when the setting sun washes the sky in pink, and the clouds to the west glow yellow. The sky is so pretty here that I use it as the profile picture for my San Diego Hikes Facebook page (**tinyurl.com/sandiegohikesfacebook**).

Nearby Activities

Turn right on Del Mar Heights Road and continue the short distance to the coastline in Del Mar. You'll be able to see the ocean almost immediately after turning. In fall and winter, it isn't too difficult to find a parking spot with access to the beach where Del Mar Heights Road hits the coast.

GPS INFORMATION AND DIRECTIONS
N32° 57.176' W117° 15.197'

Take Interstate 5 to Del Mar Heights Road and head west. Drive about 0.4 mile to Durango Drive and turn right. Houses line the right side of the street—the canyon is hidden on the left, dropping beyond the scrub growing close to the road. Follow Durango Drive 0.2 mile and park at the end, near the CREST CANYON OPEN SPACE sign.

5 La Jolla: COAST WALK TRAIL

Let spectacular views and the ebb and flow of the tide lull you on this cliffside trail in paradise.

In Brief

This easy cliffside walk offers shore views. Along with resident seabirds and seals, dolphins may be seen frolicking in the ocean. Despite the area's shops and tourism, La Jolla's coastline is still a haven for the birds.

Description

To the right and left of the cliffside parking on Coast Walk, benches overlooking the ocean offer a spectacular view. Depending on the tide, the waves crash with striking force against the cliffs or gently swell and ebb in a rolling rhythm. The area is popular among kayakers. You may spot them paddling their narrow vessels along the coastline, getting a closer look at the series of watery caves carved into the cliffs below.

The path starts to the left of the parking area, where thick stands of lemonadeberry bushes separate the trail from the cliff's edge. You'll quickly come to a plank bridge and head up wooden steps, reaching an earthen path open to the cliffs. Be careful here, especially with children.

La Jolla: Coast Walk Trail

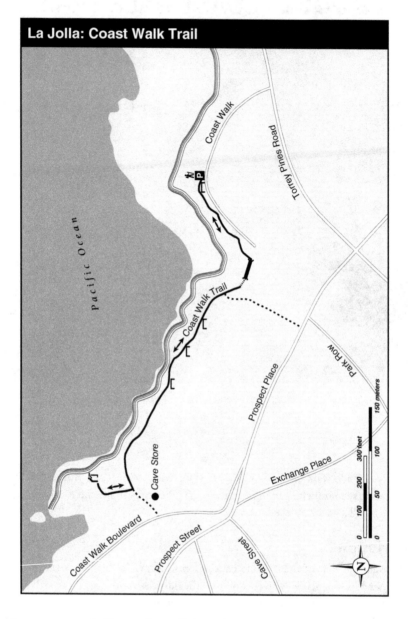

A strong ammonia-like smell may fill the air here. Birds—cormorants, pelicans, and a variety of gulls—are the culprits. They gather on the rocky cliffs in huge groups, the cormorants clinging to the sides of the steep cliffs, while the gulls and pelicans congregate in groups on the flatter rocks jutting out beyond the path.

Several benches placed along the 0.25-mile-long strip provide opportunities to sit and let the ocean lull you. The strong odor isn't as shocking after a few moments, and it's relaxing to sit here on the brink of the cliffs overlooking the vast watery expanse. The cliffside coast walk is a surprising change of pace from the hustle and bustle of tourist

LENGTH & CONFIGURATION 0.5-mile out-and-back or loop	WHEELCHAIR-ACCESSIBLE? No, due to uneven terrain alongside steep drops
DIFFICULTY Easy	
SCENERY Ocean views, birds	**FACILITIES** None
EXPOSURE Mostly sunny	**INFO** No official contacts
TRAFFIC Moderate–heavy	**SPECIAL COMMENTS** Children enjoy this hike, but watch them carefully or insist on holding hands, because sheer cliffs that drop 100 feet to the rocky shoreline can be dangerous. Though this hike is enjoyable anytime, fall and winter promise smaller crowds.
TRAIL SURFACE Packed cliffside soil, optional sidewalk add-ons	
HIKING TIME 30 minutes	
ACCESS Free	
MAPS No official ones, though Googling pulls up a number of unofficial maps.	

activity along La Jolla's shop-lined streets. But there are other surprises here. You will discover that pelicans may look a bit slow and clumsy on land, but they fly with regal elegance. In large flocks, the graceful-in-flight birds soar toward the coast, surveying the cliffs then doubling back to land among the masses that sometimes gather here.

A viewing platform near the Cave Street end of the path gets visitors closest to the birds, busily preening themselves on the rocks just a few feet beyond the railing. The clustered birds, the sparkling Pacific Ocean, and the spectacularly curving San Diego coastline make this a favorite spot for photos. You may also spot seals sunning themselves on shoreline rocks below. Even dolphins are a common site in this wonderful coastal nature enclave.

From here, you can exit the path and turn right onto Cave Street, then continue walking along the sidewalk another 0.25 mile or so with pleasant breezes, ocean views, and lovely pathways with embedded shell art. The Children's Pool beach, where seals gather to give birth to their pups, is just a short distance ahead. Or, instead, you can turn left, walking up the hill and left again onto Torrey Pines Road, meeting Coast Walk and heading around to your car. If you have the time and energy, do both. Everything is in close proximity here.

GPS INFORMATION AND DIRECTIONS

N32° 50.923' W117° 15.996'

Take I-52 West into La Jolla, where it merges onto La Jolla Parkway. Continue northwest on La Jolla Parkway for about 1 mile, where it becomes Torrey Pines Road. Continue about 1 more mile and turn right on Coast Walk, a narrow street that holds very limited cliffside parking a short distance ahead. If no spaces are open here, turn right back onto Torrey Pines Road. Travel about a 0.1 mile, then turn right again where you see a sign for Cave Street. Park curbside wherever you can—the path's opposite end can be accessed about 200 yards from the junction of Torrey Pines Road, at a grove of pine trees near the Cave Store.

6 La Jolla Shores:
TIDE POOLS WALK

A California gull enjoys an ocean view.

In Brief

The ocean breeze, rolling waves, and sand beneath your feet. Who could ask for more? But that's only the beginning—low tides mean plenty of sea creatures to marvel at.

Description

From the grassy area at the north end of Kellogg Park, where free parking is plentiful in the off-season or early on weekday mornings, head north up the beach toward the pier. You might as well kick off your shoes on this wide, sandy beach and let the surf roll in around your feet.

It's about 0.5 mile to the pier that extends from UCSD's Scripps Institute of Oceanography on the cliff above the beach (the cliff and the institute are closed to the public). Standing beneath the pier between the wide, mussel-encrusted supports, one can only wonder at man's ability to build structures strong enough to withstand the ocean's power. A short distance ahead, though, tiny creatures thrive in the ocean's ebb and flow—proving worthy design on a small scale.

As you continue north, you'll see more and more large rocks, pitted by the sea and sand, strewn along the beach. Stuff your feet back into shoes to cross a strip of piled, rounded rocks that form a hobbling path near the base of the cliffs. The larger rocks, roughened into various shapes by wind, water, and sand, clump together, leaving little sand between them.

As you hop from rock to rock, startled crabs scurry sideways into crevices. Schools of fish trapped in pools left by the receding tide swim to safety among fluttery pink and mauve sea plants. Take the time to stoop and get a closer look at what may seem at first just an empty pool. Often, you'll discover the collected water teems with life.

Squabbling over territory, hermit crabs scuttle about in temporary shell houses that are sometimes smaller than a pea. The bigger crabs carry larger shells. Notice the variety of shapes and sizes they select. Even a broken shell may be chosen by a less discerning

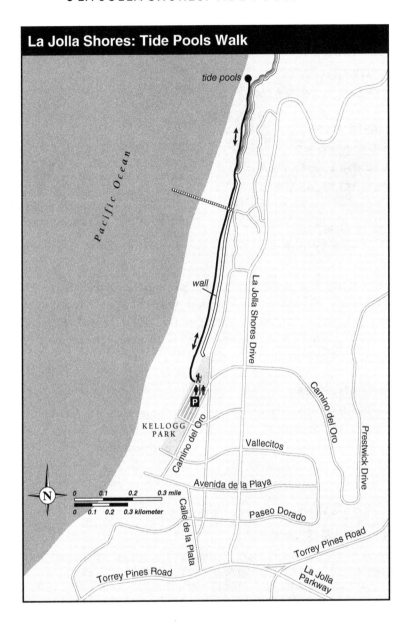

La Jolla Shores: Tide Pools Walk

hermit crab. As he haltingly makes his way across the waterscape, the shell's uneven edge catches on everything he passes. A rusty-colored sea plant suddenly moves away, and you realize it's a sea slug. Watch for a moment and see several more that have been camouflaged in plain sight advance into view. Clumps of elongated oval mussels adhere to the rocks. Sea anemones contract when touched. Gently touching the animals is permitted, but you may not collect or remove anything from the area.

LENGTH & CONFIGURATION 2-mile out-and-back	**WHEELCHAIR-ACCESSIBLE?** No, due to soft sand and rocks on the beach
DIFFICULTY Easy	
SCENERY Ocean waves, tide-pool creatures	**FACILITIES** In the parking area near the lifeguard tower
EXPOSURE Exposed	**INFO** No official contacts
TRAFFIC Moderate–heavy	**SPECIAL COMMENTS** Wear sturdy rubber-soled shoes that will cling to wet rock surfaces. You'll need protection to climb among the tide pools. Be sure to visit around low tide; find tide schedules online at weather and forecast sites.
TRAIL SURFACE Sand and surf, rocks	
HIKING TIME 1 hour	
ACCESS Free	
MAPS None needed	

From the rocky tide-pool area, you could hike about 3.5 more miles to Flat Rock, named for its shape, and access a climbing route (signed BEACH TRAIL) up into Torrey Pines State Reserve. You may spot nude sunbathers along the way: Past the rocky tide pools is the area called Black's Beach, well known as a clothing-optional zone—although public nudity is officially illegal.

Nearby Activities

If the tide pools have whetted your appetite for knowledge about the ocean and its wildlife, the nearby **Birch Aquarium,** at 2300 Expedition Way in La Jolla, is worth a visit. Consult **aquarium.ucsd.edu** or call 858-534-3474 for more information.

GPS INFORMATION AND DIRECTIONS

N32° 51.514' W117° 15.374'

From CA 52 West, merge onto La Jolla Parkway, drive 1.4 miles, and turn right on Calle de la Plata. Continue 0.2 mile to Avenida de la Playa and turn left. Drive 0.1 mile to Camino del Oro and spot the park. Drive to the north end of the parking area and park near the lifeguard tower and restrooms.

7 Lake Calavera Preserve Loops

Lake Calavera reflects the sky.

In Brief

A pleasant 3.25-mile jaunt that makes a figure-eight into local wilderness and views a lake that's surrounded by nearby homes. You're unlikely to get lost this close to civilization, and you can get the restful benefits of nature.

Description

Start out on the walkway that goes through Oak Riparian Park toward Lake Boulevard. You'll pass the restrooms on your right. Using the sidewalk along Lake Boulevard, walk west toward the signal at Emerald Drive, where you'll spot signs for Lake Calavera on the left. Steep stairs take you down onto the dirt trail, which bears right through a slough, with homes on your right.

On my last visit here, a red-shouldered hawk flew close, then headed into the thick brush and trees on the left—a perfect habitat for these hawks that can hunt from a perch for crayfish, frogs, toads, snakes, and other small animals.

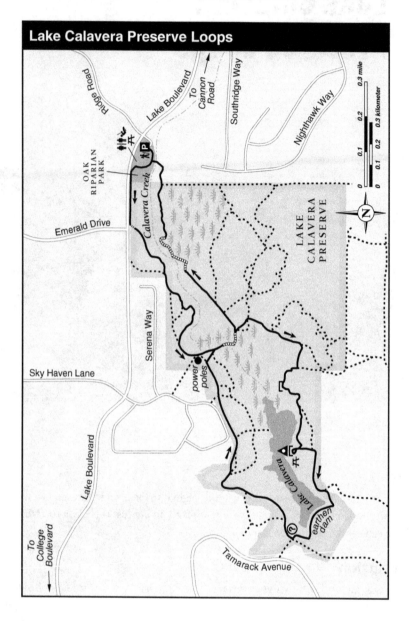

Lake Calavera Preserve Loops

A short uphill section takes you to a plateau. In the distance to your left, Lake Calavera glistens. Head toward the power poles, also to your left, where the trail dips south into a marshy area. Plank bridges, like a boardwalk, head through a shaded area. In wetter months, water trickles—an agreeable sound in this closed-in section that leads quickly back out into the open. Just past the boardwalk, turn right and continue to the lake. You could also turn left and return to Oak Riparian Park.

Head southeast to the right, uphill through a rutted section, and then make a harder right to get to the lake. If you chose to, you could follow the trail straight ahead and climb

LENGTH & CONFIGURATION 3.25-mile figure-8 with string	**WHEELCHAIR-ACCESSIBLE?** No, due to stairs, although wheelchair users could find an alternate access point using many of the numerous maps available online and navigate other portions of the trail.
DIFFICULTY Easy	
SCENERY Birds, native plants, lake view	
EXPOSURE Open to sunlight	**FACILITIES** Restrooms at Oak Riparian Park
TRAFFIC Moderate–heavy	
TRAIL SURFACE Sandy soil, some rocky areas, plank bridges	**INFO** preservecalavera.org/?page_id=512
HIKING TIME 1.5 hours	**SPECIAL COMMENTS** You'll be among dog walkers and bikers. We've even pushed a stroller here, although a few stretches required some muscling. Our group's toddler enjoyed the bumpy ride, but that wouldn't be suitable for an infant.
ACCESS Free	
MAPS No official maps; variety of unofficial maps online at biking websites	

the rough trail steeply to the 514-foot peak of Mount Calavera. The "mountain" is actually a volcanic plug. From a distance—back on the highway, for instance—it's easy to spot a gaping section that was cut into Mount Calavera back in the early 1900s when it was mined for gravel. If in a group, some could take the peak route then travel a trail down the other side, and meet up later on the lake trail near the dam.

To reach the lake's loop, take a hard right at the doggie-poop-bag dispenser and head downhill. A bench at the bottom provides a pleasant resting place with a view of the water. The trail then bears left and begins to curve around the lake.

Lake Calavera remains on your right as the narrowing trail lined with coastal sage scrub bends. You'll come to an overlook area on your right with a picnic table and benches. Beyond this, the dam comes into view, and you'll head across it to the left. Pause to look across the water. The glassy expanse acts as a mirror, reflecting blue sky and puffy clouds on the sunny Southern California days we love.

Bear right at the spillway to reach a kiosk and sign that tells of local wildlife. Turn right here. Houses soon come into view, very close on your left. Continue walking with Lake Calavera on your right. You'll spot the power poles ahead. You could go left and back to the stairs at Lake Boulevard to return the way you came, but to cover new territory, go right, back beneath the power poles, down the hill and across plank bridge again—only this time, head left at the end.

From here, walk the long flat stretch of open space. Pass some side trails to your right, where bikers abound. You'll cross another, longer plank bridge that runs through a marshy area where yerba mansa grows all around and emits a tangy scent when in bloom. In spring, a creamy pinwheel of petal bracts circle a sort of "tongue" on flowers that rise from the leathery, red-streaked green leaves. The conical center that protrudes from yerba mansa's flower is what's known as an inflorescence--a dense cluster of tiny blooms. The herb is antimicrobial and antibacterial, which has made it popular for all sorts of medicinal uses.

Overlooking calm Lake Calavera from the trail

The trail eventually passes through an oak-wooded area and spills out into Oak Riparian Park, near where you left your car. Leave the park, refreshed from time spent in this preserve that's often called "Carlsbad's hidden gem."

GPS INFORMATION AND DIRECTIONS

N33° 10.586' W117° 16.155'

From CA 78 West, exit at Sycamore Avenue. Turn left and drive 0.3 mile, then turn right on Shadowridge Drive. Travel 1.6 miles to South Melrose Drive and turn right. After 0.9 mile, turn left on Cannon Road and drive 0.2 mile. Turn right on Lake Boulevard. After 0.3 mile, come to Ridge Road and turn left into the lot of Oak Riparian Park.

From CA 78 East, exit at South Melrose and head south for 1.5 miles. Turn right on Cannon Road. Then follow the directions as above.

8 San Elijo Lagoon:
LA ORILLA TO RIOS AVENUE

In Brief

This easy stroll through nature is popular with families, walkers, and joggers. People often bring their dogs (on leashes) here.

Description

From the trailhead, proceed west past the entry kiosk through eucalyptus forest, where a variety of toadstools call the moist path home. Hummingbirds buzz in the branches overhead. The younger, spindly trees grow close together here. Their branches chafe one another in the breeze, making a squeaking noise that may have you wondering if an unusual bird is in the treetops.

At 0.2 mile, the trail moves out of the trees. Lemonadeberry, toyon, prickly pear cactus, bladderpod, and scrub oak line the path. Creeping wild cucumber vines twine over the bushes like a lacy veil. At about 0.4 mile, cross the Santa Helena side trail and continue. Mature pine trees spot the land as the trail gradually climbs. The lagoon soon comes into view on the right, about 50 yards from the path. There are always ducks here, paddling about in pairs. You might also see egrets, herons, and a variety of other birds— 295 species have been spotted here at San Elijo Lagoon.

As you continue, sweeping views of the lagoon alternate with areas where thick toyon, sumac, and scrub oak rim the trail. White and black sage grow here, releasing a refreshing scent. The red and yellow of California fuchsia and fiddleweed provide bright splotches of color.

At about 0.7 mile, a side trail loops off to the right. Follow it across a level plain that moves closer to the water. The path comes to an overlook point with a bench, then heads south and reconnects with the main trail. Go right, continuing west on the main trail. Ice plant grows in the soft sand that slows you down here.

At 1.5 miles, the trail bears right. Head around the chainlink pass-through for access to the concrete levee. Sometimes the levee is dry, and at other times (seasonally) the water trickles over the cement. Bird tracks of varying shapes and sizes form interesting patterns on the cement. Ducks paddle in and out of the marsh alongside the levee as herons and egrets wade and feed in the shallows.

The levee trail ends after 0.3 mile, where it reaches Manchester Avenue. Double back to the pass-through and continue. Pass the point where you turned right to reach the

San Elijo Lagoon: La Orilla to Rios Avenue

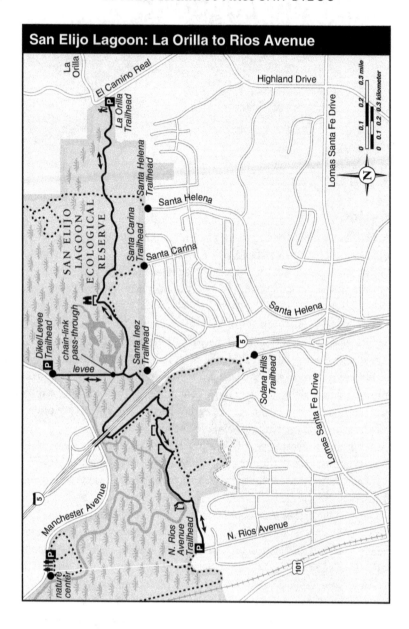

levee. Continue southwest a short distance and bear right where the trail makes a U-turn; then walk parallel to I-5 on the left for 0.25 mile or so.

At the interstate overpass, follow a narrow trail that leads under the freeway to emerge on the west side of I-5, where you'll find a high trail and a low trail. Both trails head south, paralleling the freeway for about 0.2 mile. Runners seem to favor the high trail, which is separated from the low trail by a sandbar that cushions the sound of highway traffic. If you choose the low one, notice the millions of shells filling the sand, which

LENGTH & CONFIGURATION 6.7-mile out-and-back	WHEELCHAIR-ACCESSIBLE? No, due to muddy areas and soft sand. The paved Nature Center Loop (not profiled here) is officially accessible.
DIFFICULTY Easy	
SCENERY Birds, coastal sage scrub, lagoon waters	**FACILITIES** None
EXPOSURE Sunny	**INFO** 760-436-3944, **sanelijo.org**
TRAFFIC Moderate–heavy	**SPECIAL COMMENTS** This is an ecological preserve. Leashed dogs are allowed, but bikes are not. The **San Elijo Lagoon Nature Center** (2710 Manchester Dr.; 760-634-3026), open daily, 9 a.m.–5 p.m., makes for a nice side trip.
TRAIL SURFACE Packed and soft sand	
HIKING TIME 2.5–3 hours	
ACCESS Free	
MAPS Available online at website at right	

has piled high on the left as the water has filled the trail and receded. Pickleweed grows along this stretch, which heads west through eucalyptus and willow forest. At 2.7 miles from the trailhead, you'll reach a wooden bench that faces the bird-filled marsh.

From here, the trail bends west. You'll find another bench just ahead. Continue west for another 1 mile, where the trail forks right to continue along the lagoon edge. This segment is called the Gemma Parks Interpretive Trail. You'll find more benches facing the lagoon along this stretch. Marsh plants grow low, making for good bird-watching. The Gemma Parks Interpretive Trail soon forms a junction the main route again. Turning right takes you another 0.2 mile to Rios Avenue. Some hikers choose to begin the hike at the Rios Avenue trailhead, taking the trail from the opposite end.

Nearby Activities

When visiting the levee in summer, you may notice growing fields across Manchester Avenue. A strawberry stand there sells the sweet, juicy produce.

GPS INFORMATION AND DIRECTIONS

N33° 0.588' W117° 14.386'

Take I-5 to the Lomas Santa Fe Road exit. Head east about 1 mile to Highland Road, then turn left. After about 0.5 mile, turn left on El Camino Real. Drive 0.5 mile; the trail entrance is on the left. Park in the dirt area adjacent to El Camino Real.

9 Tijuana Estuary Trail

Birds explode in flight.

In Brief

A bird-watcher's delight, the Tijuana River National Estuarine Research Reserve is a biological preserve within the city of Imperial Beach. Flat paths make the reserve a walker's haven for nearby homeowners and nature lovers, who come for rare glimpses of endangered year-round residents and the migrating shorebirds that winter here.

Description

Although San Diego is well known for its beautiful beaches, the estuary's 2,500 acres of intact coastal wetlands prove that there's more to the city's coastline than just surf and sun.

From the visitor center, head east on the sandy path past the entrance for the North McCoy Trail, which is a short, dead end overlooking a tidal channel. Continue southeast toward the opening to Grove Avenue. If you're lucky, you'll glimpse a great blue heron. My family has often seen one or more of them standing in the field just south of the path. When startled, the bird spreads its blue-gray wings to an impressive 6 feet and takes off in a slow motion lift. It will land again several yards away, as if wanting to stay safe yet close enough to watch visitors pass.

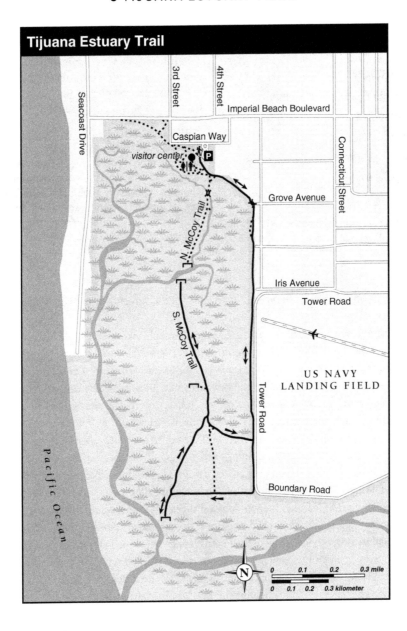

A wooden footbridge traverses the bend at Grove Avenue, then settles onto the dirt start of the southbound River Mouth Loop. You'll pass the backyards of several tract homes. At 0.75 mile, Iris Avenue meets the trail, marking another entrance point for visitors. A shaded bench provides a brief resting spot here where the US Navy Landing Field fence starts and the trail widens, changing to a fine-gravel surface. Mallards sometimes gather on the other side of the Navy's chainlink fence, paddling in water that gathers in a shallow ditch at the edge of the landing field. Maybe the water looks better than the reedy

LENGTH & CONFIGURATION
3.5-mile out-and-back

DIFFICULTY Easy

SCENERY Marsh plants, birds

EXPOSURE Sunny

TRAFFIC Moderate

TRAIL SURFACE Mostly fine gravel

HIKING TIME 2 hours

ACCESS Free

MAPS Free trail map at the visitor center and the website below

WHEELCHAIR-ACCESSIBLE? Generally

FACILITIES A visitor center with store, museum, and restrooms is open Wednesday–Sunday, 10 a.m.–5 p.m.

INFO 619-575-3613, **trnerr.org**

SPECIAL COMMENTS With identification, you can borrow binoculars at the visitor center. If you decide to venture onto trails other than this one, be aware that the signage may not match what you see on a map from the website or in the visitor center. As of this writing, new sign names aren't reflected on those.

pond that's on this side of the fence—or maybe it's the "greener" government grass that attracts them!

Continue another 0.75 mile along the fence to reach a westbound side trail that leads off to meet the South McCoy Trail. Don't turn here, though—instead, keep following the chainlink fence south until cut logs force a right (westward) turn. On sunny days, the Pacific Ocean may be visible across the vast fields of California buckwheat and lemonade-berry bushes, but on overcast weekends, you'll hear the roaring waves for half an hour before they finally come into view at this southeastern tip of the River Mouth Loop. If you're here on a weekday, the sudden view of the ocean may surprise you, the sound of it having been drowned out by the comings and goings of helicopters at the landing field.

Head west, where even on gray fall days the sunlight glints off the waters of the tidal channel and the calls of birds such as the Western grebe fill the air. Several yards of southwest-stretching trail lead to a bench—a good place to sit and watch the birds along the shore. Snowy egrets with their bright-yellow legs wade slowly along, jabbing their bills in to the shallow water to feed. The light-footed clapper rail, which is endangered in California, strolls in pairs and trios along the shore that is riddled with holes from the birds' probing bills. More than 370 species of birds have been seen here, including the least tern and brown pelican, which are endangered. Books sold at the visitor center offer more-in-depth facts about the wildlife mentioned in the center's free brochures.

From this southernmost tip of the trail, the Bull Ring, just a couple of miles south in Mexico, is visible, from this distance resembling a great stone monolith rising from the earth. The reserve is the terminus for the 1,734-square-mile Tijuana River watershed, only one-third of which lies in the United States. The other two-thirds are in Mexico, including most of Tijuana and all of Tecate. Managed cooperatively with the US Fish and Wildlife Service and the California Department of Parks and Recreation, the Tijuana Estuary is located entirely on US land.

After a breather, take the trail behind the bench; it leads north to the South McCoy Trail, which continues north about a mile past marshes and wetland areas. A bench placed halfway along the trail faces west to overlook the wetland, where a variety of waterfowl sounds like a chorus of kazoos. On the east side of the trail, wetland birds such as the snowy plover, black-bellied plover, and killdeer gather en masse. Binoculars, brought from home or borrowed at the visitor center, help you catch sight of all of them— there are sometimes thousands. Their coloration blends with the marsh, making them difficult to spot at first glance.

The smaller tern varieties are prey to the American peregrine and other large falcons that populate the area. The terns sometimes put on an amazing flight show: Looking like a fireworks display, large groups of the birds take off from the marshy feeding grounds. They school like fish, and, flying with their darker topsides to the sky, tilt and change direction to display their snowy undersides. The erratic movement serves to confuse predators. The mass of terns flies away and then back, dipping close to the path, the whirring of so many wings in flight a deafening roar.

Retrace your steps and turn left (east) onto the first side trail you come to. This takes you back to the chainlink fence, where you'll pass the ducks again and make your way north to the footbridge, then west back to the visitor center, where permanent exhibits educate guests about estuarine ecology.

Nearby Activities

If you enjoy fishing, try tossing a line over the **Imperial Beach Fishing Pier.** No fishing license is required here. Or catch a good meal at the **Tin Fish** (910 Seacoast Dr.), at the end of the pier. You might also get an exciting view of dolphins romping in the Pacific Ocean while you eat. Open daily; 619-628-8414, **thetinfishrestaurants.com.**

GPS INFORMATION AND DIRECTIONS

N32° 34.488' W117° 7.554'

Take I-5 south to Coronado Avenue in Imperial Beach and head west; Coronado Avenue becomes Imperial Beach Boulevard at the 13th Street intersection. About 2.5 miles from the interstate, turn left on Third Street, which will curve onto Caspian Way; park at the visitor center, on the right.

GUY FLEMING TRAIL

Torrey pines frame vast Pacific Ocean views.

In Brief

No hurrying allowed—fill your senses with the serenity of nature's power and beauty during an easy stroll along the Guy Fleming Trail. Puffy, gilt-edged clouds drift overhead, and a refreshing breeze guides you along the meandering path to ocean overlooks. Bring binoculars—you can often spot dolphins in the waters below. Also watch for migrating whales during the winter viewing season, or just let your mind wander as you sit on one of the many benches, letting the roar of the ocean lull you.

Description

Enter the Guy Fleming Trail just as Torrey Pines Park Road curves sharply west. You'll find a kiosk with information just a few short steps into the trail, and the loop opens to the

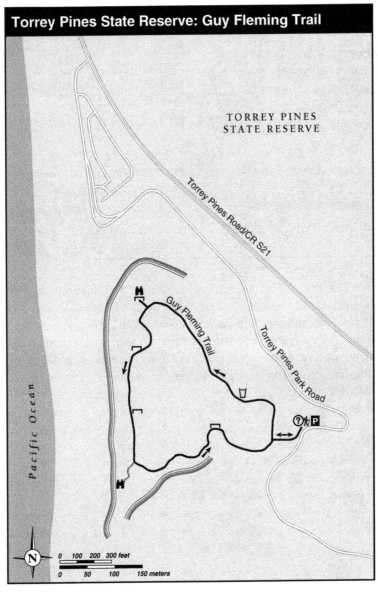

Torrey Pines State Reserve: Guy Fleming Trail

TORREY PINES
STATE RESERVE

Torrey Pines Road/CR S21

Guy Fleming Trail

Torrey Pines Park Road

Pacific Ocean

0   100   200   300 feet
0   50   100   150 meters

N

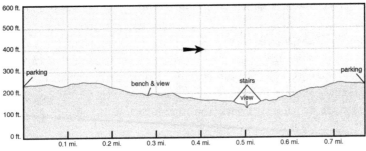

LENGTH & CONFIGURATION
0.7-mile balloon-and-string

DIFFICULTY Easy (see note at end of Description for extension)

SCENERY Sweeping ocean views, wildlife, intricate cliff erosion

EXPOSURE Mostly sunny, some shade

TRAFFIC Moderate–heavy

TRAIL SURFACE Puddles after rain, well-maintained sandy soil paths

HIKING TIME 30 minutes–1 hour

ACCESS Day-use fee to park ($10–$12 Monday–Thursday, $12–$15 Friday–Sunday

and holidays (low–high season); additional fees for buses, and on major holidays. Open daily, 7:15 a.m.–sunset (visitor center opens at 9 a.m.)

MAPS Download from the website below or obtain at the park.

WHEELCHAIR-ACCESSIBLE? No, due to uneven path, sandy soil, and steep drops. Visit the website for accessible trails.

FACILITIES Restrooms in the upper parking lot

INFO 858-755-2063, **torreypine.org**

SPECIAL COMMENTS See longer note on facing page.

right or left. Either way is fun. Go right to follow along with this description. The trail moves northwest at a very slight climb, rounding the bend into shade, where northeast views offer glimpses through the pines of Los Peñasquitos Lagoon far below. The water stretches out amid the marshy land like dark, abstractly shaped mirrors reflecting the sky. On the right, you'll catch glimpses of La Jolla, etched against the sky and sea.

As the path curves to the west, you may need to duck in places where twisty limbs of mature Torrey pines hang over the trail. At 0.25 mile, the path moves out of the forest, and an unobstructed view of the Pacific Ocean rolls out before you: Glassy, foamy-green, gray, or blue, the water's ever-changing (yet always beautiful) nature makes frequent visits to this easy path a must. Step down to the northernmost overlook point, where a bench perches you cliffside for a gull's-eye view.

From here, surf and sea mesmerize. Drink in the clear salt air, ponder the ocean's ominous power, or reflect on the softest whisper of a gentle breeze against your cheek. Benches rest at regular intervals along this western ridge that leads to another lookout point accessed via wooden steps to the right of the trail. You'll have come about 0.5 mile at this point, so reward yourself with a long pause . . . the ocean calls, its roaring rhythm like calming white noise.

North and south, the shore stretches for miles. Beachcombers move along like ants on the sand far below, and the waves decorate the shore with the lacy foam they leave in their wake.

Eventually, perhaps as the fiery sphere of the sun dips beyond the horizon, head back up the stairs and to the right on the trail, moving east, away from the coast. You may see quail, curious squirrels, or perhaps a raven or two. Regardless, you're sure to wear a relaxed and ready smile—returned by passersby as you continue along the path, closing the loop back at the kiosk and returning the way you came on this magical little trip above the sea.

A bee dives into its cactus-bloom pollen pool.

Note: No food or pets are allowed in this serene, coastal clifftop setting above the ocean. Trails are reserved for foot traffic only. Arrive in time to see the sun slipping low to the horizon, painting the sky brilliant orange, dusky purple, or flamingo pink. To extend this easy hike, you may opt to park in free stalls along the beach (as crowds permit) or in the lower lot behind the ranger booth, then walk about 1 uphill mile to the Guy Fleming trailhead.

GPS INFORMATION AND DIRECTIONS

N32° 55.388' 117° 15.325'

From I-5, exit on Carmel Valley Road and drive west about 1.5 miles till you reach the Coast Highway (US 101). Turn left and proceed along the beach for about 1 mile. The park entrance is on your right, just before the highway begins to climb the Torrey Pines grade. Parking choices include a small roadside area just outside the Guy Fleming Loop, a larger upper lot near the visitor center, the lower lot, and free parking along the beach (which adds to your hike; see note above).

THE MOUNTAINS

A red-shouldered hawk in its treetop perch

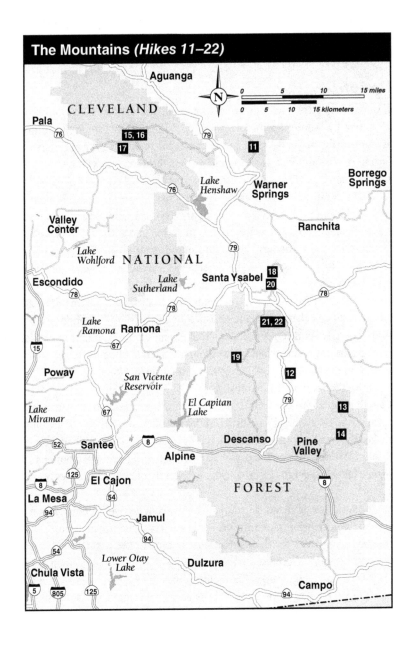

11 Agua Caliente Creek Trail

In Brief

Around the world in 80,000 steps? Not quite, but the environment ranges from arid to oasis as it travels through dry, sun-drenched country into shady woods along and across the creek—demonstrating the diversity of San Diego's land in one hike.

Description

The trail starts on a rutted, rocky dirt road past an old gate, where the sky is dotted with gliders from nearby Warner Springs Airport. Head up a gradual slope that glitters with mica fragments. After about 0.5 mile, look for a PACIFIC CREST TRAIL marker on the right. Turn here—it's almost a U-turn—and move southeast; you will begin to descend after a short distance. A view of Lake Henshaw sparkles in the distance—although California's drought conditions have diminished its glory in recent years. Rippling winds cross the vast silence of this desolate area. On hot days, the dappled shade of lemonade-berry and other small trees is a welcome gift. In spring and summer, Indian paintbrush blooms in clusters—the splotches like dollops of red paint on an artist's canvas. Mojave yucca also grows along this stretch. The blooms hang in bunches like jingling bells—but without the merry tinkle.

About 1 mile from the trailhead, you'll enter a zigzagging section that descends to an offshoot trail leading back to Lost Valley Road. Pass this offshoot to continue on a meandering, but generally southward, trail. At about 2.5 miles you'll come to oak shade and likely hear the gurgling creek, which soon comes into view. Although our recent dry years can mean that in the summer, you'll only find a tiny trickle. Go in the pleasant temperatures of spring, when water is more reliable.

Follow the trail above the creek, taking any of the small side trails down to present water if you wish. Take a break and listen to the babbling serenade—the calming atmosphere makes the relationship between the words *serenity* and *serenade* apparent.

At about 3.2 miles, the creek crosses the trail; plenty of flat-topped boulders make it fairly easy for hikers to get to the other side. Be careful, of course; the wet rocks can be slippery.

Three hundred yards ahead, a group of craggy, lichen-covered boulders on the left mark another creek crossing. Continue 0.25 mile and cross the stream again.

As on any hike, watch for snakes, particularly around the water and in springtime. You may notice small, crisscrossed tracks made by snakes on the earthen bars in the stream, or spot a hatchling or adult skimming across the water. If you sit still for a few moments you may hear an amphibious chorus among the chatter of birds, the rustle of leaves in the breeze, and the trickling of water.

Continue in the shade of the oak trees that grow close to the creek, walk through the open meadow, bear right, and continue for another 0.2 mile, then cross the creek again.

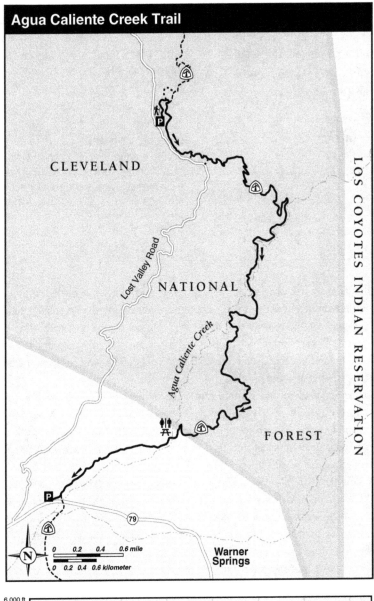

Agua Caliente Creek Trail

CLEVELAND

NATIONAL

FOREST

LOS COYOTES INDIAN RESERVATION

Lost Valley Road

Agua Caliente Creek

79

Warner
Springs

0   0.2   0.4   0.6 mile
0   0.2   0.4   0.6 kilometer

N

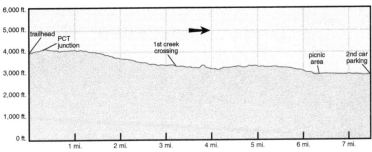

trailhead
PCT
junction
1st creek
crossing
picnic
area
2nd car
parking

6,000 ft.
5,000 ft.
4,000 ft.
3,000 ft.
2,000 ft.
1,000 ft.
0 ft.

1 mi.   2 mi.   3 mi.   4 mi.   5 mi.   6 mi.   7 mi.

LENGTH & CONFIGURATION 7.5-mile point-to-point with shuttle	**WHEELCHAIR-ACCESSIBLE?** No, due to creek crossings and length
DIFFICULTY Strenuous (for length)	**FACILITIES** Toilets are located 2.7 miles up Lost Valley Road and also near the end of the trail.
SCENERY Trees, creek, wildlife	
EXPOSURE Sunny and shady	**INFO** 619-445-6235, **www.fs.usda.gov /cleveland**
TRAFFIC Moderate	
TRAIL SURFACE Sandy soil, creek crossings	**SPECIAL COMMENTS** This is a long hike to attempt as an out-and-back, so I recommend it as a one-way trek, leaving a car parked at each end (see Directions). Although hikers might get their feet damp during particularly wet years, most often the rocks provide easy (dry) crossings.
HIKING TIME 4.5 hours	
ACCESS Free; open daily, sunrise–sunset	
MAPS Available at the Descanso Ranger District office (see Info, right); USGS *Hot Springs Mountain* and *Warner Springs*	

The trail cuts away from the stream, climbing then leveling as it heads east on a well-graded and now much wider route. The path becomes dry, with cholla and prickly pear among the spiny cactus varieties that thrive here. On hot days, even hardy hikers grow a bit weary along this section, which is open to the sun and devoid of oaks and the sound of water. You'll begin to descend at about 4.6 miles. Start to bear west to reach the creek for yet another crossing at about 6 miles.

Here, in the shade of oaks, you'll find picnic tables and a restroom. Look for tiny, funnel-shaped pits in the sandy soil—traps set by antlion larvae to catch passing insects that fall in and become trapped so the antlions can satisfy their voracious appetite for live food. As adults, the nocturnal antlions emerge from their cocoons with transparent, veined wings like a dragonfly's.

The now-flat path follows along the right bank of the creek for about a mile, and the sounds of traffic on CA 79 grow increasingly louder. Although the dappled shade provides camouflage for them, you may spot mule deer in the area—the noise from the highway can distract them from the sound of your approach. Visitors can get quite close before the beautiful animals turn tail and run.

The trail veers more westward for the last third of a mile and brings you—tuckered out—to the car you left alongside CA 79.

Nearby Activities

Consider taking a right onto CA 79 from Lost Valley Road. **Skysailing Inc.** (31930 CA 79) is less than a mile away, at the Warner Springs Airport. Sailplane (glider) rides are available for a fee, and no reservations are required on weekends. Open daily, 9 a.m.–5 p.m.; call 760-728-0404 or go to **skysailing.com** for more information.

GPS INFORMATION AND DIRECTIONS

Trailhead: **N33° 19.799' W116° 38.417'**

Shuttle parking: **33° 17.314' W116° 39.346'**

Take Interstate 15 North to the CA 76/Pala exit and turn right, heading east about 34 miles to CA 79, then turn left toward Warner Springs. Drive about 9 miles to Mile Marker 37 and park in the turnout on the right. In the second car, continue on CA 79 for a short distance (about 0.1 mile). Turn right onto Lost Valley Road at the INDIAN FLATS CAMPGROUND sign. Travel 4.6 miles on this winding, bumpy road, and park at the trailhead kiosk.

12 Cuyamaca Rancho State Park: STONEWALL PEAK TRAIL

In Brief

This easy, well-graded path leads to a panoramic view and many perching spots on sun-warmed rocks. This is the most popular hike in Cuyamaca Rancho State Park and was one of the first trails to reopen after the 2003 wildfires. Except for the last 0.2 mile to the final peak, the trail is safe and easy even for smaller children. But it's mostly couples you'll see here—out for a romantic fitness stroll through nature.

Description

This 4.4-mile hike starts with a wide, upward grade through oak forest. Autumn leaves cover the trailside ground like a thick fluffy golden blanket.

Heading up this steep section, which has the most rapid elevation gain of this hike, you'll come to the first viewpoint at about 0.15 mile—a good spot to catch your breath. Look out over the gaping valley where thick forest used to be. You can now see to the top of the mountain, the bald rock top a craggy, exposed target for the hike.

The trail leads around to the northeast and opens to a view of the sparkling, blue-gray waters of the 110-acre Lake Cuyamaca in the distance. Late in the day, the lake view can be particularly spectacular, with the shiny surface shifting to a beautiful dusky pink or purple that reflects the sunset. On this stretch of the trail, manzanita is regenerating nicely.

Woodpeckers call out like Woody the cartoon character. The resilient birds used to flutter nearly hidden among the towering incense cedar growing thickly along this part of the trail. Flying jerkily overhead, they now land in the oak trees. The craggy trees still show some effects of fire, but their recovery demonstrates nature's resiliency.

The trail begins to switchback here as it approaches the peak. Each zigzagged section gains elevation at a barely discernible rate, making this an easy stroll for inexperienced hikers or families. Split-rail fencing at various junctures encloses the path on this well-maintained trail. Some areas are a little rocky, making for a good lower-leg workout as you pick your way across the rounded, bowling ball–sized rocks.

Halfway to the top, a wall of granite comes into view, explaining the trail's name. Quartz and granite boulders jut out toward the path, providing a rich landscape to excite visitors' imaginations. You might see a smiling seal's face or a stony dinosaur nestled in the next corner of the switchback trail.

Nature has provided flat-rock seats for hikers to rest at various junctures, but most fit hikers won't need to stop for anything other than chatting or enjoying the view. If you do take a break, the absolute quiet will astound you. Voices are lost on the wind. Another

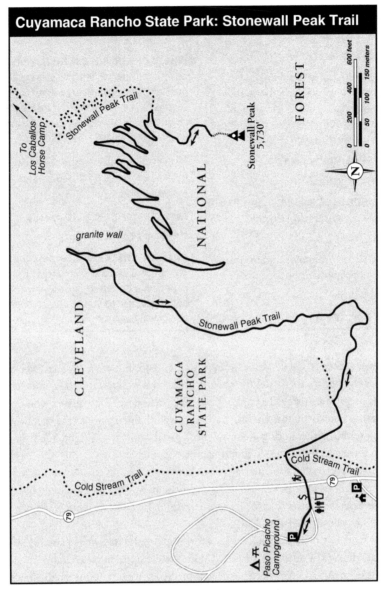

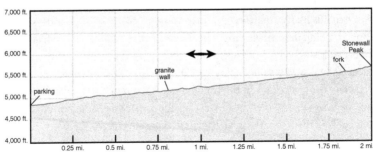

LENGTH & CONFIGURATION
4.4-mile out-and-back

DIFFICULTY Moderate

SCENERY Regrowth from fire devastation; interesting rock formations and panoramic views; spring and summer wildflowers; woodpeckers, crows, and other birds year-round

EXPOSURE Mostly sunny

TRAFFIC Moderate–heavy

TRAIL SURFACE Packed, sooty dirt with a couple of short, rocky stretches

HIKING TIME 1.5 hours

SEASON: Year-round, with rare closings in winter if snowfall is heavy

ACCESS $8 day-use fee

MAPS Available at ranger stations and at **tinyurl.com/cuyamacaranchosp;** USGS *Cuyamaca Peak*

WHEELCHAIR-ACCESSIBLE? Not officially, although wheelchair users could possibly negotiate the trail up to the last segment. The rocky spots and steepness could present a hassle, though. Restrooms in day-use area are accessible.

FACILITIES Toilets at the parking area in Paso Picacho and on the south side of the ranger station

INFO 760-765-0755, **parks.ca.gov /?page_id=667**

SPECIAL COMMENTS Because the 2003 firestorms cleared so many trees from the region, you can easily see Stonewall Peak in the distance as you approach on CA 79. Look for a bald outcropping of big rocks.

group of hikers may startle you as they round a bend, but even on busy weekends in spring when the flowers carpet the ground in purples, yellows, oranges, and reds, long stretches of golden silence are only occasionally broken by fellow hikers who disappear from earshot quickly on the winding trail. This well-defined path is easy to follow, delivering you to the marker noting Stonewall Peak just 0.2 mile to the right. You won't feel as if you've traveled 2 miles on this climbing hike designed for ease.

At the marker, it may be unclear which way to go—follow the trail to the right, then scale a few feet of rock before coming to solid footing. Where trees once blocked the edge, the expanse gapes off to the left, so be careful. If you have younger children along, consider stopping at the base of the peak.

The final section of the peak trail is a few steps up the rock ahead and slightly to the left around a bend in the stony surface. Human-made stone steps lead upward along the edge. A steel handrail offers security as you pick your way up to the small viewing platform at the top. The 5,730-foot elevation features a panoramic view. To the east, the Salton Sea extends like a vaporous blue stripe on the horizon. On clear days, you can see the ocean stretching into the distant west. Lake Cuyamaca looks more like a thimble of water than a well-stocked fishing spot from here.

Descend the way you came, enjoying views on the easy switchback route. Or, if you want, you can veer right, back at the trail marker, for a much rougher descent alongside Los Caballos horse camp, then head west on the California Riding and Hiking Trail to hike a total of 2.5 miles from the peak back to the parking lot.

Up the stone steps to the peak

GPS INFORMATION AND DIRECTIONS

N32° 57.582' W116° 34.743'

Take I-8 East past Alpine; take the CA 79 exit, turn left, and proceed north about 13 miles to the Paso Picacho campground, on the left—you'll pass the Green Valley campsite and the park headquarters before reaching Paso Picacho. Turn left and pay the day-use fee at the ranger station. Park in the lot on the right and proceed on foot across CA 79 to the trailhead, which is at the edge of the road, directly across from the ranger station. If you prefer free parking, you'll find designated roadside space 1 mile south of the trailhead.

13 Laguna Mountains:
PENNY PINES TRAIL

The desert valley stretches beyond the fragrant forest.

In Brief

Beginning along dry, rocky terrain with a desert view and creeping slowly toward forest, this route straddles two worlds, offering a unique perspective on the diverse nature of the San Diego area. Where else can you drive 50 miles from downtown and find lush mountain forest contrasting with arid desert?

Description

If you're at the north end of the parking lot, start out on the narrow trail that begins behind the signs explaining reforestation. The path treks through fragrant sage, often alive with the buzz of bees and the colorful flutter of butterflies. This trail bends to the right and joins the wider main trail. You can also access the Pacific Crest Trail directly from the south end of the parking area.

The northeasterly path leads through pine–black oak forest. Watch out for low branches with bony, fingerlike limbs that droop into the path. Pesky flies and bees are prevalent here, a nuisance on much of this hike.

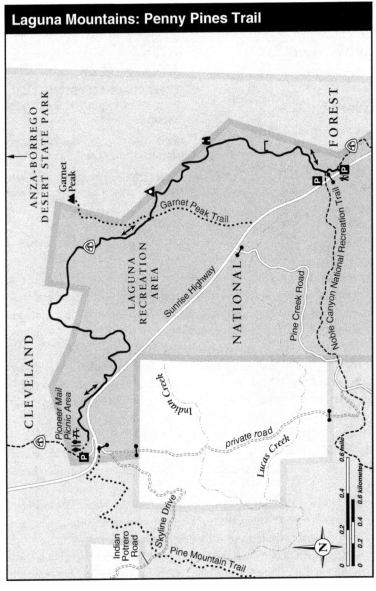

Laguna Mountains: Penny Pines Trail

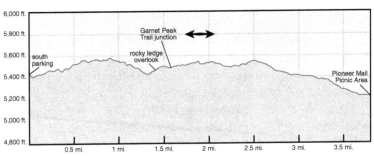

LENGTH & CONFIGURATION 7-mile out-and-back with loop option	Find out where to buy locally or online at **tinyurl.com/adventurepassvendors.**
DIFFICULTY Moderate	**MAPS** Online at **lmva.net/id3.html;** USGS *Monument Peak*
SCENERY View of desert valley, possible wildlife	
EXPOSURE Mostly sunny	**WHEELCHAIR-ACCESSIBLE?** No, due to rocks, length, and precarious edges in spots
TRAFFIC Light–moderate	
TRAIL SURFACE Terrain alternates among rocky, sandy, or leaf-littered	**INFO** 619-445-6235, **www.fs.usda.gov /cleveland, lmva.net**
HIKING TIME 5 hours	**FACILITIES** Public restrooms at the Pioneer Mail picnic area, 3.5 miles into the hike
ACCESS Parked vehicles must display a USDA Adventure Pass ($5/day, $30/year).	**SPECIAL COMMENTS** See longer note at end of Description.

After a short distance, the atmosphere abruptly changes from mountain forest to chaparral habitat that soon thins, becoming a rocky ridge trail with sparse vegetation and a breathtaking view of the Anza-Borrego Desert. Watch for the showy white blooms of the prickly poppy. From a distance, the crinkly white petals with bright-yellow centers look like fried eggs growing on spindly gray-green stems.

The trail bends left, heading generally northwest. Manzanita trees, devastated by recent fires, are regrowing here. You may notice warty red formations, like oblong berries, along the edges of some of the pale-green leaves. Insects lay their eggs inside the leaf structure, and then the berry-red galls form to encase the eggs.

At about 1 mile, the trail appears to dead-end at a rocky ledge overlooking the drab, brown desert valley. But look to the left and you'll notice that the route actually turns abruptly to the southwest. Take this fairly short switchback path that soon bends northwest again.

On this downward sloping section, tread carefully. Loose rocks can slide, causing you to fall. After another 0.25 mile, the trail heads upward again, cutting through two terrains: thick pine forest to the left and arid desert to the right.

At 1.5 miles, the trail intersects the Garnet Peak Trail, which ascends a few hundred feet on a right-hand path about 0.5 mile long. Watch for horned lizards as you move along this stretch where manzanita prevails. The rocks and sandy soil camouflage the rusty-brown lizards.

About 0.5 mile past the intersection, the trail bends west, moving gradually along a ridge, then leaving desert behind. The trail meanders south from here, then doubles back along the highway, through pine-and-oak forest. You'll notice burned areas here; the raging firestorm of October 2003 ripped through the area.

At 3.5 miles, the shaded tables of Pioneer Mail picnic area beckon you to rest. You might spot quail running in the bush along the edge of the picnic grounds.

If you're up for it, you can cross the Sunrise Highway and head 4.5 miles through meadows that ripple along like a ribbon and up into thick oak and manzanita forests, ending on the opposite side of the road back at the Penny Pines starting point. Otherwise, head back the way you came.

Note: This hike is unsuitable for young children. The trail sometimes travels along a sheer, rocky edge. Occasionally, winter snow closes the Sunset Highway (County Route S1) or makes tire chains necessary. For current conditions, call the California Highway Patrol at 858-637-3800 or check at **cad.chp.ca.gov.**

GPS INFORMATION AND DIRECTIONS
N32° 54.275' W116° 27.395'

From I-8, take the Sunset Highway exit, turn left (north), and drive for about 14 miles to the Penny Pines trailhead. Park on the right, where signs describe reforestation efforts and the "Penny Pines" moniker.

14 Laguna Mountains:
SUNSET TRAIL

A curious squirrel shares the log bench overlooking the Water in the Woods.

In Brief

This fairly short route to the water in the woods is only a portion of the Sunset Trail but provides a quick, quiet interlude with nature and all its stress-relieving qualities. Squirrels abound on this parklike hike without the pavement, joggers, or city commotion. Before you start, consider applying an insect repellent to combat biting flies.

Description

The narrow trail starts off heading north through meadowland and toward trees, climbing ever so gradually. The path is reserved for foot traffic, but you may notice (thankfully only a few) bicycle tire tracks. After a few steps, you'll come to a trail split; go left toward water in the woods.

At around 0.4 mile, the trail comes to a ridge overlooking distant golden meadows. Early mornings mean a view of the clouds settling over the valley. Later, the setting sun's rays spill orange and pink into the dusky sky. There's a rocky area along this section, but nothing difficult. Some large boulders provide resting spots for those who wish to pause and appreciate the views.

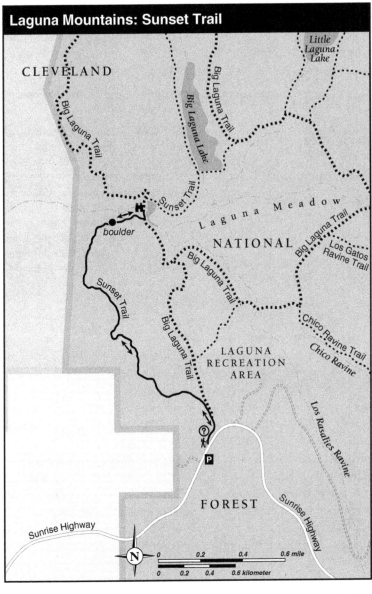

Laguna Mountains: Sunset Trail

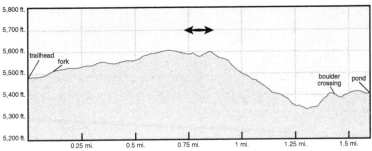

LENGTH & CONFIGURATION
3-mile out-and-back

DIFFICULTY Easy

SCENERY Forest, water, birds

EXPOSURE Filtered and full sun

TRAFFIC Moderate

TRAIL SURFACE Earthen path, some rocky areas

HIKING TIME 1.5 hours

ACCESS Parked vehicles must display a USDA Adventure Pass ($5/day, $30/year). Find out where to buy locally or online at **tinyurl.com/adventurepassvendors.**

MAPS Online at **lmva.net/id3.html;** USGS *Monument Peak* and *Mt. Laguna*

WHEELCHAIR-ACCESSIBLE? No, due to rocky patches and muddy and/or soft-dirt sections

FACILITIES None

INFO 619-445-6235, **www.fs.usda.gov /cleveland, lmva.net**

SPECIAL COMMENTS The thin air at nearly 6,000 feet can make this easy hike seem longer than the measured mileage. Occasionally, winter snow closes the Sunset Highway (County Route S1) or makes tire chains necessary. For current conditions, call the California Highway Patrol at 800-835-5247 (non-emergencies). You can also find current road information for the Laguna Mountain area at **tinyurl.com /lagunamtnroadconditions.**

Turning right takes you to a meadow dotted with trees, thick in places. Beware of biting flies wanting to make a meal of exposed skin. In the spring you'll see a variety of butterflies flitting from flower to flower—pale purple fleabane with its yellow center, bright-scarlet bugler and Indian paintbrush, sunny golden yarrow, and an array of others.

Disturbed by hikers' feet, a multitude of dull grasshoppers lying camouflaged in the dirt open their wings to reveal the vibrant orange. Fluttering away, they sound like shaking maracas.

At about 0.6 mile, the trail moves fairly steeply downhill, into black oak forest. The steep section is short and not so vertical that you must slow down. A more gradual descent stretches about a third of a mile farther. The trail then levels for a bit before climbing upward through thicker forest. The shade casts shadows, and rocks sticking up in the path might go unseen: watch your step as you pick your way through the woods.

When you come to an outcropping of rocks on the right and the path crosses the flat edge of a boulder, you'll know you've nearly reached the pond. The trail opens to a wide meadow, revealing a seasonal creek to the left just ahead. The pond teems with life. A variety of algae provides hiding places for aquatic bugs; birds come for a drink and dragonflies buzz about, then rest atop the scummy floating pads of algae.

If you want to go farther, an additional 0.5 mile or so leads to Big Laguna Lake (but thanks to drought, you can't count on the presence of water). Go left past the pond and head north to reach the lake. The Sunset Trail also continues to the north side of the lake, allowing you to connect to other trails for a long loop if you prefer (consult one of the maps listed in the box above).

Into the woods

Otherwise, sit on a log overlooking the pond. If you brought lunch, count on squirrels to pay a visit, hoping for a handout. Enjoy the reflection of the trees on the water's blue-green surface, breathe in the fresh scent of the mountain air, and relax before retracing your steps back to the highway and your car.

GPS INFORMATION AND DIRECTIONS
N32° 51.661' W116° 27.726'

From I-8, take the Sunset Highway exit, turn left (north), and drive 5.1 miles. You'll spot an observation deck and call box on the right; park on the shoulder (where there is plenty of room). The trailhead is across the street, a few hundred feet north.

15 Palomar Mountain:
FRY CREEK CAMPGROUND TRAIL

In Brief

Fry Creek Trail is a quick mountain hike that leaves the rat race behind. This trail offers a deep-in-the-woods feel even though it is easy and covers only a short distance.

Description

Being careful of traffic, cross CA S6 and enter the campground gate. Follow the narrow road about 0.1 mile to the fee station. A large display map depicts the campground and its trail, which begins directly in front of the parking space adjacent to the fee station.

The path begins as little more than an indentation in the leaves, but careful inspection reveals it heading to the right and uphill, toward S6. When the trail looks as if it bears even more to the right, you'll need to make a sharp left instead. Find the turn, which is easily missed if you're not watching for it, above some partially buried boulders. Spotting the wooden pole marker a few feet past the boulders assures you're in the right place. If you were to continue to the right, the trail leads back down to the campground road, coming out near the entrance off S6.

Having turned left, the trail bears northwest, with markers spaced every few tenths of a mile. At about 0.4 mile, the trail crosses the creek bed, which is dry and barely discernible from late summer into fall. A few steps past this, you'll come to a slatted wood bench, which makes a good spot from which to absorb the sounds of a woodpecker in the distance, intent on his work, or the gentle rush of wind through the tree leaves.

The trail undulates over hills and dales for a short distance along a ridge. In the afternoon, sunlight spills from the western sky, filtered through the tops of pine trees and splintered into rainbow prisms. The forest is thick along this section, holding moisture so that boulders are covered in fuzzy-green and rust-colored moss.

Bear right, past another marker, and come upon a second bench. The trail gets difficult to find here among the fallen leaves. A marker on a huge oak tree leads the way left to a campground, which is where we like to finish this hike. To do the entire trail instead (for a total of 1.5 miles), you'll need to locate the continuation of the loop trail, which is past the tree, looping up and around the campground then bearing left back down to an outlet near the lower restrooms.

For some odd reason, this relatively short and seemingly simple hike is disorienting—a compass often disagrees with what seems logical and apparent. Because of this, we choose to go left at the tree, making our way down the slope toward picnic tables, past camping sites, and onto the asphalt campground road. We then follow this downhill, marveling at the incense cedars' towering heights.

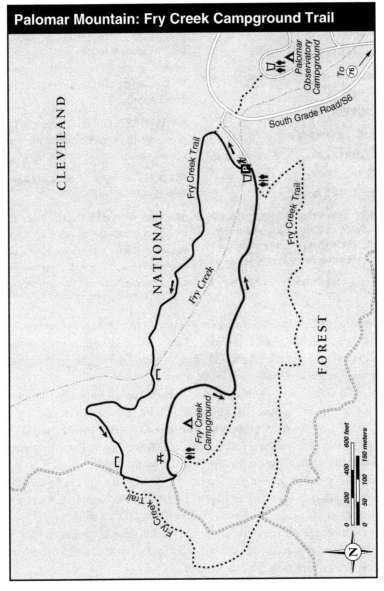

Palomar Mountain: Fry Creek Campground Trail

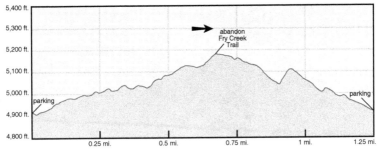

LENGTH & CONFIGURATION	**WHEELCHAIR-ACCESSIBLE?** Not as

LENGTH & CONFIGURATION
1.25-mile loop

DIFFICULTY Easy

SCENERY Cedar and oak forest, squirrels, and possibly deer

EXPOSURE Mostly shady

TRAFFIC Light–moderate

TRAIL SURFACE Loose, leaf-littered soil, asphalt

HIKING TIME 1 hour

ACCESS Parked vehicles must display a USDA Adventure Pass ($5/day, $30/year). Find out where to buy locally or online at **tinyurl.com/adventurepassvendors.**

MAPS At the trailhead; USGS *Boucher Hill*

WHEELCHAIR-ACCESSIBLE? Not as written, due to thick leaf litter and unclear trails in some areas. Wheelchair users could take the trail in reverse, traveling up the paved road portion only (see Description).

FACILITIES Public restrooms and picnic tables along the campground road are convenient.

INFO 760-788-0250, **www.fs.usda.gov /cleveland**

SPECIAL COMMENTS Despite its short length, this trail can be disorienting and sometimes difficult to find. Bring a compass and map, along with bug repellent—the small black flies have no mercy.

Along the road, poison ivy climbs smaller trees, turning them red, orange, and yellow, and looking like benign fall color from a distance. Close inspection reveals the bright splashes of this nasty plant, hiding its irritating oil within the proverbial sheep's clothing and demonstrating nature's lessons of wisdom.

Gray squirrels scuttle about in the dried leaves that carpet the ground adjacent to the road. A dried twig rolling down the asphalt sounds like a Native American rain stick or bamboo chimes. We discovered this by accident one day when a melodic sound followed us and we turned to investigate. Fallen twigs are plentiful here. Consider giving one a gentle nudge to start it rolling, musically, down the road.

Where the road levels, near public restrooms, look to the right to find the alternate longer loop trail's closing stretch ending in a steep descent here, too. A nearby picnic table offers a restful last few minutes before continuing the 0.1 mile back to your car. If you have the time, absorb the surroundings—the incense cedars with their sturdy reddish trunks standing sentry as they reach for the sky, and in autumn, the soothing *plip-plip* rhythm of falling acorns as they hit the ground.

Fall colors on the Fry Creek Trail

Nearby Activities

Mother's Kitchen restaurant, 2.5 miles back at the S6 turnoff (33120 Canfield Rd.), is a haven for hungry vegetarians. Closed Tuesday and Wednesday; 760-742-4233, **mothers kitchenpalomar.com.**

GPS INFORMATION AND DIRECTIONS

N33° 20.647' W116° 52.879'

Take I-15 to the CA 76 exit and head east (inland). Drive about 20.4 miles and note a road (marked SOUTH GRADE) forking northeast. Turn left onto this road and continue northeast for 6.5 miles to reach a T. Turn left onto S6 and drive about 2.5 miles to the Fry Creek Campground. Fry Creek is on the left, but you'll need to park in the small turnout on the right side of S6, across from the campground entrance. If you don't have an Adventure Pass, you can pay the day-use fee ($12) at the fee station, about 0.1 mile inside the park.

16 Palomar Mountain:
OBSERVATORY TRAIL

In Brief

If you're looking for woodland splendor and quietude, you'll get instant gratification here. Just a few steps from the trailhead, a dense oak-and-conifer forest envelops you.

Description

The narrow, well-defined trail moves northeast, gradually but steadily gaining elevation (about 900 feet in the first mile). I describe the difficulty level as moderate, mainly because the hike begins at nearly 4,500 feet above sea level and higher altitude, with its thinner air, makes physical activity more difficult. Plenty of benches are placed in shady resting spots along the path. You'll come to the first one just 0.3 mile into the outing.

In spring, you're likely to see lots of blooms—fleabane, goldenrod, and yellow monkeyflower, to name a few—in spots where dappled sunlight filters in through the stretching limbs of mature oaks and pines. Be wary of poison oak, which you'll likely encounter here wherever there's plentiful shade and ample moisture due to snowmelt. Stay on this trail and watch for straying branches of the plant, which sometimes encroaches on the path.

At just under 0.6 mile, an observation deck to the right of the trail overlooks lovely Mendenhall Valley. In summer, the golden meadow, dotted with small bodies of water and framed by pines, looks like the proverbial vacation postcard. In other seasons, new spring growth, fall's colors, or pure white snow makes the view a perfect greeting-card photo.

A few more steps forward bring you to a wooden plank bridge traversing a gorge that carries seasonal watershed. Manzanita grows more prevalently along this stretch, its deep-red bark contrasting with its pale, blue-green leaves. Forest shade is thicker here, too. Just 0.2 mile ahead, find another bench parked among the trees. Relish the cooler temperature here among the protective leaf cover. Some large boulders add interest. Lichen and moss decorating the large rocks bear witness to the random beauty of nature's patterns.

The trail descends along a shaded hillside. A massive seven-trunked oak stands to the left of the trail, which bends more due north at this point. Water runs in the ravine below on your right, a gurgling complement to the soothing lull of the breeze—or perhaps the unwelcome buzz of flying insects. As is the case in many mountain areas, flies and gnats can get troublesome during summer weather. A netted face cover may help.

The path begins to climb again, fresh pine scenting the air. In wetter months, you may find yourself slogging through snow, mud, or water. In drier months, you'll see evidence of moisture: rocks are stained white with water-borne minerals, and a few spiky rushes grow among the stones.

Palomar Mountain: Observatory Trail

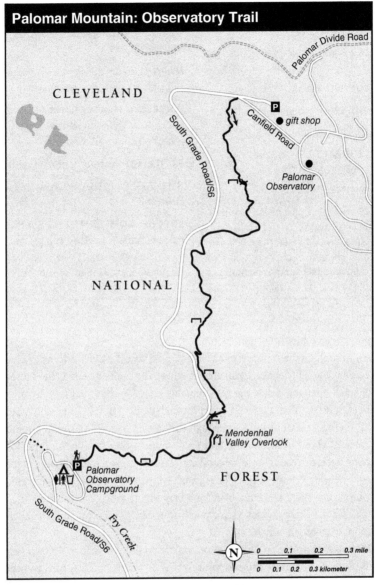

CLEVELAND

NATIONAL

FOREST

Palomar Divide Road

Canfield Road

● gift shop

● Palomar Observatory

South Grade Road/S6

Mendenhall Valley Overlook

Palomar Observatory Campground

South Grade Road/S6

Fry Creek

N

| 0 | 0.1 | 0.2 | 0.3 mile |

| 0 | 0.1 | 0.2 | 0.3 kilometer |

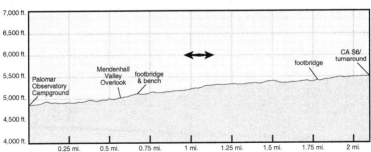

Palomar Observatory Campground

Mendenhall Valley Overlook

footbridge & bench

footbridge

CA S6/ turnaround

LENGTH & CONFIGURATION
3.8-mile out-and-back

SCENERY Pine–oak woodland, possible wildlife, valley views, observatory

DIFFICULTY Moderate

EXPOSURE Mostly dappled shade

TRAFFIC Light–moderate

TRAIL SURFACE Leaf-littered; some rocky areas

HIKING TIME 2 hours

ACCESS The trail is part of Cleveland National Forest, so you'll need a USDA Adventure Pass to park ($5/day, $30/year); find out where to buy locally or online at **tinyurl.com/adventurepassvendors.** A National Parks and Federal Recreational

Lands Annual Pass is also acceptable ($80; order online at **store.usgs.gov/pass**). Open May–November.

MAPS On trailhead kiosk; USGS *Boucher Hill* and *Palomar Observatory*

WHEELCHAIR-ACCESSIBLE? No, due to creek crossings on narrow footbridges, seasonally wet trail conditions

FACILITIES Restrooms near parking area

INFO 760-788-0250, **www.fs.usda.gov/cleveland**

SPECIAL COMMENTS Dress for the fickle mountain weather; bring plenty of water; and wear boots with good traction for possible snow, mud, or running water. Watch closely for rattlesnakes.

At just under 1 mile, the trail switches abruptly right (east), then back again. The path opens to sunlight for a short stretch, with CA S6 visible 6–700 yards away on the left. Come to a bench at a little more than a mile, where the shade begins again. Other than a couple of small hills and dales, the trail remains level for about 0.3 mile. A brief climb meanders east, then north, then east again through dense oak forest above CA S6. In late afternoon, the breezes draft up the through the trees, the rushing sound a reminder of nature's power. The trail dips again, and you'll notice the moon-white cap of Palomar Observatory peeking through the trees. Watch your step, as some fallen trees may have companions helping you up or perhaps teasing, "How was your trip?" Also be mindful of profuse poison oak along this stretch—which may trip up your comfort later.

A small plank bridge crosses a stream at just under 1.7 miles; then the trail gradually climbs again, to a shaded bench.

At 1.9 miles (per my GPS, 2.2 miles on the national-forest map at the trail's end), the path ends abruptly alongside the endpoint for CA S6. Here, at 5,500 feet, you can make your way through the parking lot and visit the observatory (see Nearby Activities, below). Or you can head back the way you came, moving quickly along on the now mostly down-hill path.

Patterns at your feet: Needles litter the rich forest floor.

Nearby Activities

Palomar Observatory, a pleasant diversion midhike, is open daily, 9 a.m.–3 p.m., until 4 p.m. when daylight-saving time is in effect. For more information, call 760-742-2119 or visit **astro.caltech.edu/palomar/homepage.html.**

GPS INFORMATION AND DIRECTIONS

N33° 20.586' W116° 52.650'

Take I-15 to the Highway 76 exit and head east (inland). Drive about 20.4 mile and note a road forking northeast off to the left (marked SOUTH GRADE). Go left onto this road and continue northeast for 6.5 miles where you'll come to a T. Turn left here, onto S6, and drive about 3.0 miles to the Palomar Observatory Campground entrance on the right. Turn in and follow the campground loop to a small turnout lot (signed) near Campsites 19 and 20.

---

17 Palomar Mountain:
OVERVIEW LOOP

Palomar Artesian Springs

In Brief

A variety of mountain landscapes on this pleasant loop include thick conifer forest, creek-side vegetation, and a pond. Opportunities to see wildlife are abundant—if you're quiet and look closely.

Description

From the parking area, you'll see an asphalt maintenance road winding northwest into the trees. Head up this road about 0.1 mile until you spot the Chimney Flats Trail marker, on the right. Turn into the dense shade of the forest, where the earthy smells of decaying leaves and fresh pines engulf you.

The trail leads down a gradual slope where fallen twigs snap and crackle under eager feet. Dry limbs intermingle with thriving greenery as dappled sunlight dances with shade like gracefully rendered strokes on a painter's canvas. Boulders set among the trees seem artfully arranged—clusters of large and small ones, with ferns growing up between them like tiny gardens within the bigger landscape.

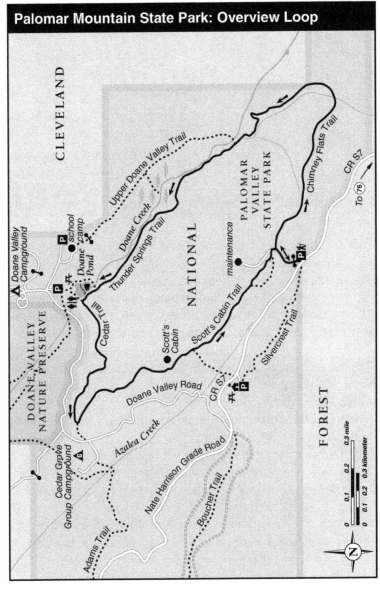

Palomar Mountain State Park: Overview Loop

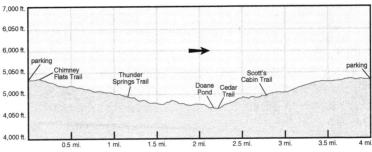

LENGTH & CONFIGURATION 4-mile loop	MAPS Download at **tinyurl.com/palomar mountainstatepark;** USGS *Boucher Hill*
DIFFICULTY Moderate	**WHEELCHAIR-ACCESSIBLE?** No, due to steep, rocky downhill section
SCENERY Forest, pond, wildlife	
EXPOSURE Mostly shady	**FACILITIES** None
TRAFFIC Moderate	**INFO** 760-742-3462, **parks.ca.gov/?page _id=637, palomarsp.org**
TRAIL SURFACE Leaf- and needle-littered soil	
HIKING TIME 2.5 hours	**SPECIAL COMMENTS** Be aware that the air is thin on this mile-high trail, increasing exertion levels. Check weather advisories, and be prepared for snow in winter.
ACCESS Free; open daily, sunrise–sunset	

After about 0.5 mile, the forest opens to a meadow of ferns. The trail then narrows to a singletrack path and continues southeast into even denser forest. Squirrels may skitter through drifts of fallen leaves alongside the path where towering, rough-barked trees play host to pale-green moss—growing on the north side, of course.

At 0.8 mile, the narrow trail becomes a steep downhill, as if nature has offered an invitation to run. Be aware that rocks cross the path in spots and smaller trees have sprung up in the path's center—if you're going fast, you may trip or smash into an unforgiving surface. The trail soon narrows to little more than the width of your foot for a short distance, slanting downhill and making slow the only way to go. The trail bears right, zigs and zags, then moves north and crosses seasonal Doane Creek. In summer, creamy blooms sprout in fragrant clusters from Western azalea bushes, their spicy, clovelike scent perfuming the air.

A short distance ahead, at 1.3 miles, the trail splits. Take the left path, Thunder Springs Trail, which heads northwest, gradually gaining elevation. The thin mountain air may make the slightly upward trek difficult. In the late afternoon, the canopy hides the sunlight.

At a little more than 1 mile from the start, the trail flattens, heading through an open meadow where the grass is golden in fall. As the meadow joins the forest, you'll cross a boggy area where mule deer like to hang out. If you're quiet, you may get a glimpse of them before they see and hear you and bound off—*boing! boing!*—into the woods.

The route briefly heads uphill again, perhaps with gnats often buzzing about, then somewhat steeply downhill again with the creek in view. Doane Pond soon enters your vision ahead. Often people stand with fishing poles or meander along the bank. Frogs escape into the water with a splash, then resurface in groups, seemingly as curious as those who stoop to look more closely at their buggy eyes staring back from the murky water. Just past the pond, a picnic table is a convenient place to rest or eat.

To the left of the pond, you'll spot the trail marked CEDAR TRAIL TO SCOTT'S CABIN. Take this steep trail uphill about 0.1 mile until it levels out in an area thick with ferns. The route remains level just long enough for you to catch your breath. Tread quietly and watch for deer that sometimes graze just a few feet from the path. Individually, the trees may look gnarled, bruised, and bent. But viewed from a distance, the forest looks flawless as a whole, as if every tree weathered the storms of nature—fire, wind, lightning—without a mark.

At 2.6 miles, nature's imperfect perfection opens to an area heavily charred by the 2007 wildfires that licked through the area. Oaks regenerate well though, as you'll see firsthand here. Amid this blazed section, some cedar trees looked completely untouched, demonstrating the chaotic nature of blazing fire, fed and tossed by wind.

At the top of the hill, you'll note Scott's Cabin Trail. Turn left, continuing steadily uphill about 0.25 mile until the trail again levels briefly. You may notice some small offshoot paths to the left, but stay on the main path that now heads southeast. Fallen twigs crunch underfoot. Before the 2007 fires, Scott's Cabin appeared as a few rough logs forming the base of the once-tall walls of an early homesteader's residence, but it's virtually unidentifiable now. What you will be able to see more easily now are adjacent residences saved by firefighters and previously hidden by thick forest.

Pass the side trail that marks the way to the ranger station, and continue toward Chimney Flats. The leveling route moves through a small meadow dotted with cedars before it splits. Either trail will take you back to the asphalt road you came in on. Follow it the short distance back to the parking area. Keep an eye out for wildlife. On a recent visit, a bobcat turned to look back at us as he slowly and confidently made his way across the road.

Nearby Activities

As you head back down CR 56, look on the right side of East Grade about 0.2 mile from the top: Spigots protrude from a stone wall. Visitors routinely stop to fill their bottles with the artesian water.

GPS INFORMATION AND DIRECTIONS

N33° 19.733' W116° 53.986'

Take I-15 to the Pala/CA 76 exit and turn right, heading east for about 21 miles. Go left on County Route S6 and drive along the steep, winding road for 6.7 miles. Turn left on East Grade, then make another immediate left—almost a U-turn, really—on County Route 57 (also marked as Palomar State Park Road). Drive 2.6 miles and park in the small asphalt lot on the right.

18 Santa Ysabel Open Space Preserve East:
KANAKA LOOP TRAIL

In Brief

Open to the public since the fall of 2006, these road-width trails through sweeping grasslands, rolling hills, and oak forest require little analysis. Bring along a friend for a leisurely stroll spent chatting or a brisk race-walk on a well-kept route covering 7 miles.

Description

Head past the kiosk and onto the trail, which begins moving easily through the rolling grassland hills typical of the Santa Ysabel area. You'll cross the seasonal stream at about 0.2 mile and continue along the westerly route. Watch for cattle from neighboring reservation lands, which roam the preserve. At 0.65 mile, an information panel describes how wildfires can affect the landscape. A patch of oaks provide shade just past the panel, and the creek runs on lower ground to the left of the trail. Wild turkeys are a common sight. About 50 made their way up the hillside on a recent visit. In spring, the males spread their tail feathers and strut noisily about, competing for the attention of the smaller females.

At about 1.5 miles, the trail bends left, leading to a shaded picnic bench, then crosses the stream again. From here the trail moves upward through scrub oaks to a second wildfire information panel at 1.75 miles. The route then bends left, moving steeply uphill for about 0.25 mile. At 2.15 miles, you'll come to a junction—head left, continuing onto the Kanaka Loop. The trail descends a little. Although trees are recovering, you'll still see evidence of the fires showing on the remaining area pines. The path climbs steadily for about 0.3 mile. Take your time and enjoy the quiet and wide-open spaces of this preserve that is so true to its name. The sky seems to go on forever above the expanse of rolling grasslands.

A long southerly stretch eventually bends west at about 3.3 miles, climbing for a short distance before descending in a long, gradual stretch that levels into a wide, grassy valley. Listen for the calls of birds and enjoy the whisper of rustling grass and breezes. At 4.3 miles, you'll cross the creek again then reach the junction of the Coast-to-Crest Trail and this loop. The Coast-to-Crest Trail extends about 2 miles, reaching the West Vista Loop Trail at the west end of the preserve; you might want to try that path another day. For now, pass through the junction, moving 0.33 mile northeast back to where you entered the loop from the main trail. On clear days, you can see the white cap of Palomar Observatory (see page 76) in the northern distance from here. Retrace your steps down the hill, past the shaded picnic bench and out of the preserve, for a total of 7 miles of easy strolling through this beautiful and peaceful addition to San Diego's public lands.

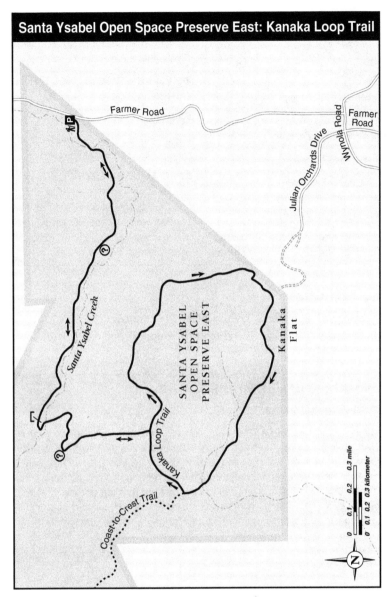

Santa Ysabel Open Space Preserve East: Kanaka Loop Trail

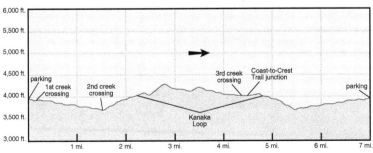

LENGTH & CONFIGURATION 7-mile balloon-and-string	**MAPS** View on kiosk near gate or download at **tinyurl.com/santaysabeleastmap,** USGS *Julian* and *Santa Ysabel*
DIFFICULTY Moderate due to length, easy otherwise	**WHEELCHAIR-ACCESSIBLE?** No, due to creek crossings
SCENERY Possible wildlife sightings, rolling hills, oak forest	**FACILITIES** None
EXPOSURE Sun and shade	**INFO** 760-765-4098 or 760-814-0208, **tinyurl.com/santaysabelpreserves**
TRAFFIC Moderate	
TRAIL SURFACE Packed soil, can be muddy after rain or snow	**SPECIAL COMMENTS** Leashed dogs are welcome on this wide multiuse trail that's fast becoming a popular equestrian spot. You're likely to encounter cattle grazing in the preserve, which has a total of 11 miles of trail.
HIKING TIME 2.5–3 hours	
ACCESS Free; open daily, 8 a.m.–5 p.m., until 7 p.m. during daylight-saving time	

Nearby Activities

Apple orchards thrive in Julian. Try the **Julian Pie Company** (2225 Main St.; 760-765-2449, **julianpie.com**) for a taste of local apples in America's quintessential dessert.

GPS INFORMATION AND DIRECTIONS

N33° 7.199' W116° 36.181'

Take I-8 East to the Japatul/CA 79 exit and turn left. Drive 2.5 miles and turn left onto CA 79 North toward Julian. Continue on CA 79 for about 21 miles, to where the road comes to a T. Turn left on Main Street and head through the town of Julian. Main Street becomes Farmer Street after passing through town (less than a mile). After 2.2 miles, turn right onto Wynola Road, travel 100 yards, and then turn left onto Farmer Road. Pass the VOLCAN MOUNTAIN WILDERNESS PRESERVE sign on your right and continue about 1 mile to the large staging area for Santa Ysabel Open Space Preserve, on the left.

19 Three Sisters Waterfalls Trail

In Brief

A trio of waterfalls known as the Three Sisters is the focal point of this hike that starts out dry and dusty.

Description

Head west past the gate on the fire road leading through chaparral that still shows some evidence of the fall 2003 firestorm that raged through San Diego's backcountry. After about 0.2 mile, the route passes through sparse oak forest not situated close enough to shade the wide, rutted path. The trail begins to narrow and move gradually downhill. In the spring, the ground is carpeted in color from a rainbow palette of wildflowers, attracting an almost equally wide range of butterflies and moths.

You may hear a scuttle and see a lizard scurrying into the brush. The horned lizard, sometimes called "horny toad," still inhabits this area, even though it has become less common in San Diego. The docile little lizard with horns looks like something out of the dinosaur era, but its sluggish nature has made it vulnerable. If you do spot one of these small horned reptiles, remember how few remain and what a rare privilege you've been given. Respect its beauty and value and let it be.

At close to 0.5 mile, you'll start to hear the waterfalls toward the south. At 0.6 mile, a stand of tall oaks provides shade. You'll see a trail on the left, leading southeast down the hill. Follow this downhill route for about 0.5 mile along the ravine that opens on your right. A few steep, slippery places make for generally slow passage until the trail levels and turns abruptly right.

Continuing, the hike takes on a different atmosphere, heading through oaks. You'll cross Sheep Camp Creek (when it's running) and move along the trail above it for a time. Be careful of poison oak along this stretch. The three-leafed plant grows in thick clumps that twine up over tree branches and form canopies that hang low over the trail. You'll need to pay attention overhead as well as where you step, being careful none of the extending vines brush against you on this narrow, shaded trail.

After walking about 0.2 more miles, the route heads uphill, sun alternating with shade. In the fall, the trees' changing colors set the land to crimson and gold. In the springtime, the bright-red flowers of Indian paintbrush stroke the air along the path, which leads uphill for a short distance, then opens into a small meadow.

From this open area, you can look down upon the cascading Three Sisters Waterfalls, or sit on small boulders if you need a rest. A narrow trail leads off to the left; follow this carefully downhill if you feel up to it. Some areas are gritty and rocky, with a 50- to 60-percent grade, causing even the most surefooted to slip, so go slowly.

Three Sisters Waterfalls Trail

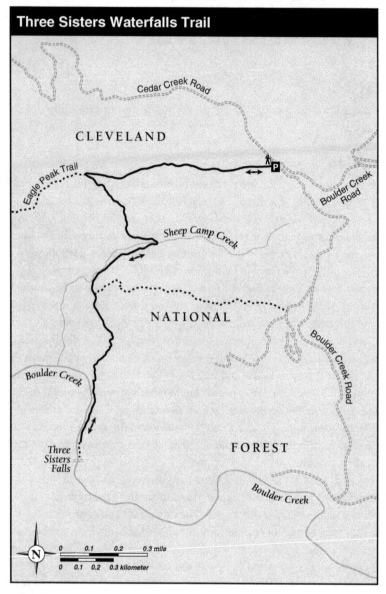

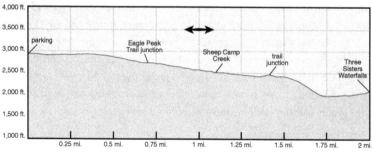

LENGTH & CONFIGURATION	WHEELCHAIR-ACCESSIBLE? No, due to
4-mile out-and-back	steep sections, seasonal creek crossings, and the near-vertical drop to the falls
DIFFICULTY Moderate; final optional section to falls is strenuous	**FACILITIES** None
SCENERY Waterfalls, oak trees, mountains, wildlife	**INFO** N/A
EXPOSURE Mostly sunny	**SPECIAL COMMENTS** This hike's remote location makes for a long drive, and with so many online meetup groups and outdoors forums, it's becoming a well-known spot. On the weekends, this means the narrow road is lined with parked cars— and the trails with people. The last section of the hike is a nearly vertical drop, though, so many turn around before reaching the actual waterfalls. Bring lots of water, especially in hot weather.
TRAFFIC Light	
TRAIL SURFACE Packed dirt; loose dirt and brush in last 0.4 mile	
HIKING TIME 3.5 hours	
ACCESS Free	
MAPS Cleveland National Forest recreation map; USGS *Tule Springs*	

After about 0.2 mile, the trail abruptly drops to a nearly vertical descent. This is where some hikers turn around, with even the promise of cool waterfalls in the distance not enough reward to climb precariously on the steep trail—and rightly so. This final, strenuous section isn't for everyone. If you choose to turn around here, you'll have logged in 3.2 miles when you return to the trailhead.

If you decide to continue, the short, perilous section will have even experienced, agile hikers grabbing at closely growing bushes for security. At the bottom, hikers can marvel at how much shorter the drop looks than it did from up above.

In the final stretch to the falls, masses of poison oak grow, so be careful what you touch. Make your way the final 0.2 mile along this route. Here at the Three Sisters Waterfalls, the sound of the pounding water can be deafening, silencing all worrisome thoughts and troubles that may have clung to you from the clamor of civilization you should have left back at your car.

If you climb up the slippery rocks around the waterfalls, step carefully so as not to fall. The middle fall is the most magnificent, with about 60 feet of water cascading into a long, curved pool.

Even if you choose not to make the final trek down to the falls, don't feel disappointed. The three falls are also impressive from the meadow up above.

Nearby Activities

If you time your travels to drive out of the area as the sun begins to set, keep your eyes peeled for deer. They're often seen grazing on the hillsides just a few feet from Boulder Creek Road. Wild turkeys are also common. Be sure to roll down the windows so you can hear their telltale *gobble-gobble.* Cows may also be crossing the road in small herds.

GPS INFORMATION AND DIRECTIONS

N32° 59.075' W116° 40.631'

Take CA 78 East past Ramona and Santa Ysabel, and turn right on Pine Hills Road. After about 1.5 miles, turn right onto Eagle Peak Road and follow it for 1.4 miles. The road bears left; after 0.3 mile, go right on Boulder Creek Road and travel south for about 8 miles (the pavement ends after 3 miles). You'll spot the trailhead where Cedar Creek Road intersects Boulder Creek Road from the west; park in the small turnout or alongside the narrow road.

20 Volcan Mountain Preserve Trail

In Brief

Leave your worries and city mentality in the car and enjoy the utter silence and beauty of Volcan Mountain.

Description

Nature author John Burroughs once said, "One has only to sit in the woods or fields, or by the shore of the river or lake, and nearly everything of interest will come round to him, the birds, the animals, the insects."

Nowhere more than at Volcan Mountain does this thought ring true. Walk quickly and you may see nothing more than tracks, but wait patiently and wildlife ventures into view.

From your car, walk up the gravel road (past homes with fruit trees) to the creative main gate, designed in part by renowned artist James Hubbell. After pausing to look at a colorful tile compass that adds to the artsy feel of this entrance, enter the preserve, where the stillness of nature wipes away the worries of the day. You'll come quickly to an information panel, added after the 2003 San Diego wildfires.

A dirt road heads north, climbing a semisteep grade about 0.3 mile before curving east. Mule deer tracks are common here. Raccoons and mountain lions are among the other animals in this habitat. Identifying tracks is easy: See the examples and information at the kiosk near the gate.

You'll come to another informative panel, then take the stone steps leading to the right up off the road and onto a side trail called the Five Oaks Trail. A short distance through the trees is a ridge path that zigzags along for 0.25 mile or so before entering thicker oak forest.

Continuing to switchback up through the trees, the path is steep in some areas, but only for short distances, offering plenty of opportunities to stop and rest or enjoy the scenery along the way. Mistletoe hangs from the branches of ancient Engelmann oaks, and sometimes the clumps are so thick you may think a new species of tree grows here—the Mistletoe Tree. Don't let this vascular parasite fool you, however: Mistletoe relies on host trees to live.

About 1 mile from the car, on an eastward bend in the path, the trees open to frame the distant mountains of the Anza-Borrego Desert. The hazy, purple-blue image is at first surprising—incongruent with the tree-filled mountain scenery through which you've come.

The oak forest thins a bit, and you'll find a stone bench at about 1.5 miles before the path levels and rejoins the dirt road on which the hike began. If you're interested in seeing

Volcan Mountain Preserve Trail

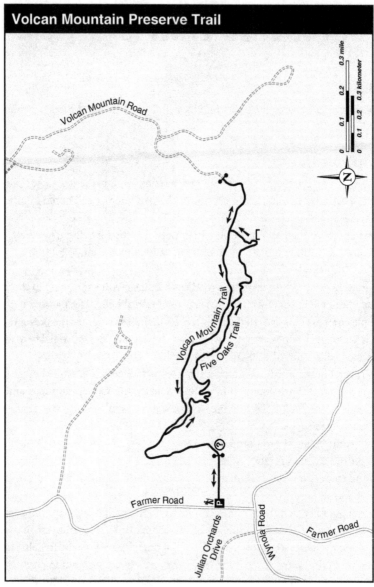

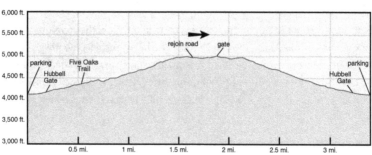

LENGTH & CONFIGURATION 3-mile out-and-back	**WHEELCHAIR-ACCESSIBLE?** No, due to stairs and steep sections
DIFFICULTY Moderate	**FACILITIES** None
SCENERY Possible wildlife sightings, oak forest	**INFO** 760-765-4098 or 760-814-0208, **tinyurl.com/volcanmountain**
EXPOSURE Sunny and shady	**SPECIAL COMMENTS** No dogs, horses, or bicycles are allowed in the preserve; this well-kept trail features undisturbed wildlife and vegetation. In the case of inclement weather (0.5 inch or more of snow or rain), the trail is closed. For more information or to find out about docent-led hikes that go farther into the preserve, visit **volcanmt.org.**
TRAFFIC Light–moderate	
TRAIL SURFACE Packed soil; can be muddy after rain or snow	
HIKING TIME 2 hours	
ACCESS Free; open daily, sunrise–sunset	
MAPS View on kiosk near gate or download at the website below; USGS *Julian*	

wildlife, this area is a good place to find a log to lean on while you wait quietly for "everything of interest" that Burroughs describes. That may be a deer stepping gingerly through the trees. Or perhaps you'll see a golden eagle soaring through the sky, its keen eyes searching for the movement of a tasty rodent—and probably well aware of your presence in its habitat.

Where the trail meets the dirt road, you could turn right and walk about 0.3 mile to a gate where the public trail ends. To return, you might retrace your steps down the narrow, zigzagging path back through the trees and rejoin the road where the trail first cut away. Or, for new scenery—which is what I usually choose!—follow the dirt road down the mountain, which is a quicker descent.

Nearby Activities

For authentic apple pie, antiques, and atmosphere, Julian's **Main Street** is the place to be. Here you'll find wet-your-whistle concoctions, fun food, and interesting shops to browse.

GPS INFORMATION AND DIRECTIONS

N33° 6.306' W116° 36.148'

Take I-8 East to the Japatul/CA 79 exit and turn left. Drive 2.5 miles and turn left onto CA 79 North, toward Julian. Continue on CA 79 for about 21 miles, where the road comes to a T. Turn left on Main Street and head through the town of Julian. Main Street becomes Farmer Street after passing through town (less than a mile). After 2.2 miles, turn right onto Wynola Road, travel 100 yards, then turn left onto Farmer Road. You'll notice the preserve sign on the right. Park here, on the road's shoulder.

21 William Heise County Park:

COMBINED TRAILS LOOP

At Glen's View

In Brief

The variety of landscape and the difficulty of this loop makes this hike a lot like a planned gym workout. You begin in a scenic forest with a moderate climb, wind your way through a rugged, strenuous portion with panoramic views, and end with an easy cool-down through lush foliage.

Description

Watch for burned areas along the route. Manzanita and other vegetation are amazing in their ability to vigorously regenerate.

From the parking stalls marked CANYON OAK, head down the hill (southwest). You will see a narrow asphalt road on the right, with signs indicating a youth area, group camping, and the Canyon Oak Trailhead. Turn right onto this asphalt path to reach the trailhead kiosk after about 400 yards.

Head left behind the kiosk, up onto the forest trail that continues north through oak forest for a short distance. The gradual uphill slope bends left, moving through thick manzanita forest, then gradually levels out.

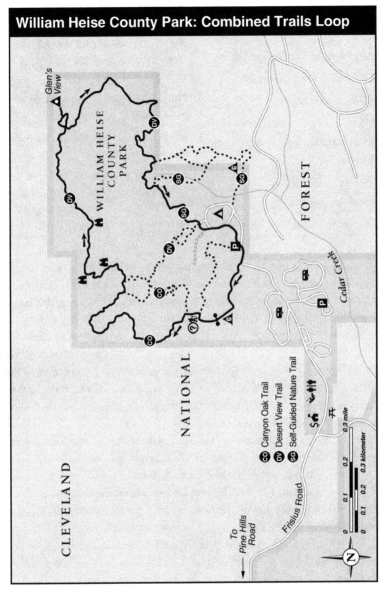

William Heise County Park: Combined Trails Loop

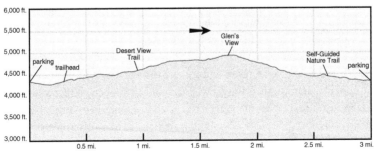

LENGTH & CONFIGURATION 3-mile loop	tinyurl.com/heisemap; USGS *Julian*
DIFFICULTY Moderately strenuous	**WHEELCHAIR-ACCESSIBLE?** No, due to rocky patches, seasonal muddy areas, and split logs in spots
SCENERY Native plants, trees, birds	
EXPOSURE Mostly sunny	**FACILITIES** Restrooms in the picnic area near cabins
TRAFFIC Moderate	
TRAIL SURFACE Earthen path, leaf litter, rocky areas	**INFO** 760-765-0650, tinyurl.com/william heisecountypark
HIKING TIME 2 hours	**SPECIAL COMMENTS** These trails can be disorienting, so bring a compass to verify that you're headed in the right direction. Leashed dogs allowed.
ACCESS $3 day-use fee	
MAPS Available from ranger and online at	

As you hike along, the wind rushes up through the mountains, making soft, rustling music in the leaves and grasses it sweeps to and fro. And what's that crackling sound? Is it raining? You might find yourself checking for drops, but the crackling, dripping sound you hear could be cicadas—if you're lucky to visit when the insects are in their active cycle. Look closely at the narrow branches of scrub oaks and manzanita trees for a lacy-winged insect with bulging eyes. The shy cicadas take three years to mature and emerge from their underground lives as nymphs, feeding on root juices. If you get close, the inch-long insects will creep behind a branch to hide. As you walk away, though, they relax again. And you'll likely hear their music start up again—the males use their abdominal noise-making organs to attract a mate.

In summer, watch for cupped mariposa lilies with their pink-speckled yellow petals along the edge of the trail. These give way to tufted, bright-green moss at about 0.35 mile, where the route, which becomes moister under a thick cover of trees, bears right and heads northeast and uphill. The trail then curves left (northwest) before straightening to lead due north. The forest opens to sky in places, and the trail alternates from wide and leaf-littered to narrow and rocky as it begins bending to the southeast.

At about 0.5 mile, the path turns abruptly right for a short distance, then southeast again, moving through hills and dales for another 0.2 mile or so. The connecting point for the Desert View Trail appears suddenly at the bottom of one of the dales. Turn left and begin moving steeply uphill. Split logs are placed at intervals of several feet. This wide, smooth area runs for several hundred feet before jagged rocks protrude into the path—some half-covered in pine needles, so watch your step.

Small turnouts serve as viewpoints along this stretch, with a view to the southeast of mountains that seem to go on forever. Butterflies are out in spring and summer. They flutter about in full color but are surprisingly well camouflaged when resting in a pile of dead leaves. Harvester ants are also common on this stretch of trail, as are darkling beetles, walking on skinny legs with their rear ends raised. Many refer to these black beetles as stinkbugs. On a recent visit we saw a pair mating—to the song of birds and the hum of bees, of course.

At more than 1 mile from your starting point, the trail bends slightly to the left now and again but generally bears right to a junction point at about 2 miles. A short trail to the left leads to the panoramic expanse seen at Glen's View. On clear days the Salton Sea gleams like a silver ribbon on the eastern desert horizon.

When your eyes have had their fill of Glen's View, go back to the junction point and head carefully downhill (south) along a rocky ridge. A canyon stretches below on the right. The trail eventually levels, curving west to make the loop and hook up with the Self-Guided Nature Trail. Turn right at the marker and head through the shady Nature Trail.

You'll come out near Campsite 91 with a clear head and a desire to return to this peaceful place. Head southwest on the narrow asphalt roads of the camping area and make your way back to the small lot where you left your car.

Nearby Activities

Consider stopping back in Julian at any of its quaint country shops or restaurants. On weekends, you can even catch a horse-drawn carriage for a fairy tale–style ride.

GPS INFORMATION AND DIRECTIONS

N33° 2.577' W116° 35.027'

Route One: Take I-8 East to CA 79 and travel north past Lake Cuyamaca (about 10 miles) into the town of Julian, then head west through the town to Pine Hills Road. Turn left and head south to Frisius Road. Turn left again and follow Frisius directly into Heise County Park.

Route Two: Take I-15 to the Poway Road exit and head inland. Poway Road ends at the CA 67 intersection. Turn left and drive (CA 67 becomes CA 78/79) to Pine Hills Road (about 26 miles). Turn right and head south to Frisius Road. Turn left and follow Frisius directly into Heise County Park.

After paying at the ranger booth, continue northwest on the main road to a small day-use parking section on the right, labeled CANYON OAK. The lot is adjacent to Campsite 63.

22 William Heise County Park:
KELLY DITCH TRAIL

In Brief

Well into spring, the thermometer may be dipping into the chilly 40s and 50s by day. Although Kelly Ditch is officially an equestrian and biking trail, you're likely to have it to yourself. Dress in layers to stay warm—or cool (temps in summer months sometimes reach the 90s). Make sure to bring plenty of water and snacks; the continuous climb on this high-elevation trail can be tiring.

Description

Even hardy hikers with 8 or more hours to spend on the trail will find an out-and-back trek taxing, so I recommend enjoying this hike one-way: Bring two vehicles, leaving one in the small area alongside Engineers Road or paying a small fee and parking at the bait station on Lake Cuyamaca; drive the second car to your starting point at William Heise County Park. Hiking the trail south–north is a little less strenuous than the north–south route, described here.

Walk south down the asphalt of the parking lot and head downhill on the rock-framed trail. Before the 2003 fires, Coulter pines shaded this strip, their heavy, 15-inch cones strewn about in carpets of pine needles. Now, only oaks that are slowly regenerating from the massive firestorms remain, providing spotty shade.

You'll come to a trail marker at about 0.3 mile. Continue southwest across a flat, barren section. Signs will soon indicate that you've entered mountain lion country. Be alert, but not necessarily worried. Although their prints are common, these elusive creatures are normally quite shy of humans (see page 13). The trail begins to climb through oak forest, then bends southeast. If you encounter other hikers, it will most likely be here, close to Heise Park, where campers wander off on short woodland treks.

At 0.7 mile, a trail sign indicates the way southeast. The trail narrows, moving gradually downhill now. The babbling of water may lure you forward as you near Cedar Creek, 1 mile from your start. Flattish rocks make for fairly easy stepping across the usually shallow creek bed—but why not stop for a moment, enjoying the atmosphere. Note the sparkle of dancing sunlight, the rushing or trickling sound of the water, and the glistening pattern on wet stones. Heading uphill on the other side, the ground may be slippery, particularly when winter snow has begun to melt. The slick mud makes one thankful (or perhaps wishful!) for sturdy, lug-soled boots.

After several yards on an easterly stretch, a series of switchbacks begins, leading along to the eventual 5,150-foot high point. Continue uphill for a physically taxing 1 mile. Fallen trees block the path in spots. Pause to rest, then climb over or under or go around

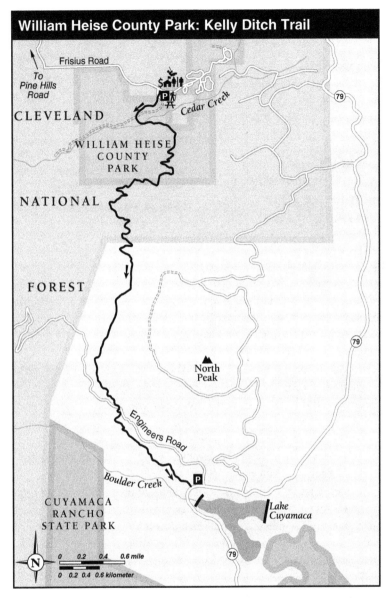

William Heise County Park: Kelly Ditch Trail

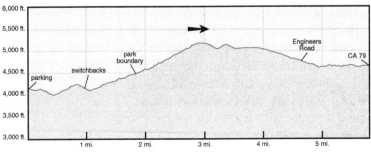

LENGTH & CONFIGURATION 5.8-mile point-to-point with shuttle	MAPS Partial map available at Heise County Park and online at **tinyurl.com /heisemap;** USGS *Cuyamaca Peak, Julian*
DIFFICULTY Strenuous	
SCENERY Oak forest recovering from 2003 fires, mountain views	**WHEELCHAIR-ACCESSIBLE?** No, due to rocky areas, strenuous uphills, and length
EXPOSURE Mostly open to sun	**FACILITIES** Restrooms at the park
TRAFFIC Very light	**INFO** 760-765-0650, **tinyurl.com/william heisecountypark.** A Junior Rangers brochure for kids is available at **tinyurl .com/heiseparkjuniorrangers.**
TRAIL SURFACE Muddy or snowy patches, leaf litter; some rocky areas	
HIKING TIME 4–4.5 hours	**SPECIAL COMMENTS** See longer note at beginning of Description.
ACCESS $3 day-use fee	

the rotting trunks. A fertile, earthy scent ripens the mountain air, broken only by the whir of breezes or the rhythmic tapping of woodpeckers.

Even in chilly weather, the steady climb provokes a sweat. Now, those clothing layers come in handy. Unzip jackets and overshirts to allow cool air to reach skin. Enjoy the scenery. On rocks and logs, moss sprouts up in a variety of colors and textures—grass green to pale silver, or edged in rusty red.

Where cedar forest was once so thick it blocked sunlight, the fires of 2003 allowed light to penetrate, fueling bushy growth that has spread over the ground. Deer have always frequented this area, but since the fires, their prints seem more prevalent on the trails themselves—perhaps because thick growth all around makes the clear paths an easier route for the animals. Be quiet and watchful, and you may see the graceful creatures. On a recent late-winter visit, a trio of does bounded off into the brush, pausing at a safe distance to look back at us with gentle eyes.

At 1.8 miles, a trail sign marks the point where William Heise County Park ends. Here, the trail is sometimes slightly more difficult to identify than the clear trek thus far. Reach the pinnacle at 2.7 miles, continuing southwest on leveler ground for a short distance, and then moving downhill into a serene meadow. In the summer, dry grasses grow bronzy yellow, making sense of California's nickname, "The Golden State." In May and June, wildflowers splash rainbow-hued patches across the land. A few small cedars remain here, lonely but beautiful reminders of the previously thick forest.

Continue on a wide-open path that slopes gradually upward again. Another trail marker stands at 3.1 miles. With less than half the mileage remaining, this is a sensible place to stop for a snack if you've packed food.

Back on the trail, the path heads gently downward. Woodpeckers continue as flighty companions. Their tireless tapping echoes and is perhaps punctuated by occasional calls to one another, as if curious about the human visitors.

At about 3.4 miles, you'll notice that the oak trees look healthier, less damaged by fire. More residences lie close to this area, and rightly so: Firefighters worked hard to save homes and their surroundings from the relentless 2003 blazes. Turn left here, traveling 0.2 mile southeast through shaded oak forest on rocky terrain, to Engineer's Road. You'll come out directly across from where the Kelly Ditch Trail picks up on the other side of narrow Engineer's Road.

The rocky downhill path moves through chaparral and scrub oak, leading around to a level, southeasterly ridge trail with a view all the way to the ocean in the distant west (on clear days). Spiny yucca and ornamental grasses grow close to the path, which soon enters the remnant of Kelly Ditch. According to local history, the ditch was constructed more than 100 years ago by men with hand tools as a means to divert mountain drain-off into Lake Cuyamaca.

The final, mostly flat mile is hiked through piled leaves in the spotty shade of oaks. The sound of cars on CA 79 grows louder, heralding your return to civilization. The trail emerges from the forest across the highway from the lake. Turn left and move 0.1 mile to your car on Engineers Road (or 0.4 mile to the bait-station parking).

Nearby Activities

Lake Cuyamaca Restaurant (15027 CA 79; 760-765-0700, **cuyamacarestaurant.com**), which serves burgers, sandwiches, steaks, and other homey fare, is a deliciously restorative stop after the hike.

GPS INFORMATION AND DIRECTIONS

Trailhead: **N33° 2.366' W116° 35.544'**

Shuttle parking: **N32° 59.508' W116° 35.166'**

Take I-8 East from San Diego (about 40 miles) to CA 79 and travel north for about 13 miles. The lake is on your right. Turn left onto Engineers Road, pull a U-turn, and park the first car alongside the road in a small strip of legal parking across from the firehouse. Or drive a little farther just past the lake and pay a small fee to park at the bait station (there are restrooms here, too). To reach the Heise County Park trailhead, drive the second car north on CA 79 to the town of Julian and drive west through town, then turn left on CA 78. Drive about 1 mile to Pine Hills Road and turn left, heading south to Frisius Road. Turn left again, and follow Frisius directly into Heise County Park. Leave your car in the lot on the right and pay at the ranger station on the left.

THE DESERT

A lazy jackrabbit resting in the sparse cactus shade.

23 Anza-Borrego Desert State Park: California Riding and Hiking Trail (p. 104)

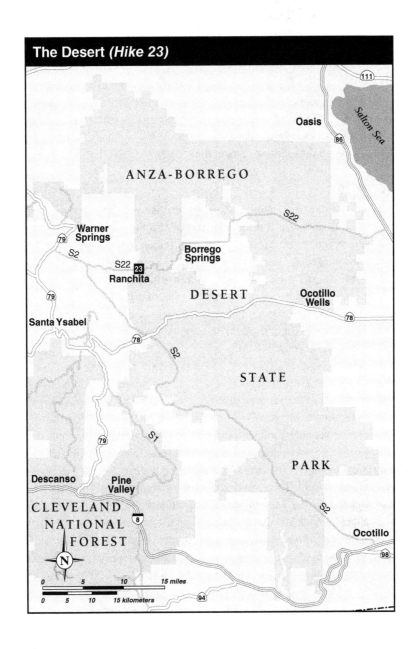

The Desert *(Hike 23)*

23 Anza-Borrego State Park:
CALIFORNIA RIDING AND HIKING TRAIL

In Brief

The vast desert swallows the sound of the human voice, making encounters with other hikers a surprise. Walking through this arid, yet remarkably vibrant, desert on singletrack corridors that aren't easily spotted from the distance, one has the sense of being little more than a dot on the infinite canvas of time.

Description

The California Riding and Hiking Trail moves northeast on flat, sandy soil through chaparral and desert plants such as the prevalent cholla cactus, which reaches with spiny arms toward (and sometimes onto) the trail—a good reason to wear long pants. Be careful of beavertail and hedgehog cactus, as well as pointy Mojave yucca.

In the springtime, the wildflowers are a much-anticipated treat. Peak bloom times vary from year to year. Call the state park's wildflower hotline (760-767-4684) for best viewing. March and April are safe bets for springtime flowers, and you'll find them carpeting the ground in a rainbow of color. Popcorn flower grows close to the ground; the thick groupings look like drifts of snow. Find tiny yellow desert sunflowers interspersed; the leafless stalks of chia rise several inches and are stacked with balls of tiny blue-violet blooms. Chuparosa, with long, leathery green leaves and a dripping spray of tubular lipstick-red flowers, often stands alone on the trail edges, as does the desert globemallow, which grows into a spreading bush with ruffled leaves and cupped, coral-colored flowers.

After about 0.3 mile, the trail dips and bends to the left, then climbs, bearing right again. The route continues, dipping then climbing, meandering slightly back and forth past an odd variety of boulder formations that make the huge rocks look like dinosaur eggs or stacked sandwich bread. There's even a truck-size "horned lizard" at about 1.5 miles from the trailhead. Rattlesnake weed grows in fluffy clumps, filling in the space around smaller boulders along the trail. You should watch for actual rattlesnakes, too, especially in spring when they are most active. Another snake common to the area is the long, thin whipsnake, which is brown or black with a creamy stripe running its length. If you do encounter this nonpoisonous snake, which hunts with its head held up to spot its prey (mostly lizards), you'll likely get little more than a glimpse as it disappears lickety-split into the brush to escape you. However, the shy whipsnake will be aggressive if cornered.

At about 1.7 miles, a great wall of rock nestles among a "city" of rocks. You'll encounter another rock city a short distance ahead. At about 2 miles, the route begins to descend

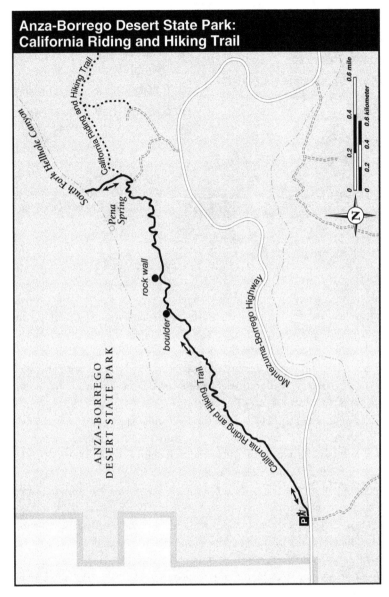

Anza-Borrego Desert State Park: California Riding and Hiking Trail

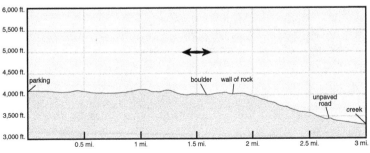

LENGTH & CONFIGURATION 6-mile out-and-back	**WHEELCHAIR-ACCESSIBLE?** No, due to narrow and rocky sections, as well as seasonal mud and/or snow. Other trails in the state park are officially accessible.
DIFFICULTY Moderate	
SCENERY Spring wildflowers, desert vegetation, views of the desert valley	**FACILITIES** Only at the visitor center
EXPOSURE Sunny	**INFO** 760-767-5311 or 760-767-4205, parks.ca.gov/?page_id=638
TRAFFIC Moderate	
TRAIL SURFACE Sandy soil, some rocky areas	**SPECIAL COMMENTS** Desert temperatures can be extreme, so dress in layers and bring lots of water. Consider a spring hike (mid-March–mid-April is best) to see the colorful palette of desert wildflowers.
HIKING TIME 3.5 hours	
ACCESS Free	
MAPS At the visitor center, about 8 miles north of the trailhead; USGS *Tubb Canyon*	

more quickly, with a view of the Culp Valley opening on your right and the Borrego Valley spreading in the distance ahead (north). Puffy clouds leave sweeping shadows on the flat valley floor, the image vaguely reminiscent of photographs of Earth from space.

You'll begin to encounter more people along this stretch, some of whom may be venturing up from the Culp Valley Primitive Campground or the Pena Spring turnout off the Montezuma Highway. When you reach the bottom, turn left and continue 0.25 mile through a flat washout area toward Pena Spring.

If you prefer, you can continue on the California Riding and Hiking Trail, which extends north for nearly 6 more miles. You could do this entire trail one-way by leaving a car in the large parking area near where the trail comes out on Montezuma Highway, about 0.5 mile south of Palm Canyon Drive.

Assuming you turned left toward the spring, you might see running water—most likely in winter or just after rain. Near Pena Spring, flat boulders and sandy banks provide places to sit and enjoy the quiet, boulder-strewn landscape. Here in the flatland, the tissue-papery dune evening primrose blooms on prickly, sawtooth-leafed plants. From a distance, the large white blooms with yellow centers look like fried eggs.

The enormous land stretches for miles, the only sounds the wings of a hummingbird hovering curiously close, as if mistaking a colorfully dressed hiker for a nectar-filled flower.

Retrace your steps, awed by a deep appreciation for the desert's unique beauty.

For more desert enjoyment, see my book *Day & Overnight Hikes: Anza-Borrego Desert State Park* (Menasha Ridge Press, 2007), which features 32 hikes within the park.

Bees swarm in the spring to make new colonies.

GPS INFORMATION AND DIRECTIONS

N33° 12.638' W116° 29.463'

Take I-15 North to the CA 76/Pala exit and drive east for 33.6 miles to CA 79. Turn left, traveling 4.1 miles to CA 52, where you'll turn right and drive another 4.6 miles to Montezuma Valley Road (commonly called Montezuma Highway by San Diego natives). Turn left. Drive 6.8 miles to the trailhead, marked by a yellow-tipped wooden pole on the left. (It's across the street from the slightly better marked Jasper Trail, on the right.) You can park in a small turnout area at the Jasper Trail and cross the highway, or park in the turnout on the left, about 0.2 mile past the trailhead.

INLAND NORTH

Mallard pond at Daley Ranch (see Hikes 28 and 29)

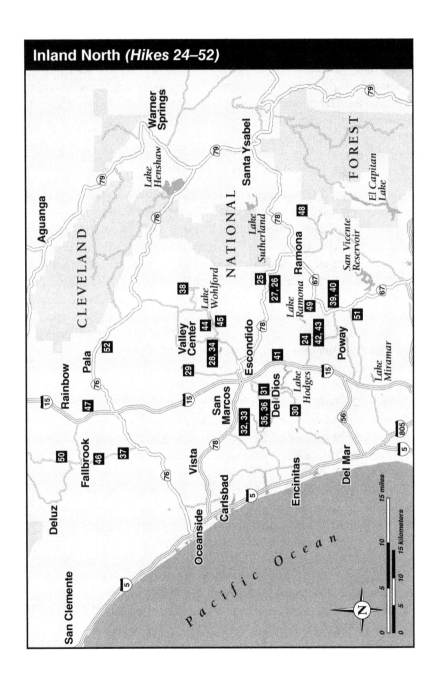

Inland North *(Hikes 24–52)*

24 Blue Sky Trail to Lake Ramona

In Brief

Oak woodland, riparian habitat, coastal sage scrub, and chaparral lend variety to this oasis near the suburbs of Poway. The first 1.5-mile stretch is a flat walk through dappled shade in woodland recovering from fire, which makes the Lake Ramona trail fork a logical turnaround point for anyone not wanting an uphill hike.

Description

Park in the lot and head south along the street for a few yards before turning to the left (east) down the dirt road that begins this trail. Very close to the trailhead, old oaks that once allowed only small patches for a view of the sky—and made one wonder about the reserve's name—are now recovering from fire, so provide less shade. On this nice flat stretch, enjoy the growing evidence of the stately oaks' regenerative powers.

At about 0.25 mile, you'll notice a narrow trail descending on the left side of the wide main trail. Take the side trail down toward the creek that runs along the north side of the trail. You will see an ancient grove of oaks to the left. Sunlight filters through the canopy in glints of gold, producing a hazy, enchanted atmosphere. Baby oaks stand like spindly weeds, while their towering parent trees reach with outstretched limbs as if gathering the seedlings under protective wings. Be careful to stay on the trail to avoid trampling the young oaks. You'll note the 2007 fire's devastation, which has thinned the canopy, but the enchantment remains.

Listen to the frogs' chorus rising from an underlayer of fallen leaves and limbs tangled with the vines of wild roses and poison oak. Alongside the narrow trail, strewn with acorns and decaying oak leaves, clusters of fat toadstools sprout from a fluffy orange carpet of leaves, dropped in the fall by the Western sycamores growing immediately adjacent to the stream. Look for toadstools on the other side of the trail, too. A variety of them grow here in the cool forest shade. Flattened and with fluted edges, or round as buttons, or shaped like a beanie cap, they burst from the ground, making the moist dirt clump form a tiny earthen fence around the fleshy stems.

At about 0.5 mile from the hike's start, the 0.3-mile streamside trail reconnects with the broader main route, where horses are allowed. Pass the side trail, marked Lake Poway, off to the right. Another 0.2 mile brings you to an area that, before the fires, held picnic tables—at the time of this writing not yet replaced. You've come 1.1 miles from your car. When you reach the sign pointing left to Lake Ramona, turn left. (The main trail leads to a water tower and pump station, and beyond that a private residence—none of which are public areas.)

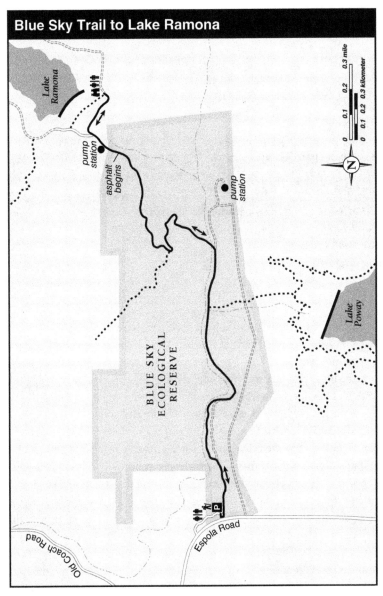

Blue Sky Trail to Lake Ramona

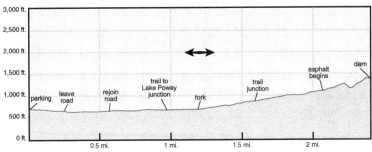

LENGTH & CONFIGURATION 4.5-mile out-and-back	**MAPS** Free at kiosk beyond trailhead and at the website below; USGS *Escondido*
DIFFICULTY Easy	**WHEELCHAIR-ACCESSIBLE?** Not officially, due to silty areas and some uneven trail, but hardier wheelchair users could probably navigate most, if not all, of this trail.
SCENERY Views of Lake Ramona, distant Lake Poway, birds, creek lined with syca-mores, oak forest, and a variety of flower-ing plants along the upper trail	
EXPOSURE Shady with some dappled sunlight on entry trail; full sun on trail to lake	**FACILITIES** Portable toilets near entry, in picnic area, and above Lake Ramona
	INFO 858-668-4781, **blueskyreserve.org**
TRAFFIC Heavy	**SPECIAL COMMENTS** Horses and leashed dogs are permitted (on main trail only, not the creekside trail); bicycles and motor vehicles are not.
TRAIL SURFACE Packed dirt, leaf litter on creekside trail	
HIKING TIME 2.5 hours	
ACCESS Free; open during daylight hours year-round	

After turning left at the Lake Ramona fork, emerge into sunlight. Bring drinking water, even in moderate spring and fall weather. You'll hear the roar of the pump station, which comes into view as the trail begins its gradual, 400- to 500-foot ascent to Lake Ramona to the northeast. The trail gets steeper for a short distance, switching back to the west. Don't let the wide, somewhat barren dirt trail fool you into thinking this will be a dull hike. As the path switches back, climbing steadily and gradually to the east, surpris-ingly delightful foliage awaits. Blooming with tiny white flowers well into autumn, wild cucumber twines up into the branches of laurel sumac growing along the trail. Bright-orange clumps of parasitic California dodder, more commonly called witch's hair, wind around both the cucumber and the laurel sumac. The knotty orange tangles thrive at lower elevations, disappearing as the trail climbs higher. Lupine and a variety of mint begin to appear in bushy tufts along the inner edge of the trail, resting against the rocky face where the road has been cut into the mountain. This hiking route is actually the old Green Valley Truck Trail but is no longer open to motor traffic.

At just shy of 2 miles, asphalt replaces the dirt road. Getting closer to the lake, a wall of rock rises ahead to the east. Here, closer to the water, tree tobacco grows. Its narrow yellow flowers seem to drip from the ends of spindly stalks. The road becomes asphalt where Blue Sky Ecological Reserve land ends and the Ramona Water District begins. Pause and look to the southwest, where the trail etches down the mountain. Lake Poway, about 2 miles away, sparkles in the sunlight. Turkey vultures circle overhead, giving par-ents an opportunity to tease any children who are tuckered out from the hike—maybe those vultures are circling above a weary hiker who collapsed! You will pass another pump station on the left before the asphalt road bends to the south. Avocado groves growing above the road come into view, and as you reach the top, the plumed branches of commercially grown palms line the hillsides to the southeast.

To work out a different set of muscles, or just for fun, walk backward on this last, smooth stretch of asphalt. Once at the top, enjoy a view over the vast blue waters of Lake Ramona from the guardrail. You'll have come 2.25 miles. The dense quietude is interrupted only by the quack and flutter of ducks gathered near the lake's shore, or by an occasional small airplane heading east to the airstrip in Ramona.

The trip back down feels entirely different than the climb, which can be tiring, especially in warmer weather. But passing breezes will cool your damp shirt as you make your way back down with the help of gravity. My family likes to stop at the picnic area on the way out of the reserve, eating the lunch we packed for the trip.

Nearby Activities

A treat for both the eyes and the taste buds can be found at the **Hamburger Factory.** Old-fashioned memorabilia, a friendly neighborhood atmosphere, and an inexpensive menu that includes barbecued chicken, ribs, and much more than the name implies offer diners an experience sure to satisfy. From Blue Sky Ecological Reserve, turn left onto Espola Road; drive about 3 miles and turn right on Twin Peaks Road. At about 0.8 mile, turn left on Midland Road. The restaurant is about 0.5 mile down on the right, at 14122 Midland Rd. in Poway; 858-486-4575, **hamburgerfactory.com.**

GPS INFORMATION AND DIRECTIONS

N33° 0.961' W117° 1.421'

From I-15, exit at Rancho Bernardo Road and travel east for 3.5 miles, noting that the road becomes Espola Road at the Summerfield intersection. Watch for the blue sky ecological reserve sign on the left, and turn into the nearby parking lot. The trailhead is to the right.

---

25 Clevenger Canyon North:

EAST TRAIL

A rock doorway to the west begins the descent into Clevenger Canyon.

In Brief

This tasking hike includes 3 straight miles of uphill walking on a sometimes narrow trail. Experienced hikers will enjoy the challenge, with its rewarding views.

Description

In autumn one can see the bright, yellow-orange leaves of the Western sycamore trees stretching out in the valley below CA 78 like a ribbon, marking the Santa Ysabel Creek, which runs through Clevenger Canyon. Fall and spring are the best times to visit because of the more moderate weather, but foot traffic on the portion of trail leading down to the creek can be heavy even in the heat of summer.

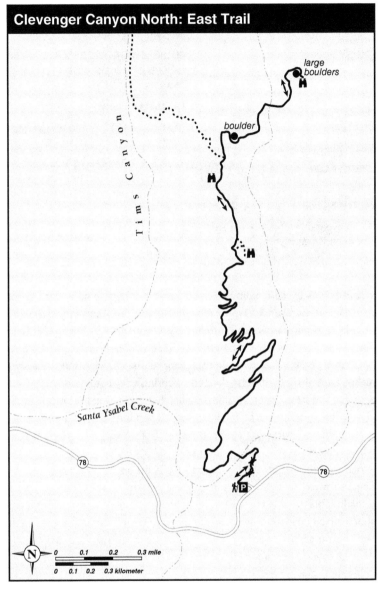

Clevenger Canyon North: East Trail

large boulders

boulder

Tims Canyon

Santa Ysabel Creek

78

78

N   0   0.1   0.2   0.3 mile
    0   0.1   0.2   0.3 kilometer

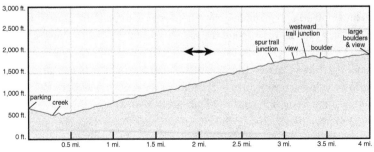

LENGTH & CONFIGURATION 8-mile out-and-back	**MAPS** Online at **tinyurl.com/clevenger canyontrails;** USGS *San Pasqual*
DIFFICULTY Strenuous	**WHEELCHAIR-ACCESSIBLE?** No, due to creek crossing and steep, rocky, uneven sections
SCENERY Views of the San Pasqual Valley and the canyon; large boulders	
EXPOSURE Sunny, with a small section of shade at creek	**FACILITIES** None
	INFO 858-674-2275, **sdrp.org/wordpress /trails**
TRAFFIC Moderately heavy	
TRAIL SURFACE Packed soil, often loose and slippery	**SPECIAL COMMENTS** Tote in lots of water, especially on hot days. Not suitable for children under age 10; use your best judgment regarding the stamina of a child 10+. For that matter, this route is unsuitable for anyone who isn't used to uphill hiking.
HIKING TIME 4 hours	
ACCESS Free; parking lot at staging area open daily, sunrise–sunset	

The trail begins by descending west between two large boulders, then continues down well-placed natural rock steps. Walk west a few yards and the trail bears to the northeast. The leisurely descent lulls unknowing visitors into believing that this will be an easy hike—and easy it is on this 0.3-mile section down to the creek, which flows year-round. No bridge crosses the creek, and the area can be dangerous after heavy rainfall. Water rushes around the granite rocks and towering oak, cottonwood, and sycamore trees, becoming almost stagnant in summer. This shady respite at the bottom of the valley is a good sack-lunch spot, with huge, lichen-covered granite rocks for sitting. In spring, you may see tadpoles swimming about. Be careful of poison oak, which is sometimes plentiful here. Rattlesnakes are also common.

The real workout begins where the trail picks up on the other side of the shaded creek. The narrow footpath stretches in a zigzag pattern up the mountain, with only a few, tiny shade spots provided by a curved boulder or scrub oak, prominent members of the southern mixed chaparral plants common here. While resting for a moment in the shade, listen for the squawking of scrub jays, or for the repetitive chirp of the small brown towhee that also makes its home here among the chaparral.

On these unprotected trails winding up the canyon, cautious parents may be fearful that a gust of wind will blow small children right off the trail, which is one reason why I don't recommend bringing young children along. Also, scratchy chaparral and foxtail frame the trail, which narrows in areas to less than a foot in width and drops to a semi-sheer edge in this steeply sloped canyon. The trail also winds through bush and rock, which makes getting separated from exuberant children who may run ahead an issue. If you do bring children, consider two-way radios and establish rules beforehand about one adult staying at the front of the pack and one at the rear. Mountain lions and bobcats use this canyon to travel, and, although hikers aren't likely to see these shy animals, safety is never a wasted effort.

At about 2.5 miles up the canyon trail, the path edges around the west side of the mountain to a small plateau that overlooks a beautiful patchwork display of the Escondido orange groves far below.

Continue north on the trail for 0.2 mile, where another trail that heads west intersects the main trail. Pass this by and continue for about 0.3 mile. Here, a huge, precariously positioned outcropping of granite boulders marks an "almost there" point—only 1 more mile to the end. Many turn back here, though, because the trail all but disappears. A sign pointing straight up through a tunnel in the shed-sized boulders seems a practical joke. Agile climbers can clamber up through the stone tunnel and over the rock formations. But for the less adventurous, retracing one's steps a few yards reveals an overlooked side path that runs a slippery and steep, but more logical, route up to the continuing trail. Take this slippery section of loose dirt north up around the boulders then head east. Another 15–20 minutes of flatter trail brings you to a cluster of huge, house-sized sitting rocks marked viewpoint.

From this 1,937-foot vantage point, CA 78 twists by like a narrow snake in the distance. Listen closely for the barely discernible hum of cars, a reminder that civilization is nearby. High on the north side of the canyon, the environment can feel desolate. Because of its narrowness and poor condition, the Northeast Clevenger Canyon Trail—especially here at the very end—isn't as heavily trafficked as some other trails that are also close to the urban inland. Before reaching this stretch, many hikers will have grown weary of the climb and turned around. One can rest here on a granite rock warmed by the sun and feel all alone, with only the scuttling sound of curious Western fence lizards to distract you from your thoughts. Enjoy the solitude—and catch your breath—before retracing your steps.

Nearby Activities

The **San Diego Zoo Safari Park** is 5.3 miles west on CA 78. Twenty times the size of the San Diego Zoo, this 1,800-acre facility offers visitors a chance to see animals in herds, living as if in their natural habitats. For more information, call 619-231-1515 or visit **sdzsafaripark.org.**

GPS INFORMATION AND DIRECTIONS

N33° 5.088' W116° 54.989'

Take CA 78 east to the staging area, which is on the left, 5.3 miles east of the San Diego Zoo Safari Park. Turn left (north) into the lot and park. The trailhead is located at the northeast corner of the parking area.

26 Clevenger Canyon South:
EAST TRAIL

Westerly view of San Pasqual Valley from the trail

In Brief

This moderately steep ascent makes for a vigorous aerobic workout on well-defined trails. The thick chaparral, manzanita, and aromatic sagebrush are still recovering from the devastating 2007 fire. Previously bush-framed trails are more open. The topmost viewpoint is sprawling, but it's the sweeping serenity along the entire hike that makes this somewhat taxing trek a favorite.

Description

From the trailhead, look southeast and spot a prominent triangular boulder atop the hills. After climbing 1,000 feet, you'll have reached that massive formation and still have roughly half a mile to go to trail's end.

If you hike midafternoon, the sunlight will be over the crest of the canyon, leaving the trail a cool, shady path that begins to work its relaxing magic just a few yards from the parking lot. That's not to say that this hike is a breeze: Gentler than the steeper slopes on the northern trails of Clevenger Canyon (see page 114), the path is, however, an uphill

Clevenger Canyon South: East Trail

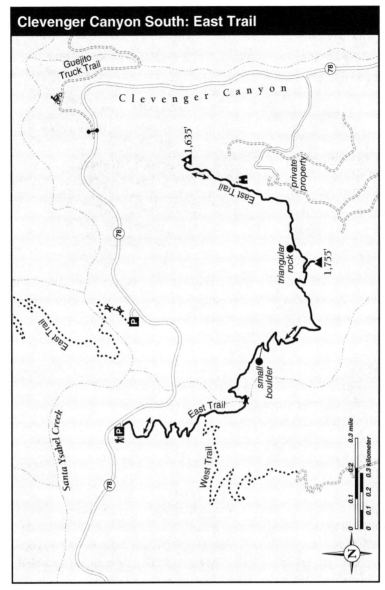

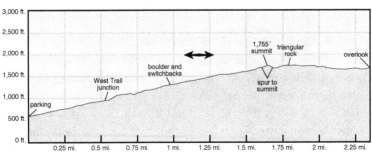

LENGTH & CONFIGURATION 4.4-mile out-and-back	**MAPS** Online at **tinyurl.com/clevenger canyontrails;** USGS *San Pasqual*
DIFFICULTY Moderately strenuous	**WHEELCHAIR-ACCESSIBLE?** No, due to creek crossing and steep, rocky, uneven sections
SCENERY Views of the San Pasqual Valley, city of Ramona, trees, and chaparral	
EXPOSURE Open to sunlight	**FACILITIES** None
TRAFFIC Light to moderate	**INFO** 858-674-2275, **sdrp.org/wordpress /trails**
TRAIL SURFACE Packed soil, some rocky areas	**SPECIAL COMMENTS** Tote in lots of water on hot days. Leashed dogs allowed.
HIKING TIME 3 hours	
ACCESS Free; parking lot at staging area open daily, sunrise–sunset	

one, ascending 1,000 feet. But as you head up into the canyon along a gusty southbound trail, the quietude of nature embraces you. Birds such as the towhee and scrub jay call for you to join them far away from the stresses of your busy life.

Prior to the 2007 fire, the trails were framed in impenetrable thickets of high, fragrant chaparral, making the trail like a secret path up the mountain. Now, sweeping views in all directions delight the eye. As the road below grows smaller and smaller to your sight, the climb offers a sense of accomplishment that builds with each step.

From the start, the southeast trail switchbacks up to the 0.5-mile point, where a marker signals the beginning of the west trail—one you may choose to hike another day. Continue moving on a stretch of south trail descending into a wooded ravine shaded by live oak. On hotter days, this is a wonderful place to stop and rest in the cool shade. Though you've come only about 0.6 mile, the steady ascent plays tricks on your sense of distance, making it seem you've hiked twice as far.

At the base of the ravine, cross a small footbridge over a seasonal stream. The trail switches north again, working its way upward through granite boulders and recovering foliage. Wild cucumber twines and stretches, reaching out to brush your legs as you pass. Aromatic black sage fills the air with its minty scent. In spring, its light-blue flowers extend like tiny orchids from knotty outgrowths on slender stems.

Curve northeast for several yards on open trail. Look to the west, where you can glimpse your car back in the parking lot. It looks like a child's toy, as do the cars buzzing 1,200 feet below along CA 78. The trail dips to the southeast again, curves to the north, and then continues southeast. At about 0.9 mile, a rounded washing machine–sized boulder marks a sharp westward switchback, leading upward a few yards to the 1-mile point then switching back again to the southeast.

Continuing on, a wide, flat stretch overlooks Ramona to the southeast, then narrows again near the 1.5-mile marker, heads south uphill, then bends to the northeast again. A little farther, a trailer-sized boulder with several smaller, good-for-sitting boulders at its base marks the "almost there" point for the first scenic view. Follow the trail several yards, keeping an eye out for a narrow path heading off to the right, which leads to a 1,755-foot summit. Catch the view of the sycamores—bright green in the spring and summer, and yellow in fall—stretching like a colorful Chinese dragon's tail through the canyon and across CA 78. Then amble back down to the main trail and head north, where a meadow opens up on a gradual downhill slope. The yucca's tall stalks mark the way like flowering staffs, earning the plant its nickname, "Our Lord's Candle."

Here, close to the top in the open space, the wind gets gusty. At about 1.6 miles, you'll pass the massive triangular rock (on your left) that you will have spotted from the outset. A short distance farther, the route bends more north, and passes near private property on the right.

At 2.1 miles, the viewpoint marker comes as a surprise. Another tenth of a mile brings you to the end, where you can look back across the canyon to the parking lot below and marvel at how this is the longest 2.2 miles you've ever hiked. The distance seems much further than its actual length. Trail fatigue gives way to playful exuberance as the setting sun reveals a brilliant red-orange palette in the Western sky.

If you've begun the trail in midafternoon to avoid the direct sunlight, any dalliances now pose a threat. As the sun begins to set on the ocean's horizon, coyotes yip. But don't worry too much. Although it could easily have taken more than 2 hours to reach the trail's endpoint, little more than an hour is needed for the return hike. To be on the safe side, however, allow an hour and a half. Although swift steps and gravity carry you downhill almost like flowing water, the fun ends if an attendant starts honking his car horn from the parking lot below. I know, because my family has raced down the mountain with darkness closing in, bats flitting about in the twilight, and the fresh dung of coyotes awakened from their day naps marking the trail.

Nearby Activities

San Pasqual Battlefield State Historic Park, about 3 miles west on CA 78, honors soldiers from the Mexican-American War of 1846. The site is meant as a reminder of the human ideals, passions, and actions that can lead to bloodshed. The 50-acre park has a visitor center with video and interpretive displays and a 0.5-mile nature trail and picnic tables. In early December, volunteers reenact the battle, complete with costumes and cannon firing. Free admission; open weekends 10 a.m.–4 p.m. November–March, 10 a.m.–5 p.m. April–October. For more information, call 760-737-2201 or visit **ci.escondido .ca.us/glance/uniquely/battlefield.**

GPS INFORMATION AND DIRECTIONS

N33° 5.111' W116° 55.336'

Take CA 78 east to the staging area, which is on the right side of the road, a little more than 5 miles east of San Diego Wild Animal Park. Turn right (south) into the paved lot and park.

27 Clevenger Canyon South:

WEST TRAIL

Blue skies, golden hills, and sage scrub greet you west of the trail's outset.

In Brief

A steady, though fairly gradual, ascent makes this a brisk workout on well-defined trails where chaparral and aromatic sage provide a thick habitat for birds. The birdsong-filled atmosphere makes this hike seem farther into wilderness than it actually is.

Description

A small trail leads off the east edge of the parking lot, then south past a gate before heading up a steep hill. The first 0.5 mile is shared by hikers taking the southeast trail (for details, see the previous hike). The trail splits near a cluster of flattish boulders with an eastern view, offering a good place to pause.

Once you've had your fill of the view and caught your breath from the initial 300-foot ascent, head right. The westward trail affords a view of the parking lot and your tiny car. The route will continue to climb steadily but gradually, zigzagging upward for an additional 550-foot gain in elevation.

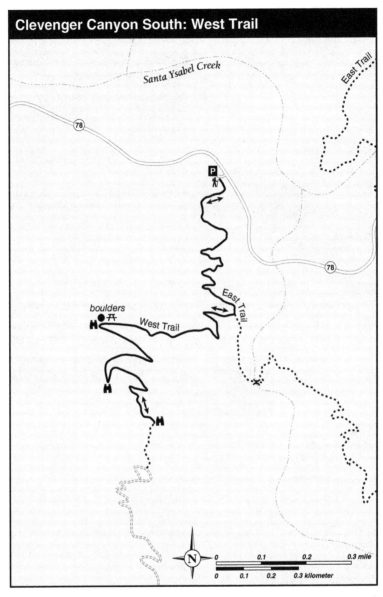

Clevenger Canyon South: West Trail

Santa Ysabel Creek

78

East Trail

boulders

West Trail

East Trail

78

N

0   0.1   0.2   0.3 mile

0   0.1   0.2   0.3 kilometer

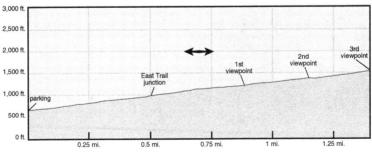

3,000 ft.
2,500 ft.
2,000 ft.
1,500 ft.
1,000 ft.
500 ft.
0 ft.

parking

East Trail junction

1st viewpoint

2nd viewpoint

3rd viewpoint

0.25 mi.   0.5 mi.   0.75 mi.   1 mi.   1.25 mi.

LENGTH & CONFIGURATION 2.8-mile out-and-back	**ACCESS** Free; parking lot at staging area open daily, sunrise–sunset
DIFFICULTY Moderate	**MAPS** Online at **tinyurl.com/clevenger canyontrails;** USGS *San Pasqual*
SCENERY Views to the east and west; views of nearby orange groves, chaparral, and birds	**WHEELCHAIR-ACCESSIBLE?** No, due to narrow trail width and uneven terrain
EXPOSURE Mostly sunny	**FACILITIES** None
	INFO 858-674-2275, **sdrp.org/wordpress /trails**
TRAFFIC Moderate; less traffic than trails accessed via the northern trailhead	**SPECIAL COMMENTS** Use caution when bringing children—the singletrack trail moves along some steep, open slopes. Leashed dogs allowed.
TRAIL SURFACE Packed soil	
HIKING TIME 2 hours	

After you've walked a short distance on the first westward stretch, the path turns sharply left and levels for an easy southward stroll, then heads right again, moving gradually uphill. The narrow trail is angled, slanting downhill in spots, as if the mountain wants to throw you off. Watch your step, but enjoy the fresh air and scenery. When I hiked this trail in early spring 2008, after the fires of 2007 had cleared away much of the larger chaparral plants, the space was filled with a variety of colorful wildflowers. The carpet of blooms was so lush that a sudden appearance of Julie Andrews and the children of *The Sound of Music* wouldn't have seemed extraordinary. The brush is now recovering nicely.

Yucca grows here, too. Amid the round, clustered boulders, a single, smooth-skinned rod rises from the center of the spiky-stemmed plant. In late summer, the stalk matures, shooting upward 2–3 feet and erupting into purple-tinged bloom.

The trail continues to zigzag for a bit before turning west toward a viewpoint spot at 0.8 mile. Here, a large, flat boulder beckons picnickers. On winter mornings when the sun heats the inland mountains, fog may blanket the valleys below, providing hikers a shrouded view. To the south, a great boulder resembles a giant bear, rhinoceros, or pig—depending on whose imagination is doing the conjuring. To the north, across the highway, notice that the south-facing canyon's slopes are much more barren than these north-facing ones, offering a good example of how exposure affects habitat. The south-facing slopes get more sunlight and heat, requiring vegetation that is more drought-tolerant. The north-facing slopes get less sun, thus retaining more life-giving moisture for ferns, lichen, and denser chaparral.

At 1.1 miles, the trail cuts a sharp left. The path narrows, heading uphill, then zigzagging to the end marker at an even better viewpoint at 1.4 miles. Before retracing your footsteps for an easy downhill return, allow the quiet of nature to envelop you as it does the land. Birds share their gift of music and send the mind wandering. You've found yet another perfect natural spot.

GPS INFORMATION AND DIRECTIONS

N33° 5.111' W116° 55.336'

From southeastern Escondido, take CA 78 East to the staging area, on the south side of the road just a little more than 5 miles east of the San Diego Wild Animal Park. Turn right (south) into the paved lot and park.

28 Daley Ranch:
COMBINED TRAILS LOOP

A tranquil morning at Daley Ranch

In Brief

This easy combined-trails loop offers the best of Daley Ranch, with its wide-open spaces, rustling grasses, and ponds. The description below takes you back to a central point, allowing you to leave out sections for a shorter hike, if you prefer.

Description

Start by heading north under the arching daley ranch sign and begin walking up the paved road. You'll encounter signs identifying native plants such as Ramona lilac and Mojave yucca on this uphill stretch of asphalt. As the city sounds fade, listen for the piercing cry of a hawk soaring overhead, the repeating *chip-chip* call of the California towhee as it forages in the bushes, and the high-pitched buzz of masses of cicadas. The insects' whirring sound is similar to the ominous warning of rattlesnakes—also found at Daley Ranch and

126

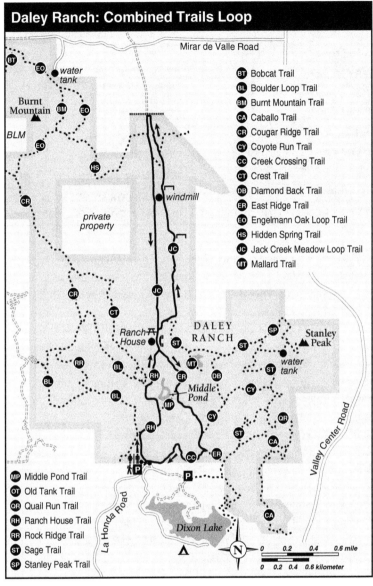

Daley Ranch: Combined Trails Loop

Mirar de Valle Road

water tank

Burnt Mountain

BLM

private property

windmill

DALEY RANCH

Ranch House

Stanley Peak

water tank

Middle Pond

Valley Center Road

La Honda Road

Dixon Lake

BT Bobcat Trail
BL Boulder Loop Trail
BM Burnt Mountain Trail
CA Caballo Trail
CR Cougar Ridge Trail
CY Coyote Run Trail
CC Creek Crossing Trail
CT Crest Trail
DB Diamond Back Trail
ER East Ridge Trail
EO Engelmann Oak Loop Trail
HS Hidden Spring Trail
JC Jack Creek Meadow Loop Trail
MT Mallard Trail

MP Middle Pond Trail
OT Old Tank Trail
QR Quail Run Trail
RH Ranch House Trail
RR Rock Ridge Trail
ST Sage Trail
SP Stanley Peak Trail

N

| 0 | 0.2 | 0.4 | 0.6 mile |

| 0 | 0.2 | 0.4 | 0.6 kilometer |

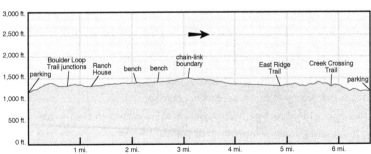

3,000 ft.

2,500 ft.

2,000 ft.

parking
Boulder Loop Trail junctions
Ranch House
bench
bench
chain-link boundary
East Ridge Trail
Creek Crossing Trail
parking

1,500 ft.

1,000 ft.

500 ft.

0 ft.

1 mi. 2 mi. 3 mi. 4 mi. 5 mi. 6 mi.

LENGTH & CONFIGURATION 6.3-mile loose figure-8	MAPS Available in kiosk boxes at trailhead and at **daleyranch.org/explore /hiking**
DIFFICULTY Easy	
SCENERY Chaparral, ranch house, rock formations, ponds	**WHEELCHAIR-ACCESSIBLE?** Partially—the asphalt road and Jack's Creek Loop portions are wheelchair- and stroller-friendly.
EXPOSURE Sunny	
TRAFFIC Moderate–heavy	**FACILITIES** Restrooms are located near the ranch house.
TRAIL SURFACE 1.1-mile asphalt entry, then silt; some rutted areas	
	INFO daleyranch.org
HIKING TIME 3 hours	**SPECIAL COMMENTS** Hikers must yield to bikers and horseback riders.
ACCESS Free; open daily, sunrise–sunset	

most often seen in spring and summer. Keep your eyes open for them. On a recent visit, one large snake didn't bother to rattle a warning at all as it cautiously slithered past—and others tell of similar tales. The snakes may be getting used to people in this place that's often busy with foot traffic, so be on the lookout.

A bench sits in the shade on the right at about 0.3 mile, after which the road begins sloping downhill. You'll spot a side route on the right leading to Middle Pond. This short path goes past the water to another trail that you will take on your way out. If you can't wait, take a side trip to the pond now. The connection of many trails that cross one another within Daley Ranch makes this an easy area to explore. Consult the official trail guide, available at the parking lot kiosk, for a complete map.

Assuming you've stayed on the asphalt road, you'll pass Engelmann and live oaks and large laurel sumac bushes closely enough to enjoy their spotty, welcome shade. The road continues north, bending to the west where it meets the entry and exit for the Boulder Loop, which you might want to explore another day. Also growing along the road are light-purple flowered fleabane, coastal sagebrush, black sage, and even some wild roses.

At 1.1 miles, you'll reach the green ranch house, which has been preserved since the late 1800s. A pay phone stands across the road. (When was the last time you saw one of those?) Adjacent to the house is a grassy picnic area with benches shaded by towering oaks. Don't miss the opportunity to loll in the shade, letting your mind wander back to what this historic ranch may have been like 100 years ago. You can almost hear the mooing of cattle and the pounding of hoofbeats as hands rounded up strays. Close to the house, outbuildings are unstable and off-limits to visitors.

From the picnic area, you'll spot the 3.4-mile Jack's Creek Meadow Loop. Enter the loop via an eastern trail on the right instead, allowing you to enjoy the breezier part of the loop on the north after you're warmed from exercise.

Head up the rutted dirt path through sparse eucalyptus forest, where swaying willows and oaks also mingle. The wide trail passes the entrance to the Sage Trail on the right, then moves north. Spotty tree shade alternates with wide views of the meadow,

Shady spot along the entry road trail at Daley Ranch

running lower along the left. About 2 miles from the parking lot, an east-facing bench allows restful viewing of odd rock formations on the hill. Look for one easily recognized boulder nicknamed "Muppet Rock." Its stony profile looks like the late Jim Henson's creations. Another bench, shaded by stately oaks, is 0.3 mile ahead.

Turn the corner of the Jack's Creek Meadow Loop at about 2.7 miles, near the chain-link boundary, and head in the opposite direction (south) along the straightaway. The wide trail undulates over hills and dales for a short while. You'll pass a rusting windmill on the left and see the Hidden Springs route on the right—another of the many Daley Ranch trails you may wish to eventually explore. Continuing south, notice the hushed whisper of the grasses, and see the road stretch out before you, seemingly endless before the restful-looking ranch house finally comes into view again.

Jack's Creek Meadow Loop closes back at the picnic area, marking 4.5 miles of hiking so far. Head south past the ranch house and take a trail on the left marked east ridge, which will lead you gradually uphill toward the southeast.

In creative imaginations, boulders on the hillside to the trail's left take on the shape of giant frogs or other creatures. The path begins sloping downward again. After walking about half a mile on the East Ridge route, you may notice water out to the right. This is Middle Pond—although it's been dry on recent visits. California's drought conditions are evident here at Daley Ranch. A side trail leads past and hooks up with the asphalt Ranch House road you entered on. You'll remember seeing the entry to this short connector path on your way in. Skip the side route and continue southeast on East Ridge. A short distance ahead, you may again see water. If present, it will be on the left, closer to the trail.

Past this area lies a steep hill, but the 0.1-mile distance up makes grip-soled shoes and a willful burst of speed and energy all that's necessary to reach the top, where the path levels. You'll spot the secondary trail, Coyote Run, on the left, and also see Lake Wohlford Dam in the southeastern distance. When the trail begins heading downhill again, watch for a rutted side trail on the right. This is the Creek Crossing Trail, and your way out. It's unmarked as of this writing, except for a wooden pole where the trail begins. Head right. You'll soon see Dixon Lake on the left. Eventually, the dirt parking area where you left your car also comes into view. On weekends, the sounds of merrymakers picnicking at the lake will serenade (or perhaps annoy) you as you head toward the parking lot and end your hike.

Nearby Activities

If seeing the old ranch house started you thinking about some tasty old-fashioned barbecue flavors, try the **Wrangler Barbecue Pit,** where slowly smoked meats and original recipes keep the locals coming back. The restaurant itself is definitely no-frills, but the food is the real deal. From the intersection of El Norte Parkway and La Honda Drive, go 0.3 mile west on El Norte and turn left on North Midway Drive. Continue 1.1 miles to East Valley Parkway, then turn right and drive 0.4 mile. The restaurant will be on the right, at 1644 E. Valley Pkwy. in Escondido. Call 760-746-2399 or visit **facebook.com/wranglerbbqpit** for more information.

GPS INFORMATION AND DIRECTIONS

N33° 10.004' W117° 3.124'

Take I-15 to the El Norte Parkway exit. Travel east on El Norte for about 4 miles to La Honda Drive, and turn left. Follow La Honda Drive to the top and turn left into the dirt parking area directly across from the entrance gate to Dixon Lake.

29 Daley Ranch:

ENGELMANN OAK LOOP

Stretching oak branches form a canopy of shade over the trail.

In Brief

This truck-width trail is well graded and offers views to the north, east, and southwest. With only a few steep areas and the promise of quail, a variety of other birds, and even the glimpse of a coyote, Engelmann Oak Loop is an easy-to-get-to choice for a family day hike.

Description

To reach the Engelmann Oak Loop, start by heading east on the Cougar Ridge Trail, which begins at the Cougar Pass Road entrance. Follow this wide, flat trail shared by mountain bikes, horse riders, and hikers through a meadow dotted with young coast live oak trees. Stands of laurel sumac, with its unique red-tinged leaves, add color to this flat section of Cougar Ridge.

At about 0.6 mile, the trail dips and heads southeast, continuing through a stretch of mature oaks with branches reaching across the path, nearly blocking the sunlight. Except

131

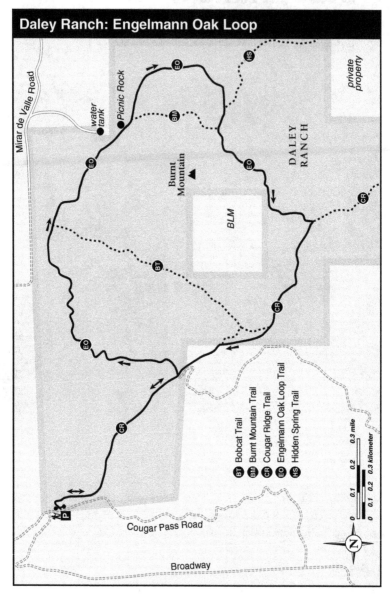

Daley Ranch: Engelmann Oak Loop

BT Bobcat Trail
BM Burnt Mountain Trail
CR Cougar Ridge Trail
EO Engelmann Oak Loop Trail
HS Hidden Spring Trail

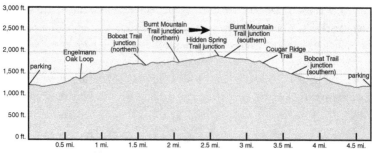

LENGTH & CONFIGURATION 4.7-mile loop	**ACCESS** Free; open daily, sunrise–sunset
DIFFICULTY Easy–moderate	**MAPS** Free in map box at Cougar Pass Road entrance and at **daleyranch.org /explore/hiking**
SCENERY Scenic views to the north, east, and southwest; Engelmann and coast live oaks; and a variety of wildlife	**WHEELCHAIR-ACCESSIBLE?** No, due to creek crossing and steep, rocky sections
EXPOSURE Half-sunny and half-shady	**FACILITIES** None
TRAFFIC Light on weekdays; heavy weekend use	**INFO** daleyranch.org
TRAIL SURFACE Packed earth with some rocky and rutted areas	**SPECIAL COMMENTS** Hikers must yield to bikers and horseback riders. Leashed dogs allowed.
HIKING TIME 3 hours	

on the hottest summer days, hikers may feel most comfortable in sweaters on this chilly, shaded section where runoff water collects, crossing the path after rainfall. You may hear the steady hum of honeybees, hinting at hives hidden in the branches towering over the path. Curiosity sometimes causes hikers to stand here with their necks bent, straining to locate an elusive hive above.

At just under 0.5 mile from the entrance, the first trail marker comes into view, identifying the Engelmann Oak Loop intersection. Bear left and take this path to the north, through steep sections littered with fist-size rocks. These uphill sections get the heart pounding and are interspersed with short plateaus that allow a moment's cool-down as hikers pace forward. Yucca is prevalent here, blooming in profusion during spring and summer, and then receding to spiky green skeletons in fall and winter.

The trail bends to the east, opening into meadows sprinkled with tall oak trees. Closer to the trail, small oaks offer cover for the Western scrub jays that flutter by, giving hikers a glimpse of vibrant blue wings before they disappear into the larger trees. Stop for a moment to enjoy the silence and clear views of Fallbrook to the north and the Palomar Mountain area to the east.

Fewer hikers will be seen in this northern end of 3,500-acre Daley Ranch, which was purchased for multiuse trails by the City of Escondido in 1996. It often feels desolate. Horses leave behind their fertile evidence, but most riders are out in the early-morning hours. Mountain bikers yield to horses, but not that many bikers are encountered on the Engelmann Oak Loop trail itself. Those on foot should yield to both bikes and horses.

Continuing the hike, Engelmann Oak Loop intersects the secondary 1-mile trail called Bobcat, then curves to the southeast. A water tower stands at the halfway point. Coyotes are common in the hills that rise beyond the trail to the east. Even at midday, you will sometimes see the contrasting gold tint of their sandy-colored coats as they lope through the dark green yucca and rosy laurel sumac on the hillside. Coyotes are more often spotted in the early morning, though, or during the dusky hours near sunset.

Just beyond the water tower, a flat grouping of rocks that visitors call Picnic Rock offers a partially shaded respite. Hikers, who recline like lizards, are often lulled by the sun-warmed rocks. The spot's nickname changes to Nap Rock at a snore's notice. Don't relax too long, though. Nodding off means you miss out on the twittering of wild finches often seen among the velvety gray-green sage that grows thick across the western meadow.

A few yards ahead, a trail marker identifies the northern end of Burnt Mountain Trail, which is 0.4 mile you won't want to miss. Use this cutoff to shave about 0.5 mile off the hike and reconnect with the Engelmann Oak Loop on the other end. Or, if you're feeling energetic, pass up this northern entrance, continue around the loop past the intersecting Hidden Springs Trail, and enter Burnt Mountain Trail from the southern end. From this entrance, a slight ascent on this path that is little more than a ditch takes you up into the chaparral, where quails run into the bushes and cottontails hop for cover. Iridescent green and red hummingbirds rest in groups on the branches of an Engelmann oak that stands out among the shrubs beyond the path. Some hover close, curious about the visitors. After the short upward slope, Burnt Mountain Trail travels downhill in this direction, making it an easier hike than the northern entrance. Pick up the Engelmann Oak Loop trail near Picnic Rock and retrace your steps around to the southwest, or trek back up over the shorter 0.4-mile Burnt Mountain Trail.

Continuing on the Engelmann Oak Loop, ancient coast live oak trees are prevalent and they reach out with twisting branches to block the sunlight, making this area cool and refreshing in the heat of summer. The trail is usually muddy in fall, winter, and spring. Beyond the trail, the song of crickets echoes among the cottage-size boulders that form stony villages among the trees.

At the southwestern tip of the Engelmann Oak Loop, a marker signals the intersection with Cougar Ridge, which will complete the loop for this hike. Go right to make your way back to the entrance and the parking area. This rutted, downhill ridge trail travels above a picturesque valley. Beyond that, the city of Escondido stretches out in the southwest. Pass the southern entrance to Bobcat Trail and continue down through the shady trees. After heavy rainfall, water runs along the east side of Cougar Ridge for a short stretch, leading up to the marker that led you off onto the Engelmann Oak Trail earlier, to make the loop. Continue past it this time, retracing your steps along the path that now leads northwest, back to the heralding buzz of the beehives still hidden in the trees, and up across the flat meadow to the gate.

GPS INFORMATION AND DIRECTIONS
N33° 12.589' W117° 5.139'

Take I-15 to CA 78 East. Follow CA 78 east to the traffic signal, which intersects Broadway, and turn left. Travel north on Broadway about 4 miles and go right on Cougar Pass Road. One mile up this twisting dirt road, you'll see the Daley Ranch entrance gate on the right. Park in the turnout on the left.

30 Del Dios Gorge, Dam, and Lake Hodges Trek

Feathery eucalyptus grows along sparkling Lake Hodges.

In Brief

Here, where the San Dieguito River is close, the twanging call of red-winged blackbirds may fill the air, setting a relaxing tone for your 11-mile out-and-back hike. The multiuse trail has both modern and historical interest, and pleasant views of the lake.

Description

The initial 1.1-mile stretch of this hike is included in my book *Easy Hikes Close to Home: San Diego.* When I first wrote the hike profile in the summer of 2009, much of the trail construction past the new bridge at Del Dios Gorge wasn't complete. Now, the full trail links Del Dios to the lake. Or, if you're really adventurous, you could hike an additional 4.5 miles by linking with Hike 41, Lake Hodges: North Shore Trail (page 175).

From the staging area, head uphill on the pavement toward a gate, which is an alternate entrance to The Crosby residential community. Before reaching the top of the hill, you'll spot the marked Del Dios Gorge trailhead on your left. On the right side, you'll

Del Dios Gorge, Dam, and Lake Hodges Trek

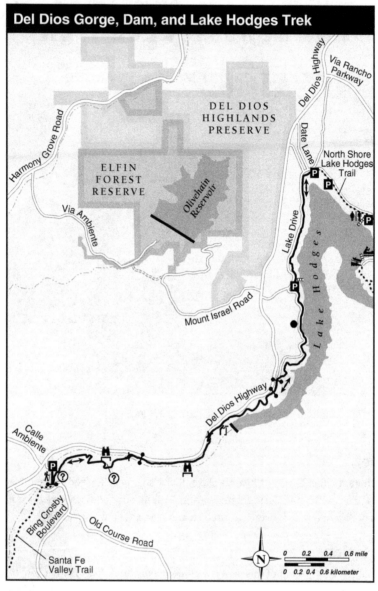

DEL DIOS
HIGHLANDS
PRESERVE

ELFIN
FOREST
RESERVE

Olivenhain Reservoir

Harmony Grove Road

Via Ambiente

Mount Israel Road

Via Rancho Parkway

Del Dios Highway

Date Lane

North Shore Lake Hodges Trail

Lake Drive

Lake Hodges

Del Dios Highway

Calle Ambiente

Bing Crosby Boulevard

Old Course Road

Santa Fe Valley Trail

N

0   0.2   0.4   0.6 mile
0 0.2 0.4 0.6 kilometer

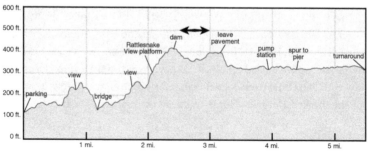

600 ft.
500 ft.
400 ft.
300 ft.
200 ft.
100 ft.
0 ft.

parking
view
bridge
view
Rattlesnake View platform
dam
leave pavement
pump station
spur to pier
turnaround

1 mi.   2 mi.   3 mi.   4 mi.   5 mi.

LENGTH & CONFIGURATION 11-mile out-and-back	**WHEELCHAIR-ACCESSIBLE?** Not officially. Initial portions of the trail include some silty and rocky areas.
DIFFICULTY Moderate one-way, strenuous round-trip	**FACILITIES** Portable toilet at 4.3 miles, in the staging area
SCENERY Lake views, historical interest, chaparral	**INFO** 858-674-2275, **sdrp.org/wordpress/trails**
EXPOSURE Mostly open to sunlight	
TRAFFIC Moderate weekdays, heavy weekends	**SPECIAL COMMENTS** Consider making this a point-to-point hike for your group by driving two cars: Leave one at the turnaround spot on Lake Drive and then shuttle people in the other to the starting trailhead. Especially on weekends, be aware that the path east of the truss bridge is popular with bicyclists. Closer to this trail's endpoint, you're likely to see people on horseback, too. Leashed dogs allowed.
TRAIL SURFACE Sandy soil, finer near lake	
HIKING TIME 5 hours	
ACCESS Free; open to hikers, bikers, and equestrians daily, sunrise–sunset	
MAPS Online at **tinyurl.com/deldios gorge;** USGS *Escondido*	

notice another trailhead—for the Santa Fe Valley Trail. On another day, perhaps you'll want to explore that 3.7-mile round-trip excursion through mixed rocky and flat terrain that climbs to a viewpoint.

For now, move up the gradual northerly grade of the Del Dios Gorge portion of this trip, where information panels describe how the land regenerates after fire—an ongoing process here since the 2007 wildfires. The path bends left and settles into a nearly flat, easterly walk. In spring, the flat paddles of the prickly pear cactus erupt in sunrise-pink blooms that appear to glow. Thistle is another thorny plant that grows here. Its purple spring blooms dry as the year wears on, their color fading to a drab yellow-brown that fits California's "Golden State" moniker. Also see creamy California buckwheat blooms frosting the tops of the small-leaved bushes, and California poppies growing in bright butterscotch-orange clusters in spring. Even an occasional mariposa lily pops a pale-pink head from the brush.

At about 0.4 mile, the trail jogs right and then back left again as it heads slightly uphill. Across Del Dios Highway on the left, remnants of an old aqueduct system held up by trellis platforms come into view—reminders of days gone by. These bits of history are sections of the Lake Hodges Flume, built in the early 1900s to connect Lake Hodges to the San Dieguito Reservoir.

At about 0.8 mile, there's seating straight ahead. Stop if you need to, but you'll also find a bench with a good view just after the trail turns to the right. The path climbs a little more, then passes an information panel about bats that expounds on the benefits of these wild creatures, which eat pests and get a bad rap as spooky. At the top of the hill, turn left—east again—and head downhill.

Passing by the dam

You'll reach the 180-foot steel truss bridge at 1.1 mile, which was completed in 2007. Enjoy the view east and to the reedy depths below before moving on. Beyond the bridge, you'll head slightly upward and pass through a gate. There's an opening out to Del Dios Highway here, and some use this spot as an entry point. You'll see a trash can here, along with a doggie-poop-bag dispenser. Beyond the gate, the newer trail is easy and well maintained. Native grasses sway in the breeze.

At 1.5 miles, encounter a narrow uphill stretch. Be aware of bicyclists who might be speeding down the hill. While most cyclists are considerate, weekends bring them in large groups.

At 1.7 miles, you'll find a bench, which is a good place to stop and look down at any water in the gorge below. Years of meager precipitation have diminished the flow of water here. Come after a rain, when the chaparral soaks up moisture and releases its herby scent.

At just shy of 2.1 miles, you'll reach the Rattlesnake View platform, which was completed in 2011 with grant funds. Native rock in the curving shape of a snake forms the seating for this overlook point. At the stone snake's rattle, a pipe scope points out views of the river below, the spillway, and the dam.

Beyond the lookout, the path leads upward, close to the road again, to a point used as another entry off Del Dios. The path travels alongside the road for about 0.3 mile. You'll be relieved to veer to the right again above the dam, leaving the passing traffic behind. Pause for some close glimpses of the massive structure, which was built in 1918. As you walk along the easy path, pause to enjoy restful views of sparkling Lake Hodges through the patchy-barked trunks and wispy branches of eucalyptus trees.

At 3 miles, pass through a yellow gate onto pavement and continue a short distance where, past another yellow gate, the pavement ends. Skip the chainlink gate you'll see straight ahead. Instead, veer to the right on a narrow dirt path toward the lake. The water glitters like diamonds in sunlight. Spark of light dance across the surface, leaving no doubt that water's benefits go beyond hydration to speak to the soul.

Pass a pump station on your left at 3.9 miles, and continue forward with the watery expanse on your right. At 4.3 miles, there's a staging area with a portable toilet near Hernandez' Hideaway restaurant. Since 1972, this local pit stop has occupied an old building constructed around the same time as the dam. It originally served as a stagecoach stop, but rumor has it that over the years, the building once housed a brothel.

Continue along on narrow trail that stretches beneath the shade of California pepper and eucalyptus trees, with quiet Lake Drive and its waterfront homes on your left. The yellow-and-orange splashes of nasturtiums growing in the shade may catch your attention. The leaves on some of these edible plants here near the lake grow as large as dinner plates. You'll encounter more-casual meanderers as you get closer to this hike's endpoint—the lake entry at 5.5 miles. This is where you'll turn around—or end your hike if you've taken two cars. Assuming you've opted for the out-and-back, rest up at a picnic bench in the shade of big California pepper trees before retracing your steps to the starting point.

GPS INFORMATION AND DIRECTIONS

Trailhead: **N33° 2.299' W117° 9.404'**

Shuttle: **33° 3.974' W117° 4.097'**

Route One: From I-5, exit on Via de la Valle and drive 7.5 miles east. Turn right at the unmarked entry road across from the Cielo development.

Route Two: From I-15, exit at Via Rancho Parkway and drive west for just under 4 miles to Del Dios Highway. Turn left and continue 5 miles. Just before reaching the Cielo development, you'll see The Lemon Twist, a fruit stand, on the left, and turn down the adjacent entry road just past the stand.

Route Three: Exit I-15 at West Valley Parkway and drive west. After about 2 miles, West Valley Parkway becomes Del Dios Highway. Continue another 5 miles and then turn left. There's a staging area on the right, several hundred yards off Del Dios Highway/Via de la Valle.

To do this as a one-way hike, take the West Valley Parkway exit off I-15, drive west for 2.5 miles, and turn left on Date Lane. Drive approximately 0.4 mile to Lake Drive. You'll turn left and park one car alongside the road. In the second car, proceed south on Lake Drive for 1.4 miles. Turn left on Del Dios Highway and proceed approximately 3.1 miles. Turn left just past the Lemon Twist stand to reach the staging area.

31 Del Dios Highlands Preserve Trail

In Brief

An ever-steepening trek on a wide, well-defined dirt road up into the Del Dios–area highlands offers a taxing climb rewarded by panoramic views. At the top, the trail hooks into the Elfin Forest Recreational Reserve system, which allows for all-day hiking if you choose.

Description

From the staging area, head past the kiosk up the wide dirt road. The trail immediately begins climbing, gradually at first, and then dips and levels, providing a brief interval of ease before the real climb begins. You'll spot gleaming Lake Hodges to the distant southeast, reflecting the sky's blue or perhaps cloudy gray depending on the day's weather.

The trail soon begins to climb again. Small oak trees planted trailside evoke an imaginary shady respite, which over the years will grow into reality. Pass the 1-mile marker pole and continue climbing. Enjoy the fragrant sage and other plants in our native chaparral. In spring, look for vibrant red monkey flower, purple vetch, and the soft, straining pink blooms of a succulent called chalk live-forever. The official county maps show viewpoints, as yet unmarked, but the entire trail serves as a viewpoint, really. Each bend offers a slightly different vantage point over Escondido. The slashing zigzag of Elfin Forest Recreational Reserve's Way Up Trail cuts into the hills to the southwest. To the north, hills roll into a corridor that forms the wide, high valley of Escondido.

The incline will lessen for a bit, allowing you to catch your breath, and then it grows steep again, bending southwest to reveal another large body of sparkling water. Olivenhain Reservoir glistens to your left and remains in view for a short, level stretch to the endpoint (marked 1.3 miles but measured by my GPS as 1.2 miles). Here, Del Dios Highlands Preserve intersects Elfin Forest Recreational Reserve land. Continue on into the reserve if you wish, or perhaps linger for a bit to rest, then head back down the hill the way you came. Either way, this hike may become a favorite for those seeking an uphill aerobic workout amid the serenity of the Del Dios–area highlands.

Nearby Activities

Authentic Mexican cuisine in a casual lakeside atmosphere with a full-service bar await you at **Hernandez' Hideaway.** Drive 1.6 miles west of the trailhead on Del Dios Highway, turn left, and find the restaurant 0.2 mile ahead on the left, at 19320 Lake Dr. Call 760-746-1444 for more information.

Del Dios Highlands Preserve Trail

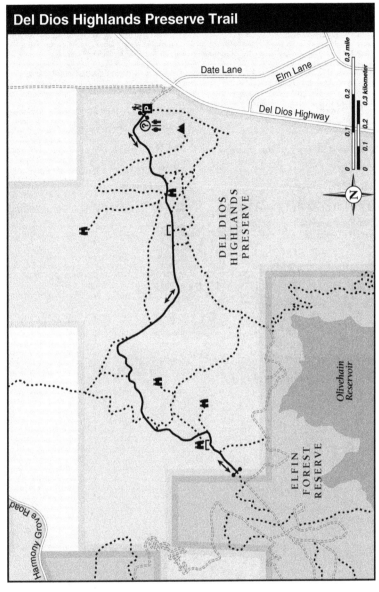

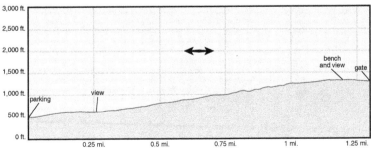

LENGTH & CONFIGURATION
2.6-mile out-and-back

SCENERY Panoramic views of Escondido, Lake Hodges, Olivenhain Water Reservoir, Elfin Forest

EXPOSURE Open to sunlight

TRAFFIC Light–moderate

TRAIL SURFACE Sandy soil, some graveled areas

HIKING TIME 1.5 hours

ACCESS Free; open daily, year-round. Opens at 8 a.m.; parking lot closes

"one-half hour before sunset," which is interpreted loosely by rangers—check the kiosk for specific closing times.

MAPS Online at **tinyurl.com/deldios highlands;** USGS *Escondido*

WHEELCHAIR-ACCESSIBLE? No—this route is too steep for a wheelchair.

FACILITIES None

INFO 760-745-4379, **tinyurl.com /ddhpreserve**

SPECIAL COMMENTS Leashed dogs allowed

GPS INFORMATION AND DIRECTIONS

N33° 5.095' W117° 7.220'

From I-15, exit on Valley Parkway and drive west. Valley Parkway becomes Del Dios Highway at about 2 miles. Drive a total of 2.6 miles to the Del Dios Highlands entrance, on the right (across from Date Lane, which is on the left).

32 Discovery Lake and Double Peak Trails

Looking west from the high point at Double Peak Park

In Brief

Rising almost 700 feet from the lake to Double Peak Park, this well-maintained trail climbing through open space within urban San Marcos is a quick getaway to nature's refreshment. Spectacular views from Double Peak Park at the top, combined with close proximity to the city, make this a favorite for many.

Description

From the parking lot, make your way past the gate and enter the asphalt roadway adjacent to the park. Be aware that caretakers in trucks may occasionally drive slowly by. The lake stretches out on your left. Just past it, the road forks. Turn left for the lake loop—a flat, paved route of 0.8 mile—or take the route uphill toward the peak. Here, we're exploring the 4.02-mile round-trip peak trek, so head up the hill. This first climbing stretch is the warm-up for the nearly 700-foot ascent to Double Peak Park, at an elevation of 1,644 feet.

Discovery Lake and Double Peak Trails

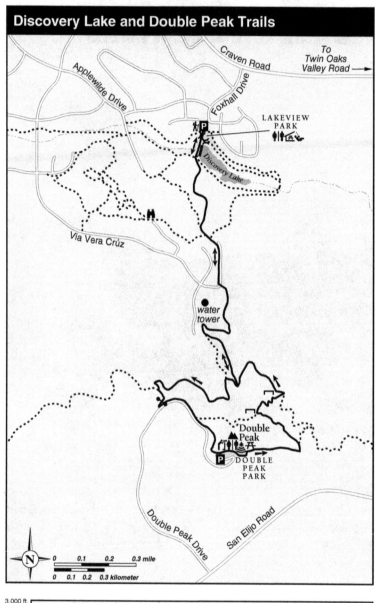

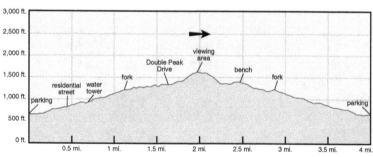

LENGTH & CONFIGURATION 4.02-mile balloon-and-string	**MAPS** Online at **tinyurl.com/discovery lakedoublepeak;** USGS *Rancho Santa Fe*
DIFFICULTY Moderately strenuous	**WHEELCHAIR-ACCESSIBLE?** Partially. The loop around the lake is fully accessible to wheelchair users.
SCENERY Birds, flowers, lake and panoramic views	
EXPOSURE Open to sunlight	**FACILITIES** Restrooms at Double Peak Park and at Lakeview Park
TRAFFIC Moderate	**INFO** 760-744-9000, **tinyurl.com/san marcosparks**
TRAIL SURFACE Pavement and earthen road, some rocky singletrack areas	**SPECIAL COMMENTS** Especially at the lower elevations near the lake, you'll see dog walkers, joggers, and even groups of parents with children, and seniors groups out for strolls. Leashed dogs allowed.
HIKING TIME 2–2.5 hours	
ACCESS Free	

You'll bend left with the road, ignoring offshoot trails to your right, and enjoying the view of Discovery Lake, ever decreasing as you ascend. At about 0.4 mile, the route joins a residential street. Pass through the space between the poles onto the street. Then move to the right, up the dirt path that runs alongside the road. A short distance ahead, this path ends and the trail reopens on the left. After several uphill yards, the route levels and passes a water tower to your right. On the left, the charred hills are evidence of the 2014 fire that ravaged the area. This spot lets you see just how close to these homes the flames licked up the previously dense brush.

The wide dirt road steepens as it moves up the mountain; it can be slippery, so hold on to the pole fencing. For more secure footing, walk in the cement ditch that runs the length of the dirt road.

At about 1.1 miles, turn right to stay on the wide, well-defined trail. Early in the year, when there's moisture in the air, you'll spot some moss growing on the shady portions of the trail. A variety of California wildflowers will cheer you as well. Watch for birds, too: the California brown towhee, mockingbirds, and hummingbirds with their twisting call.

For now, ignore any narrow offshoot trails leading up through the chaparral. The wide trail bends in a westerly course that eventually curves southeast and meets Double Peak Drive. You could use the sidewalk for the final ascent, or you could take the steeper narrow rutted path in the dirt to the left of the road for a more direct route to the top.

The narrow, rutted path delivers you to a viewing area with picnic benches, a scope, and some informative panels. On a clear day, you might see Catalina Island in the western distance. At the very least, you'll see the flat-topped tower of the Encina Power Station on the Carlsbad coast jutting into the sky, and the blue band of the Pacific Ocean beyond. Looking east, Palomar Mountain is visible, and more to the north, the San Jacinto and San Bernardino Mountains.

After a breather at the peak, take a few steps to the east to the front of diminutive Double Peak Park. There are restrooms here. Continuing eastward, you'll pass the park's little amphitheater on the left. Just past that, find the start of a rocky downhill path. The steep route here requires care but soon spills onto flat space at the bottom. Turn left, then look down to the right: The sparkling blue-green of South Lake peeks from the distance.

After just a few steps, you'll see a narrower hillside trail that opens on your left. Take that, moving into the brush. As you follow the northwesterly, sometimes zigzagging path downward, enjoy the sky—a bright overhead strip of light as you move along within the shade of tall chaparral that consists predominantly of scrub oak and ceanothus. The slanting singletrack trail rejoins the main one. Retrace your steps down the wide earthen road to Discovery Lake, being careful on the steep parts again.

At the lake, the happy sounds of children in the playground mix with the tooting of ashen coots squabbling as they paddle about on the lake. On some days, all you'll hear is the gentle lapping of water along the shore. Herons or egrets prowling for fish or frogs in the shallow water may stand as still as statues, cautiously watching as you come near.

Lulled by the birds, a gentle breeze, and your hike toward the sky and back, you may be startled by the piercing call of a soaring hawk overhead. . . . Time to get on with your day, back to the urban civilization that, for a few moments, you forgot was so close.

GPS INFORMATION AND DIRECTIONS
N33° 7.497' W117° 10.715'

From CA 78, exit at San Marcos Boulevard. Drive west for 0.5 mile to Bent Avenue, then turn left. Almost immediately, Bent becomes Craven Road. Travel 0.3 mile and turn right on Foxhall Drive. Proceed another 0.2 mile and turn right into the parking lot for Lakeview Park, where you'll begin.

33 Discovery Lake and Hills Loop

It's a duck parade at Discovery Lake.

In Brief

An urban trek that varies in appearance from park to greenbelt to open chaparral, this loop is used by locals as an exercise route. Local retirement centers bring seniors here to walk the paved lake path, where they mingle with neighborhood families.

Description

Follow the asphalt to the right of the parking lot for just a few steps to reach the lake. From the bridge, watch a heron or egret fishing, their long legs and necks the perfect tools for wading and dipping their beaks into the water, seemingly effortless in their habits.

Alive with ducks, coots, fish, and frogs, the small lake glistens in the sun. Despite the nearby houses and human activity, the animals appear at ease in an environment surrounded by tall reeds, where they can easily retreat. According to City of San Marcos information, bobcats and deer have also been spotted here. Early morning hours are probably best if you hope to see these more elusive creatures.

Across the bridge, you could continue on the paved lake path, curving left and looping around the lake for a short, 0.8-mile walk. For this longer trek, however, go right

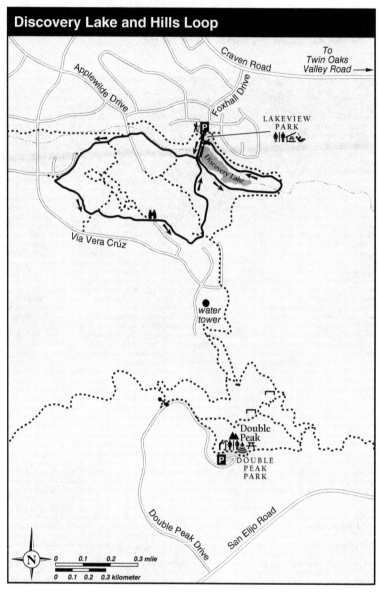

Discovery Lake and Hills Loop

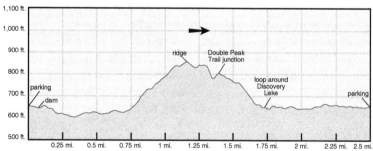

LENGTH & CONFIGURATION 2.5-mile loop	**WHEELCHAIR-ACCESSIBLE?** Partially. The loop around the lake is fully accessible to wheelchairs.
DIFFICULTY Moderately easy	
SCENERY Waterfowl, lake, surrounding homes	**FACILITIES** Restroom at Lakeview Park
	INFO 760-744-9000, **tinyurl.com/san marcosparks**
EXPOSURE Sunny	
TRAFFIC Moderate	**SPECIAL COMMENTS** It can be quite hot on these trails, which are mainly surrounded by blacktop streets in a newer neighborhood where vegetation isn't yet mature. Bring water and be prepared for lots of kids, joggers, and dog walkers around the lake itself—especially on weekends.
TRAIL SURFACE Asphalt and soft soil	
HIKING TIME 1 hour	
ACCESS Free	
MAPS Available at the trailhead kiosk at Lakeview Park and online at **tinyurl.com /discoverylakehills**	

instead, on the downward sloping dirt trail past the bridge. The path will curve left toward nearby houses. Oak trees offer some shade on this section. A side trail leads off to the left, but you'll pass this by and continue along with the creek on your right; off-season, the creek may be dry.

At about 0.75 mile, you'll come to a paved road that heads into the housing complex. Be careful of cars as you cross a street, then hook up with a dirt path on the opposite side. Ignore that right fork that crosses the creek, instead going uphill. Bushy chamise grows abundantly. Also notice straggly tree tobacco, with its smooth bluish-green leaves and cylindrical yellow-green blooms that may appear year-round. Its spindly limbs sway in even the gentlest of breezes—which may be all you get inland on hot days.

At a little over a mile, the trail splits off into the housing tract on the right. Take the left path uphill; do the same when the path splits again. These plentiful side routes make the paths convenient for nearby residents. Continue to the left, heading up the moderately steep hill that curves to follow the route of Via Vera Cruz, the vehicle road down below. Here, on the chaparral-covered hillside, the hike begins to feel more rural. After little more than a third of a mile, the path delivers you along the ridge with views to the east, beyond the quarry, and into the mountains. On clear days, you really can see forever—or close to it. Unfortunately, clear skies mean a view of brown smog as well, sometimes hanging like a dismal tent above the earth in the distance.

You'll pass houses very close on the right. Continue east, moving downhill with the view on the left and fenced backyards on the right. When you reach pavement again, head left to go back down the hill toward the lake. If you're feeling adventurous, hook up with the Double Peak Trail (see previous hike) to the right. Leading about 1 mile to an elevation of 1,644 feet, Double Peak affords panoramic views of the Pacific Ocean to the west and mountains to the north and east. Assuming you've turned left, Discovery Lake comes back into view. The blue-green oasis contrasts sharply with the barren adjacent area that used to be a working quarry. The quarry closed in 2008, silencing its hulking machines with their loud rock-crushing. Watch for a park in the near future, which is planned for at least part of the quarry area.

At the bottom, head right for a 0.8-mile trip around the lake before going back. The pleasant loop is lined with berry bushes and native plants (marked with signs), and the calls of the coots splashing on the lake fill the air. The ashen-colored birds splash noisily about, quarreling endlessly among themselves—but they're also very smart. According to a recent University of California Santa Cruz study that was published in the journal *Nature,* the birds can count and keep track of how many eggs they lay. Coots who don't win prime nesting spots don't give up their chance to have offspring either. They lay their eggs in other birds' nests—maybe that's what all the squabbling is about!

Where the lake loop bears left, make the curve around to the other side. Back near Lakeview Park, you'll notice a small gate leading to a dock where people sometimes feed the ducks and coots.

Nearby Activities

If you're hungry after your hike, turn left on San Marcos Boulevard and drive about 1 mile to San Marcos's restaurant row. Cuisines run the gamut from Thai to Mexican to seafood.

GPS INFORMATION AND DIRECTIONS

N33° 7.497' W117° 10.715'

From CA 78, exit at San Marcos Boulevard. Drive west for 0.5 mile to Bent Avenue, then turn left. Almost immediately, Bent becomes Craven Road. Travel 0.3 mile and turn right on Foxhall Drive. Proceed another 0.2 mile and turn right into the parking lot for Lakeview Park, where you'll begin.

---

34 Dixon Lake:

SHORE VIEW TRAIL

Within the safety of the lake, a cormorant suns itself upon a rock.

In Brief

There's something about ambling along a large body of water that calms the spirit. Unbelievably peaceful on weekdays, Dixon Lake is a slice of inland paradise: sage scrub, wildflowers, birds, and water all combine to make this an easy, rewarding hike.

Description

From the parking area, proceed northeast and find the trail marker near the vehicle road. The rock-edged path heads south, just above the grassy picnic area, and continues a short distance past some small pines and acacias where scrub jays flutter. The trail gets a little rocky as it gradually descends, bringing the northwestern edge of the lake into view. A wooden footbridge crosses Jack's Creek, which slows to a trickle in summer and fall.

Past the footbridge, the trail heads around the cattail-filled Jack's Creek Cove and bends to the left toward the pier. A breathtaking view of the entire lake stretches out to the east, making it feel as if you've stumbled into paradise. The brilliant blue-green water is alive with squabbling American coots. The birds hunt for a meal alongside the anglers,

151

Dixon Lake: Shore View Trail

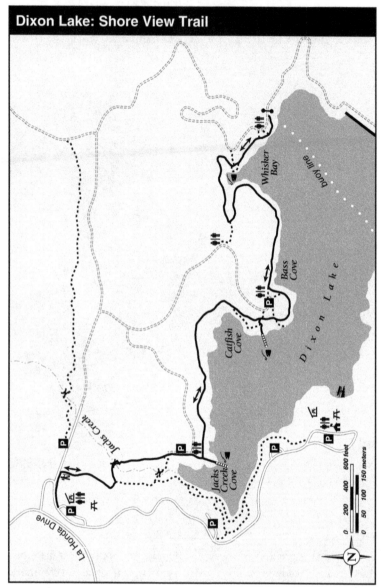

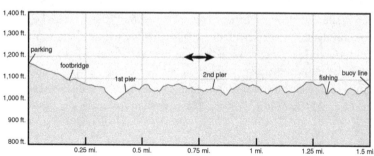

LENGTH & CONFIGURATION 3-mile out-and-back	**WHEELCHAIR-ACCESSIBLE?** No, due to narrow trail width and uneven terrain
DIFFICULTY Easy	**FACILITIES** Public restrooms at the parking lot near picnic area; portable toilets along the trail
SCENERY Lake, birds, chaparral, wildflowers	
EXPOSURE Mostly sunny	**INFO** 760-839-4680, **escondido.org/dixon -lake.aspx**
TRAFFIC Heavy on weekends; light on weekdays	
TRAIL SURFACE Packed dirt	**SPECIAL COMMENTS** The difference in weekend and weekday traffic is like night and day; for a peaceful commune with nature, hike this easy, family-friendly trail on nonholiday weekdays. As always when near water, be alert and supervise children.
HIKING TIME 1.5 hours	
ACCESS $5 parking fee on weekends and holidays; open daily, 6 a.m.–sunset	
MAPS At the ranger station; USGS *Valley Center*	

who pose like statues in their boats. The lively coots are fun to watch. Tread lightly, though. The ash-dark birds with bright-white bills glide away in a V of gentle breakwater as you near. If you're quiet and catch one unaware, you may see a bird dive through the clear water to the lake bottom, grab a tasty crustacean, and paddle to the surface to eat.

You can walk out onto the first pier to see anglers hanging their poles out for a catch. Continuing on the trail, you will find lots of areas where you can easily get closer to the water and sit on large rocks along the shore. A second pier lies just past Catfish Cove. There is a portable toilet in the parking area, a few short steps from the trail.

The sage scrub thins, and you'll come to a drier section where the trail is higher above the water. The coots like to hang out here, near Bass Cove, where they're hidden from view of the path. You'll hear them, though. With a series of short clicks, they warn of your presence; the birds pass the signal from one to the next. These sounds intersperse with longer, higher notes. Close your eyes and the birds' more-excited squabbling may conjure the image of a child's bicycle horn.

Head on around to Whisker Bay, where people fish from the shore. When you reach the bench at a fork in the path, go right. You'll pass through a cool, shady area where ferns cascade down the decomposing granite alongside the trail, and willows and overgrown laurel sumac tangle with wild berry and wild cucumber vines. Sage and mint grow in abundance on this stretch as well, pleasantly scenting the air.

The trail widens into an open rock face approaching the buoy line, which marks the end of the hike. Dusky-brown cormorants balance on the cable line and atop the oblong red buoys, drying their not-quite-waterproof wings in the sun. With their long necks outstretched, they keep a cautious eye on anyone watching them. It's difficult to get a photograph of these ultrawary birds. They will fly away even as you aim your camera. Enjoy the cormorants for the time you can—they serve as a good reminder to enjoy every moment, a mentality that will serve you well while hiking.

Calm water mirrors the sky.

As you head back, focus on the vegetation. Mesmerized by the water, you may have missed it on the way. From early spring through late summer, you will likely see skullcap, with its upright, dark-purple flowers. California fuchsia, sometimes called honeysuckle trumpet, blooms in profusion here. I've seen the narrow, orange-red flowers right into fall here at the lake. California lilac offers delicate clusters of pale blue–purple flowers that contrast with the dark-green leaves of the shrub. When you reach the bench at the trail fork, you can turn right and head west up to the vehicle road. The trail ends here, where there are two portable toilets, and you can walk along the vehicle road, if you choose.

GPS INFORMATION AND DIRECTIONS

N33° 9.982' W117° 3.050'

Take I-15 to the El Norte Parkway exit. Travel east on El Norte for about 4 miles to La Honda Drive, then turn left. Follow the road to the top and turn right into the gate for Lake Dixon. Make an immediate right and park in the lot.

35 Elfin Forest Recreational Reserve: BOTANICAL LOOP

In Brief

This well-maintained trail offers a quiet, easy loop that makes it perfect for any age. The "Botanical Trail Guide" published by reserve staff lends an educational element that makes this foray into nature even richer.

Description

To access the Botanical Loop Trail, head south across the cement creek bridge as if to hike the Way Up Trail (see next hike), which is marked by a sign near the reserve's entrance. Once across the cement, turn right and walk uphill for about 200 feet. The trail bends east, connecting with the Botanical Loop Trail after about 0.5 mile.

Take a "Botanical Trail Guide" from the box on the left and head down the hill onto the loop trail. Numbered marker poles correspond with informative paragraphs in the guide. You'll see hollyleaf cherry, a bushy plant with hollylike leaves. And the guide will identify things you may have wondered about. Notice the reddish-brown "fruit" often seen hanging from scrub oak. They're not oak apples, oak oranges, or any other oak fruit. The ping-pong–sized balls are "galls" made when the California gall wasp lays its eggs in the stem. When the larvae emerge from their eggs, they release a chemical that causes the stem to swell into a gall. The gall provides food and protection for the tiny wasps.

Some plants aren't included in the guide. You may also notice clumps of thistle. In years past, the plant with its "milk"-splattered leaves was prevalent. On recent visits, the drought seems to have thinned them. The tangy, herbaceous scent of black sage wafts up as the trail levels and heads east through the partial shade of oak trees growing along the path.

Continuing, the route turns left (north), beginning the loop formation, and gradually descends at an easy grade. The ground is rocky through this section but not dangerously so. You'll find a bench in the shade along this stretch.

Make the curve to the left and head west, moving into the denser shade of thicker oak forest. You'll hear the creek running, and within a few more steps, spot water gurgling over the large, flat rocks you'll use to cross. Heed the posted warnings. The creek crossing is a natural one and can be dangerous when the water is high. Use common sense and caution.

Once across, notice the arroyo willow, with its feathery blooms that turn to cottony fuzz. On windier late-spring days, you may find yourself in a fuzz storm. You'll see a road on the right that leads to a second parking lot. Pass this and continue west to the reserve's entrance. The path ahead, framed by placed rocks and pole-and-cable fencing, leads the way back to the marker for the Way Up Trail, the entrance, and your car.

Elfin Forest Recreational Reserve: Botanical Trail

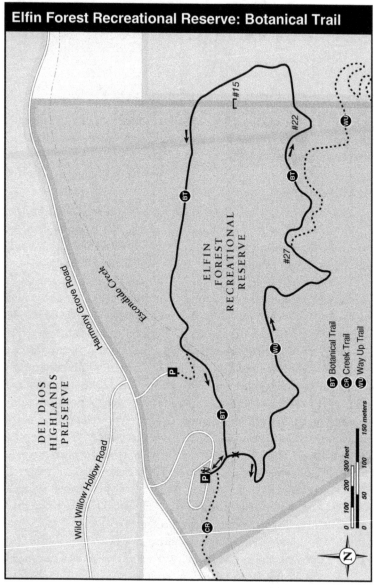

DEL DIOS
HIGHLANDS
PRESERVE

Wild Willow Hollow Road

Harmony Grove Road

Escondido Creek

ELFIN
FOREST
RECREATIONAL
RESERVE

#15

#22

#27

WU

BT Botanical Trail
CR Creek Trail
WU Way Up Trail

0   100   200   300 feet
0   50   100   150 meters

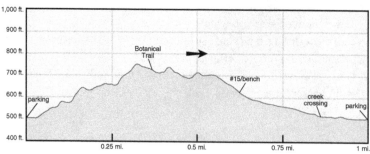

1,000 ft.
900 ft.
800 ft.
700 ft.
600 ft.
500 ft.
400 ft.

parking

Botanical
Trail

#15/bench

creek
crossing

parking

0.25 mi.   0.5 mi.   0.75 mi.   1 mi.

LENGTH & CONFIGURATION
1-mile balloon-with-string

DIFFICULTY Easy

SCENERY Native plants, described with interesting facts in the "Botanical Trail Guide," available in a box at the trail's start or online at **tinyurl.com/elfinforest maps** You can also find a bird-watcher's guide at this URL.

EXPOSURE Sunny and shady

TRAFFIC Moderate

TRAIL SURFACE Earthen path, leaf litter

HIKING TIME 45 minutes

ACCESS Free; open daily (except December 25 and rainy days), 8 a.m.–30 minutes before sunset. Check the trailhead kiosk for specific daily closing times.

MAPS Available at kiosk near parking area or online at **tinyurl.com/elfinforestmaps**

WHEELCHAIR-ACCESSIBLE? No, due to creek crossing and steep, rocky sections

FACILITIES Restrooms near parking area; visitor center

INFO 760-632-4212, **olivenhain.com /elfin-forest-recreational-reserve**

SPECIAL COMMENTS The Botanical Loop is designated for hikers only and includes a creek crossing.

GPS INFORMATION AND DIRECTIONS

N33° 5.194' W117° 8.717'

From I-15 South, take the Auto Parkway exit and turn left. Then turn left on Ninth Avenue, at the traffic signal. Proceed on Ninth, across the Valley Parkway intersection; the road bends sharply left. Ninth Avenue becomes Hale here. Continue on Hale to Harmony Grove Road. To stay on Harmony Grove, you must make the first two left turns; otherwise, you'll end up on Enterprise Street or Kauana Loa Drive. Past the second left turn, proceed on Harmony Grove Road to Elfin Forest Recreational Reserve, which appears on the left 1.5 miles past Country Club Drive. Turn left into the parking lot.

36 Elfin Forest Recreational Reserve: WAY UP AND EQUINE INCLINE TRAILS

Overlooking the reservoir on a misty morning

In Brief

Delicate springtime flowers in this rugged terrain may surprise you. The Way Up Trail earned its namesake because of its continual uphill tread leading into the Equine Incline, which heads first down and then up, looping back to the Way Up Trail.

Description

Immediately past the information kiosk, you're likely to hear the water rushing down year-round Escondido Creek.

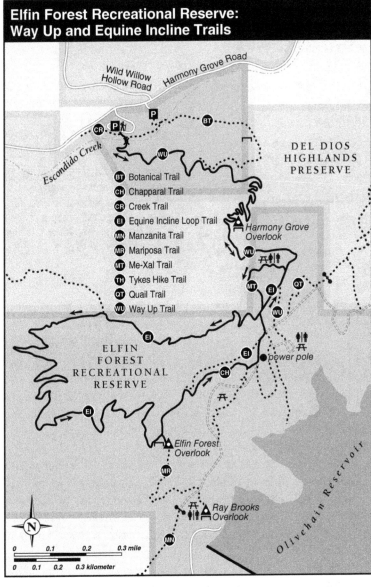

Elfin Forest Recreational Reserve:
Way Up and Equine Incline Trails

BT Botanical Trail
CH Chapparal Trail
CR Creek Trail
EI Equine Incline Loop Trail
MN Manzanita Trail
MR Mariposa Trail
MT Me-Xal Trail
TH Tykes Hike Trail
QT Quail Trail
WU Way Up Trail

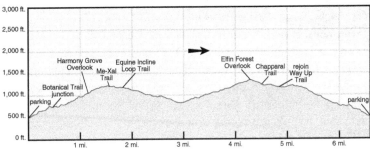

LENGTH & CONFIGURATION
5.6-mile balloons-and-string

DIFFICULTY Moderately strenuous
(uphill sections)

SCENERY Wildflowers in spring and
summer, rock formations

EXPOSURE Sun

TRAFFIC Moderate–heavy on weekends

TRAIL SURFACE Earthen path, mostly
well packed

HIKING TIME 3–3.5 hours

ACCESS Free; open daily (except December 25 and rainy days), 8 a.m.–30 minutes
before sunset. Check the trailhead kiosk
for specific daily closing times.

MAPS Available at kiosk near parking area
or online at **tinyurl.com/elfinforestmaps**

WHEELCHAIR-ACCESSIBLE? No, due to
steep, rocky sections

FACILITIES Restrooms near parking
area and also near reservoir overlook.
Visitor center.

INFO 760-632-4212, **olivenhain.com/elfin
-forest-recreational-reserve**

SPECIAL COMMENTS Bicyclists and
dog lovers frequent this multiuse trail.
On weekdays and nonholidays, dogs are
allowed off-leash at the top of the Way
Up Trail (see signs at park); dogs must be
leashed in other areas.

Spot the sign marked way up trail and head south across a cement creek bridge. If
you haven't brought along your own, consider borrowing one of the walking sticks placed
here for visitor use—it might come in handy in the steeper areas. Turn right and head
uphill about 200 feet. The trail curves left (east). Look for miner's lettuce growing on trail
edges. The leaves are edible and supposedly taste good either raw or boiled and salted. No
collecting is allowed on reserve land, but the plants were easy picking for Indians and
others traveling through the area in historical times. Thick and green in early spring, with
a tiny white flower blooming in the center of the leaf bowl, the succulent's color turns a
rusty red as spring's moisture fades in summer heat.

Also prevalent here are the pearly purple-white blooms of morning glories. The
trailing herb that is common to Southern California's chaparral twines over rocks and
bushes, forming a lacy backdrop for the monkey flowers' bright splashes of red and
orange. Another bright, orange-red flower found here is fringed Indian pink, with its
slashed ("fringed") petals and sticky, hairy stems that discourage ants and other small
crawling insects.

Continuing, the route bends to the right (south) again, and meets with the Botanical
Loop Trail at 0.4 mile. Pass this by, climbing steadily south, with small bends in the route.
These curves tighten into short, steep switchbacks with views of chaparral and interesting rock formations. In spring, lizards dart about as you pass, disturbed from their sunning spots on solar-heated rocks along the trail.

Reach the Harmony Grove Overlook at about 0.9 mile, perhaps stopping to rest on the
shaded bench. Another 0.3 mile brings you to a hard right turn, which will lead to another
side trail, the Me-Xal Trail, at 1.25 miles. Turn here to avoid the traffic of the main trail. The
0.2-mile spur loop takes you past a picnic table and benches without shade but with a southern view of Escondido and beyond. The path then loops back to the Way Up Trail.

Turn right, back onto the Way Up Trail, and proceed north just a few yards to where trail splits into a Y. Choose the right-hand path to enter the Equine Incline (going left takes you closer to a view of the reservoir, which is a rewarding turnaround point for those not wanting to hike much farther). On the Equine Incline, a steep, rocky stretch soon settles into a more gradual downhill clip, zigzagging in places. You'll travel about 1 mile, with high chaparral on either side of the narrow downhill path.

What goes down must go back up, and you'll begin the return climb at about 2.5 miles from the original trailhead. After climbing steadily uphill for about another mile, you'll reach a right turnoff leading to the Elfin Forest Overlook. On warm days, the shaded benches will beckon you. Once sufficiently rested, head back to the trail, moving to the right. The reservoir soon comes into view, a vast blue expanse on the right.

At 3.75 miles, you'll come to the Chaparral Trail, which is a 0.25-mile spur that curves back to the Equine Incline. Take this short stretch for a better view of the water, which glistens with the brilliance of a zillion diamonds on sunny days, and calls to mind (and heart) the life-giving properties water holds for us.

The Chaparral Trail leads out onto a dirt-surface maintenance road. Turn left, heading past the massive power pole that only mars the natural features if you focus on it. You'll soon spot a side trail on your left, where the Equine Incline meets the road. And a few feet ahead, take the second opening for the Equine Incline, which will deliver you back to the Y point of the Way Up Trail and beyond. Retrace your steps from here, continuing along the Way Up Trail, which leads you back down to the trailhead. Return any borrowed hiking sticks. On warm days, you'll want to stop near the creek and enjoy the shade of oak trees and the babble of the running water.

Nearby Activities

If you're hungry and heading back to the freeway, look for several drive-through and traditional restaurants near the Valley Parkway and Auto Parkway intersection.

GPS INFORMATION AND DIRECTIONS

N33° 5.194' W117° 8.717'

From I-15 South, take the Auto Parkway exit and turn left. Then turn left on Ninth Avenue, at the traffic signal. Proceed on Ninth, across the Valley Parkway intersection; the road bends sharply left. Ninth Avenue becomes Hale here. Continue on Hale to Harmony Grove Road. To stay on Harmony Grove, you must make the first two left turns; otherwise, you'll end up on Enterprise Street or Kauana Loa Drive. Past the second left turn, proceed on Harmony Grove Road to Elfin Forest Recreational Reserve, which appears on the left 1.5 miles past Country Club Drive. Turn left into the parking lot.

37 Heller's Bend Preserve Trail

In Brief

This peaceful 27-acre preserve offers a short jaunt into natural surroundings where the cares of the day are easily forgotten. It's a lovely spot for families looking for a short, easy foray into nature.

Description

Just on the other side of the white fence that runs along Heller's Bend Road, the croaky refrain of frogs and toads making their homes around Ostrich Farms Creek drowns out the sounds of city life. A few yards down the hill from the entrance, you'll see the year-round creek running east to west. The path runs east before quickly bending southward. On the right a bench nestles in the shade of oaks near some boulders. If you care to pause awhile and let the preserve's serenity calm you, this is a convenient spot.

On the other side of the cement bridge, the path begins ascending, bending east, then south again through a jungle of oak forest tangled in wild grapes and guarded by a variety of spiky-leafed thistle. Sunlight filters in through the stretching branches of the mature live oaks as you make your way up the trail. At about 0.3 mile, the oak forest thins, letting in sunlight. The passage levels a bit, leading you through the remnants of old orange and avocado groves full of mostly nonproducing trees. In early spring, the orange trees bloom, releasing a gentle, tangy scent.

At about 0.4 mile, a short offshoot on the left takes you to an eastern lookout point, which is only about 50 yards off the path. The main trail continues steeply uphill for a short distance, then levels abruptly. At the top, which is 0.5 mile from the gate, benches overlook the rolling hills of Fallbrook to the northeast. This is the end of the trail, offering an eagle's-nest view.

Descending is quicker than climbing the 0.5 mile, but take time to enjoy the scenery. Both the laurel sumac, with its red-tinged leaves, and a variety of sage bushes grow all along the route, giving off a spicy scent.

On the way back, if you're up for a little more exploring, look for trails stretching east on either side of the creek. The first is a sandy, single-track offshoot just before the creek crossing. It leads east less than 0.1 mile to the water's edge.

If you prefer, sit for a few moments on the cement bridge itself. On the west side, the water enters large corrugated pipes, the low, rushing sound similar to that of a train moving rhythmically along its tracks. On the east side, the water gushes from the pipes, spilling out into the creek that slows and ripples its way into the trees.

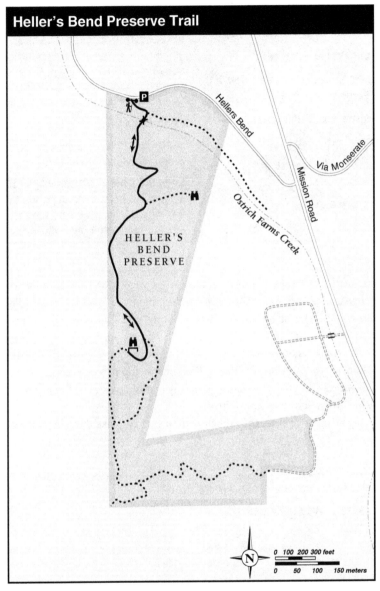

Heller's Bend Preserve Trail

HELLER'S BEND PRESERVE

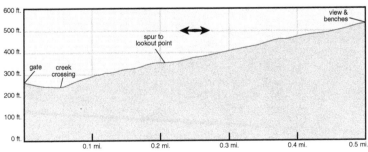

LENGTH & CONFIGURATION 1-mile out-and-back with side trails	**MAPS** Google map at website below
DIFFICULTY Moderately easy	**WHEELCHAIR-ACCESSIBLE?** Not at this writing. The trail itself is navigable, but a small opening in the preserve's fence—the gate is kept locked—is blocked by a pole that you have to walk around.
SCENERY Birds, stream, trees, view of the city of Fallbrook	
EXPOSURE Mostly shady, some sunny	**FACILITIES** None
TRAFFIC Light	**INFO** 760-728-0889, **fallbrookland conservancy.org/hellers-bend**
TRAIL SURFACE Asphalt; optional side trails are sandy soil.	**SPECIAL COMMENTS** Although not a traditional horse park where riders can trailer in their horses, the preserve is used by equestrian enthusiasts who live nearby.
HIKING TIME 30 minutes	
ACCESS Free	

Wait quietly, and frogs and toads hidden in the vegetation will serenade you. Triggered by one leading call, their music rises to a symphony of mingling croaks. Then, just as suddenly as the chorus began, the song abruptly ends—you can almost imagine an amphibious bandleader demanding silence with a sweep of his baton.

Past the creek, another offshoot trail stretches east for about 0.2 mile. Walk this sandy path beneath towering sycamores. From its treetop perch, a red-tailed hawk may utter its displeasure at your presence—especially at dusk, when he's hungry for a rodent that may hide when it hears your footsteps.

When you amble back up the asphalt path to your car, take the calm of the preserve with you.

GPS INFORMATION AND DIRECTIONS

N33° 18.907' W117° 14.050'

Take I-15 North to the Pala/CA 76 exit and go left (west) 4.9 miles to Mission Road, then turn right. After 1.4 miles, turn left on Heller's Bend. The preserve sign and entrance are on the left, at 0.3 mile. Turn around where safe and park on the shoulder of the road, outside the gate.

38 Hellhole Canyon Open Space Preserve Trail

Starting out on the Hellhole Canyon Trail

In Brief

Members of the Friends of Hellhole Canyon organization know that Hellhole Canyon is heavenly. If you like wide-open spaces and don't mind the heat, you will agree that this 1,907-acre preserve is an earthly paradise.

Description

Though not far, the lovely country scenery on the two-lane road to Hellhole Canyon gets nature-loving hikers into a relaxed mood before they step foot onto the trail.

A kiosk at the trailhead holds maps and information about Hellhole Canyon. From here, walk north on the easy path, which quickly changes to a steep descent through manzanita and scrub oak, as of this writing still in a pattern of regrowth after the firestorms of fall 2003. After about 0.1 mile, find a topographical map molded from metal sitting atop a stone pillar. Placed in 2001, the map shows preserve trails and elevations.

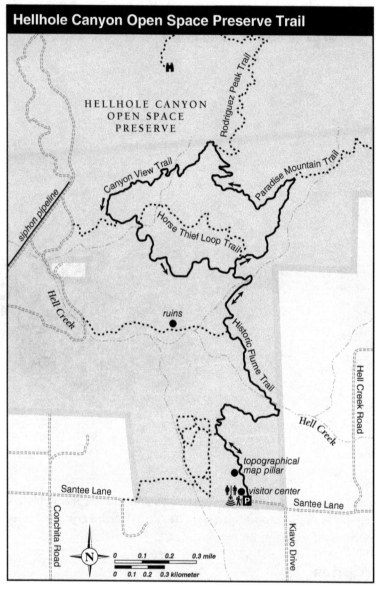

Hellhole Canyon Open Space Preserve Trail

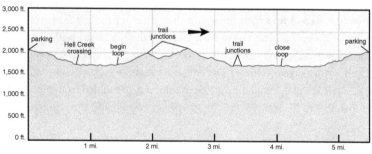

LENGTH & CONFIGURATION 5.5-mile balloon	**MAPS** Free from the box at the trailhead kiosk or online at **tinyurl.com/hellhole canyonmap**
DIFFICULTY Easy–moderately strenuous	
SCENERY Trees, chaparral, wide-open space	**WHEELCHAIR-ACCESSIBLE?** No, due to steep and rocky areas
EXPOSURE Mostly sunny	**FACILITIES** Public restrooms at trailhead
TRAFFIC Heavy on first mile	**INFO** 760-742-1631, **tinyurl.com/hellhole canyonpreserve**
TRAIL SURFACE Packed dirt, some rocky areas	
HIKING TIME 3.5 hours	**SPECIAL COMMENTS** The trail is shared by equestrians and pedestrians. Bring plenty of water, even in moderate and cool weather. Wear a hat. Leashed dogs allowed.
ACCESS Free; open Friday–Monday, 8 a.m.–sunset. Closed during August due to extreme heat.	

At 0.75 mile, the path flattens and becomes sandy, leading around granite boulders to seasonal Hell Creek. The creek used to run year-round, but lack of adequate rainfall in recent years means water is present only after winter and spring rains. The riparian landscape of Western sycamores and twisting oaks provides welcome shade all along the creek bed. If there is a flow, stop for a few moments and listen to the gurgle of water, or simply appreciate the cool air and serenity of nature here under the spreading oak canopy. Be careful of poison oak.

The creek area is a favorite of many who come to Hellhole Canyon Open Space Preserve just for the entry trail. Others hike farther into the canyon, stopping to rest in the shade on their way back to civilization. A stone wall above the creek bed provides adequate seating beneath the trees, although there is quite a drop; watch children carefully—or clumsy dogs. A young pup of ours nearly took a spill on our last visit! The tree limbs stretch out over the creek and reach across the trail. Dapples of filtered sunlight glint rainbowlike in the shade.

The route down to the creek and back is the most traveled portion of the canyon. Emerging from the shady creek area, the level trail travels in the open for about 0.2 mile, then narrows and bends northeast through the spotty shade of chaparral and oak trees. The hillside rises on the right as well, also providing shade. Wild cucumber grows in a thick net on outstretched manzanita branches, charred by the fire. The route bends northwest again and reaches a fork leading either left or right into the loop trail. This is a logical turnaround spot for those ready to go back.

Hardy hikers who are unafraid of dry heat can turn right at the trail marker and begin climbing. The first 0.5-mile section of the loop gains 200 feet in elevation on a rocky, red-dirt trail reminiscent of the Red Planet. The only water here is in your toted-in bottles, which you'll need even in moderate fall or spring weather here at Hellhole Canyon.

Turn left at the trail marker and travel 0.7 mile of steep switchbacks over lighter-colored, rocky soil to an elevation of 2,475 feet. Watch for locusts. The plentiful insects blend in with the rocky dirt, and often don't move until you're right upon them, at which time they burst from the ground in a buzzing flurry—sometimes right up to your face. The insects may be the only signs of life you spot out here where fewer hikers venture.

On these higher segments of the loop trail, the chaparral grows smaller due to the drier soil. This becomes even more evident near the end of the next segment of trail, reached by bearing left at the next marker. This third, southwesterly 0.8-mile section of the loop starts out steep, and then descends more gradually to an elevation of 1,820 feet. The surroundings grow greener as you descend. Wild cucumber vines twine onto the path, and aromatic sage springs up near yucca and prickly pear cactus.

At the next trail marker, turn left onto the 0.7-mile closing segment of the loop. This mostly sunny, very gently climbing trail has a couple of sections where trees grow on either side. Pause at these three- and four-yard oases where the wind ruffles the leaves and birds come to call.

Turn right at the trail marker back onto the entry trail and retrace your steps past the creek and up through the manzanita forest.

Nearby Activities

Back on Woods Valley Road, you'll find **Bates Nut Farm** and shady picnic areas where you can watch ducks, geese, chicken, goats, and sheep in nearby pens. Inside the store among dried fruits, nuts, and other goodies, a bag of feeding corn costs pennies and keeps the critters coming to the fence for a pat by eager children. Handicrafts are sold here by local artisans on some weekends, and in the fall there are hayrides and a pumpkin patch. For more information, call 760-749-3333 or visit **batesnutfarm.biz.**

GPS INFORMATION AND DIRECTIONS

N33° 13.005' W116° 56.037'

From I-15, take the Valley Parkway exit and travel east toward Valley Center about 9 miles. From Valley Parkway, turn right on Woods Valley Road, which becomes Paradise Mountain Road at Lake Wohlford Road. From the start of Woods Valley Road, travel about 7 miles to a five-way intersection. Make a right on Los Hormanos Roach Road, then an immediate left on Kiavo Drive. Travel north 0.5 mile. Turn left at the hellhole canyon sign and park in the gravel lot at the top of the hill.

39 Iron Mountain Peak Trail

Close to the sky at Iron Mountain Peak   PHOTO: RORY McGREGOR

In Brief

The mountain is named for its iron ore content, but the moniker could just as easily refer to the brute strength it takes to get to the top of this winding trail. The 2,696-foot peak allows hikers to touch the sky.

Description

From the parking lot where CA 67 meets Poway Road, follow the short spur trail leading southeast to the main trail. The very gently up-sloping path leads through rows of small oak trees. Although scorched in the fall 2003 firestorm, the trees survived. The cool shade they provide increases with each year of growth. Pass by the side trail you'll spot after about 0.25 mile; the north-stretching trail leads to the Ellie Lane staging area, which is popular with the equestrian crowd. Continue east on the silt-soil path that grows rockier from here, typical of much of this hike.

After about 1.5 miles, you will come to an intersection; head south (right). The path moves southwest up a well-maintained but rocky path that zigzags through air pleasantly scented by wild sage. Orange, yellow, violet, and peach wildflowers bloom through late spring; yuccas stretch upward, their tall central shaft bursting into bloom-adorned flags. In some areas the ground is an ashen black, reminders of fires that roared through this

Iron Mountain Peak Trail

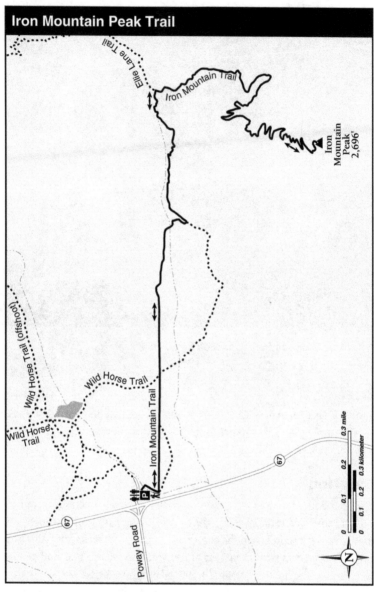

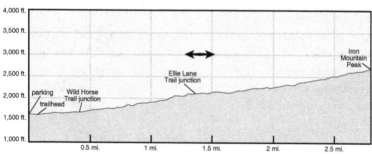

LENGTH & CONFIGURATION 5.6-mile out-and-back	at **tinyurl.com/powaytrails;** USGS *San Vicente Reservoir*
DIFFICULTY Moderately strenuous	**WHEELCHAIR-ACCESSIBLE?** No, due to steep and rocky trail
SCENERY Panoramic views	**FACILITIES** Portable toilet on the entry trail
EXPOSURE Sunny	
TRAFFIC Heavy	**INFO** powaytrails.com
TRAIL SURFACE Rocky soil	**SPECIAL COMMENTS** Climbing to an elevation of 2,696 feet, this trail is not recommended for unconditioned or inexperienced hikers. Consider bringing a hiking stick. Binoculars come in handy to enjoy panoramic vistas from the peak. Leashed dogs allowed.
HIKING TIME 3.5 hours	
ACCESS Free; open daily, sunrise–sunset	
MAPS Available at trailhead and online	

area—one in 1995, and another in 2003. Logs placed at right angles on the path guard against erosion and help with footing. Small children will need to stoop for handgrips occasionally along the rocky and sometimes steep path.

Watch for runners making their way swiftly down the mountain. Others pass with hiking poles—especially useful on the way down. Leashed dogs pass, tongues lolling, with kind owners who dribble bottled water into cupped hands from which their dogs gratefully lap.

About 1 mile from the intersection you'll spot manzanita, which tends to grow at higher elevations. The path continues for another 0.7 mile to the peak, alternating between steep, rocky sections and soft-soiled plateaus that appear just when hikers run short of breath.

At the peak, a picnic bench and several boulders offer a restful reward in the form of spectacular views. The lookout is especially magnificent near sunset, when the sky turns a red-purple hue. Before trekking back down the mountain, watch a crow glide peacefully overhead and ponder your place in the universe. From this vantage point, the world of limitless possibilities stretches below.

Nearby Activities

For a fresh bite to eat, stop at **Ichizen Sushi & Japanese Cuisine** (13307 Poway Rd.). I always get the bento box; you might like sushi, soup, or a seafood bowl. Call 858-486-4558 for more information.

GPS INFORMATION AND DIRECTIONS
N32° 58.652' W116°58.360'

Take I-15 to the Poway Road exit and travel 8.8 miles east to CA 67. Continue straight at the light, through the intersection into the large parking area.

40 Iron Mountain to Lake Ramona Overlook and Pond

In Brief

About the same length as the trail to Iron Mountain's peak, this loop has a wide-open feel; the mountains seem to part, the trail cleaving a path into the wilderness.

Description

From the parking lot where CA 67 meets Poway Road, follow the short spur trail leading southeast to the main trail, and continue east on the gently up-sloping path as described in the previous hike. When you reach the intersection at 1.5 miles, go left. The path slopes downhill, curving more northward, with mountains on either side damping the noise from CA 67. You'll note the effects of the 2003 fires here, but chaparral regenerates well, which you'll note here. About 0.25 mile past the trail intersection, switchbacks lead uphill. The trail reaches the overlook point after another 0.25 mile. A sign directs visitors several yards to the right for a view of Ramona.

Here the path joins the 2.8-mile Ellie Lane Trail and leads west across dry, rocky land. A long southwestward stretch is almost level, zigzagging in spots. After about 1 mile, the trail turns north again. Side trails stretch west toward the eucalyptus trees and a pond. Continue north. The route becomes steep and slippery, an undulating pattern on rocky ground that soon levels and turns west again. Hundreds of huge boulders dwarf passersby. Some of the massive rocks sit in piles of flaked stone. When the flames whipped through this area in the fall of 2003, the speed of the stones' natural flaking process was increased because trapped air expanded quickly, causing the boulders' outermost layers to burst and fall to the ground. Some is powdery now, owing to exposure and the passage of time.

You'll notice Table Rock on your left. The interesting formation looks as if it were plucked straight from the Flintstones' cartoon kitchen. A short distance ahead, a scorched oak tree shows signs of regrowth and promises increasing shade as its leaves regenerate.

The trail dips southwest to join the 1.2-mile Wild Horse Trail—tiring to contemplate after having hiked so far already. Enjoy the pond with its rustling reeds. Perhaps spot frogs escaping in a splash when you approach, or see a duck or two paddling lazily in the sparkling water.

When you reach the Iron Mountain Trail, turn right and head back toward the trailhead. If you look closely, you may spot rabbit tracks in the soft soil along the oak-lined entry trail.

Iron Mountain to Ramona Overlook and Pond

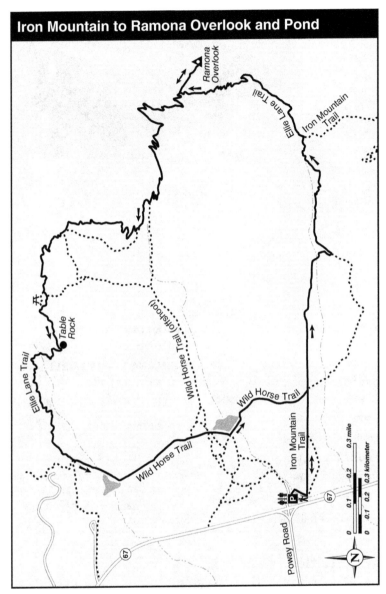

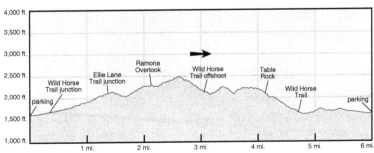

An American coot floats merrily along

LENGTH & CONFIGURATION
6-mile balloon-and-string

DIFFICULTY Moderately strenuous

SCENERY Interesting rock formations; possibility of wildlife, waterfowl at pond

EXPOSURE Sunny

TRAFFIC Light–moderate

TRAIL SURFACE Rocky soil

HIKING TIME 3.5 hours

ACCESS Free; open daily, sunrise–sunset

MAPS Available at trailhead and online

at **tinyurl.com/powaytrails;** USGS *San Vicente Reservoir*

WHEELCHAIR-ACCESSIBLE? No, due to steep and rocky trail

FACILITIES Portable toilet on entry trail

INFO powaytrails.com

SPECIAL COMMENTS Bring plenty of water and choose mild weather days to best enjoy the trek. After rains, an abundance of running water transforms this hike into a watery wonderland. Leashed dogs allowed.

Nearby Activities

Not that you'd *want* to go . . . but the **Poway Bernardo Mortuary,** featured on the old A&E reality show *Family Plots* (now resurrected on hard-to-get DVDs), is located on Poway Road.

GPS INFORMATION AND DIRECTIONS

N32° 58.652' W116° 58.360'

Take I-15 to the Poway Road exit and travel 8.8 miles east to CA 67. Continue straight at the light, through the intersection into the newly constructed parking area.

41 Lake Hodges:
NORTH SHORE TRAIL

The lake stretches out like a shiny ribbon.

In Brief

This easy hike is overrun by bicyclists on the weekends, but weekdays (aside from fishing season) are quiet and serene.

Description

From the parking lot, head south on the paved walkway that makes the first section accessible for people with disabilities. Interstate 15 runs along the right of this paved area for about 0.5 mile. Sage scrub, black sage, and California buckwheat grow close to the trail, scenting the air. On windy days, the rustling of grasses in the meadows to the left sounds like ocean waves and dulls the roar of traffic on the adjacent interstate.

The walkway bends to the right, ducking under the freeway. In the spring, cliff swallows gather by the thousands, swooping to and from their mud nests beneath the freeway. The paved walkway bears right in the cool shade where cyclists speed by (be careful!) and heads north for a short distance until the pavement ends and the dirt trail begins.

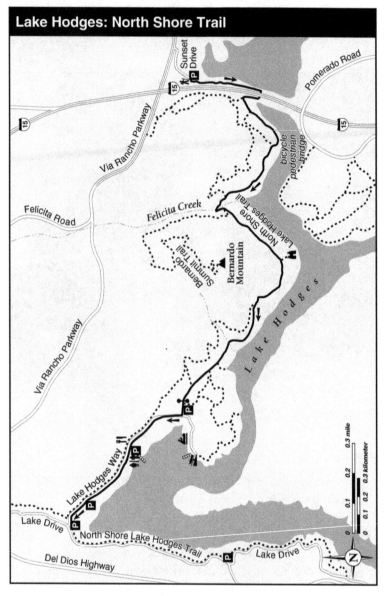

Lake Hodges: North Shore Trail

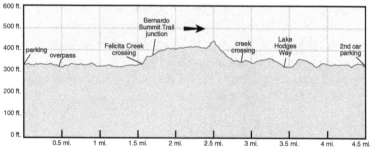

LENGTH & CONFIGURATION 4.5-mile point-to-point with shuttle	**WHEELCHAIR-ACCESSIBLE?** Just the first section; the rest is inaccessible due to a creek crossing.
DIFFICULTY Easy	
SCENERY Views of the lake, birds, and a creek	**FACILITIES** Portable toilet across the street from trailhead, restrooms near concession stand, and another portable toilet along the lake—they're open only during fishing season, though.
EXPOSURE Mostly sunny	
TRAFFIC Heavy on weekends	
TRAIL SURFACE Sandy dirt	
HIKING TIME 3.5 hours	**INFO** 858-674-2270, **sdrp.org/wordpress /trails**
ACCESS Free	
MAPS Online at **tinyurl.com/north shorelakehodges;** USGS *Escondido*	**SPECIAL COMMENTS** During fishing season, a concession stand is open near the picnic area. Leashed dogs allowed.

Turn left onto the level trail to head southwest. Notice that old cracked asphalt clings to the ground in some places, remnants of Old Highway (US) 395, which served as the main vehicle road until the interstate was built.

The route bends right, heading northwest, and the freeway sounds begin to fade, leaving the airwaves open to birdsong. Quails, startled from their foraging in the brush, may flutter across the path, and finches twitter from the bush.

Another 0.25 mile bring the trail to an oasis of sorts, with sprawling oaks and palm trees growing near Felicita Creek. Use rocks to cross the creek (bicyclists splash right through), then head uphill about 50 yards. The trail turns left, climbing southwest for a short distance.

You'll soon come to the turnoff for Bernardo Mountain Summit Trail, worth a short side trip if you have time. Or, come back another day. It's just shy of 2 miles to the viewpoint at the top.

Continue southwest on the wide, flat trail, which will soon bear to the right (northwest) again. Even in drier years, you'll begin to see the lake water along this stretch. Follow the route downhill; a 0.5-mile stretch runs closer to the water. Cottontails may dart out onto the path here, and roadrunners hop out of the prickly pear cactus that grows in massive clumps. Bright-orange California dodder and wild cucumber vines top the cactus formations like zany wigs.

A metal gate leads to the parking lot, concessions, and restrooms—facilities are open only during fishing season, which is generally March–October. The hike continues from the northwest corner of the parking lot, but if you like to picnic, this is a logical stopping point. Grassy areas hold tree-shaded picnic tables.

Continuing the hike, you'll turn right and follow the asphalt path a short way. Watch for the dirt trail on the left and follow the path with a view of the lake for about 0.25 mile. There is another parking lot here; this one has a portable toilet and a cement pathway leading down to the lake through stands of mulefat, leather root, and other tall bushes.

Back on the trail, you'll pass another parking area and reach a shady area and parking lot near Lake Drive.

Nearby Activities

Back at the Sunset Drive trailhead, you can cross the road to see the **Sikes Adobe Farmhouse,** which was built from adobe bricks in the late 1800s and is one of the oldest structures in San Diego County. Except for the adobe walls, it was burned to the ground in 2007. It's since been restored, with regular visiting hours 10 a.m.–1 p.m. Tuesdays, Wednesdays, and Saturdays and 10 a.m.–4 p.m. Sundays. The farmhouse can also be toured by special appointment or used for special events. Call 760-432-8318 or visit **sdrp.org/wordpress /sikes-adobe** for more information.

GPS INFORMATION AND DIRECTIONS
N33° 3.974' W117° 4.097'

To do this as a one-way hike, take cars on I-15 to Via Rancho Parkway and head west for 3 miles. Turn left on Lake Drive and park about 0.9 mile from the Lake Drive turnoff. In the second vehicle, travel back up to Via Rancho Parkway and head east for about 3.5 miles. Turn right on Sunset Drive and follow it less than 0.1 mile to the end, where you'll find a small parking lot at the trailhead.

42 Lake Poway Loop

Lake Poway stretches out beneath the picnic park.

In Brief

The Lake Poway Recreation Area offers boat rentals and fishing, a walk-in campground, and a grassy picnic area. For day hikers, even busy weekends in this spacious area let you feel close to nature and far from the city.

Description

A sense of pride pervades the city of Poway and spills over into its countryside and public recreation areas. With its pristine picnic areas and lake views reminiscent of a European vacation spot, hikers can immerse themselves in the relaxation of a long holiday, if only for an hour or two.

From the parking area, walk north past the office building on the left and look for the trail entrance to the left of the snack bar. You'll head north for several yards and get a view

Lake Poway Loop

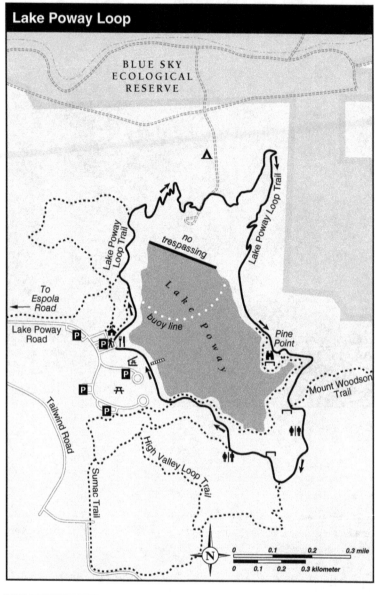

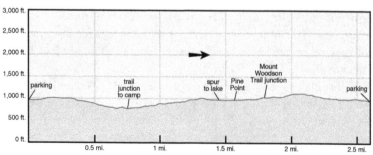

LENGTH & CONFIGURATION 2.6-mile loop	**MAPS** Online at **poway.org/502/trails-hiking** and **tinyurl.com/lakepowaytrails**; USGS *Escondido*
DIFFICULTY Moderate	
SCENERY Lake and waterfowl, picturesque views of boats atop the glistening water, chaparral, wildflowers	**WHEELCHAIR-ACCESSIBLE?** No, due to steep and rocky areas
EXPOSURE Open to sunlight	**FACILITIES** Public restrooms near parking lot; chemical toilets along the trail
TRAFFIC Moderately heavy	**INFO** 858-668-4770, **powaytrails.com**
TRAIL SURFACE Well-packed dirt, some areas of slippery loose dirt	**SPECIAL COMMENTS** The trails are shared by equestrians and bicycle riders. Children under age 10 may need a hand on the few steeper areas, especially in summer when the dry soil is loose.
HIKING TIME 1.5 hours	
ACCESS Parking free for Poway residents year-round, $5 for nonresidents weekends and holidays. Open daily, 6 a.m.–sunset.	

of the boat dock and the lake on your right, to the east. The wide trail, flanked by smallish pine trees that smell like Christmas all year, bends west and leads up a short, steep section before gradually descending northwest. Look for skullcap with purple blooms in spring and summer and wild cucumber and curly dock—all growing among sparse laurel sumac and sage scrub, which have been regenerating since the 2007 wildfires. Since those fires, this already spring-bloom-heavy lake loop is all but carpeted with flowers. Zillions of golden poppies intersperse with spring's rich color palette. Watch for fleabane (a natural flea repellent); its lavender daisies with yellow centers grow on spindly stems. Bluedicks— a member of the lily family—bloom as early as January, with showy yet delicate clusters that sway atop 1- to 1-foot, grasslike stems.

At about 0.5 mile, the trail gets steeper and a series of short switchbacks leads you down to the base of the dam. Smaller children might need a helping hand here, especially in dry months when loose ground gets slippery. Look to the northwest for a triangle of rocks peeking between the hills. It's the dam for Lake Ramona, about 4 miles away. When you get to the bottom of the downhill slope, you'll see a water trough for horses, and perhaps a few dragonflies hovering near. A creek runs here at the base of the dam, too, and you'll likely notice the creamy yellow flowers of Hooker's evening primrose during spring and summer. The festive blooms that grow on hairy stalks may be "dressed to kill," but their name doesn't refer to anything tawdry: They were named for a 19th-century botanist. At about 1 mile from the trailhead, a path on the left leads off to the campground area.

The trail continues to the right, climbing gradually upward from the dam. At about 1.5 miles, you'll start to see the dam again. A little farther and the lake is back in view as the trail gradually descends. On weekends, the glistening water is dotted with picturesque rowboats, and you make your way down to the water. On weekends, you'll likely hear laughter drifting across the lake from the picnic park near your car. As you get closer to the water, you'll hear the clicking and squabbling of the American coot, which gathers in groups on the lake. My family has nicknamed this ever-present bird the American "toot," because its voice is so similar to a child's bicycle horn.

The trail meanders around the northernmost inlet, and then comes to a fork. Keep heading to the right around the lake and bypass the Mount Woodson Trail opening to the left. You'll start to climb again, but at just more than 2.0 miles, the trail slopes downward and heads past a side trail that leads to the lake's southern shore and the boat dock. Take this if you choose, or head up the trail, at times lined with milk thistle. The spiny plants sprout purple blooms in the summer. When you reach the picnic park, head across the grassy knolls to your car. In the spring, my daughters like to pluck the clover blooms that grow profusely in the lawn, tying them together for a natural chain that brings back childhood memories for me. Press the chains into a book to hold onto the memory of a pleasant day at Lake Poway.

Nearby Activities

Old Poway Park is a historical gem with a museum, an operating steam train, and a Saturday farmer's market. From Lake Poway, turn left onto Espola Road. Drive just over 3 miles to Twin Peaks and turn right. At about 0.8 mile, turn left on Midland. The 4.75-acre park is about 0.5 mile on the right at 14134 Midland Rd.; call 858-679-4313 or visit **poway .org/452/old-poway-park** for more information.

GPS INFORMATION AND DIRECTIONS
N33° 0.408' W117° 0.812'

From I-15, take Rancho Bernardo Road and head east. Rancho Bernardo Road becomes Espola Road after about 2 miles. Travel slightly less than 5 miles and turn left on Lake Poway Road. Proceed to the entrance booth and park in the lot.

---

43 Lake Poway to Mount Woodson Peak Trail

Glistening Lake Poway shrinks in the distance as you head up the trail.

In Brief

The beautiful and serene Lake Poway Recreation Area is the starting point for this strenuous hike, which climbs about 2,300 feet to reach the boulder-crested peak of the nearly 2,900-foot-high Mount Woodson.

Description

Park at the rear right edge of the lot, since the hike begins at the kiosk near the upper restrooms, at the far edge of Lake Poway Park. From the kiosk, head southeast down the dirt road that runs to the right of the lake, where a view of the shimmering water gives the surroundings a relaxed air. Even on weekends, when sports activities and picnickers charge the area with a clatter of excitement, catching sight of lazy rowboats atop the glistening water brings a sense of peace. As you get farther from the grassy knolls and the sounds of picnickers, the squabbling of the coots, paddling about on the water in search of food, becomes more noticeable.

Lake Poway to Mount Woodson Peak Trail

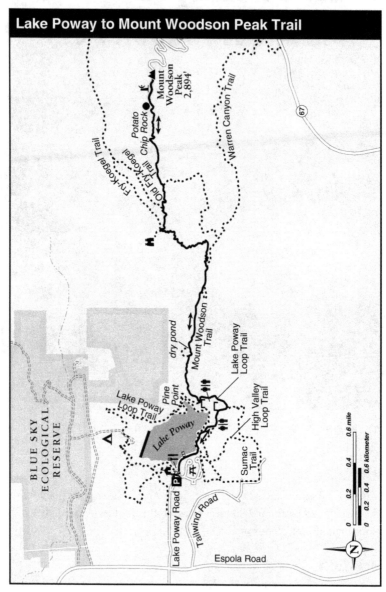

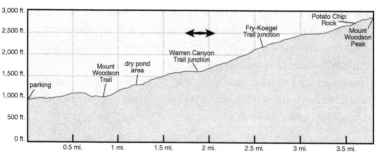

LENGTH & CONFIGURATION
7.6-mile out-and-back

DIFFICULTY Strenuous

SCENERY Picturesque view of the lake, interesting boulder formations, wild-flowers, and panoramic views

EXPOSURE Mostly sunny

TRAFFIC Moderate (heavy on the lake portion of the trail on weekends)

TRAIL SURFACE Well-packed dirt, some areas of rocky or slippery loose dirt

HIKING TIME 4.5 hours

ACCESS Parking free for Poway residents year-round, $5 for nonresidents weekends and holidays. Open daily, 6 a.m.–sunset.

MAPS Online at **poway.org/502/trails -hiking** and **tinyurl.com/lakepowaytrails**; USGS *Escondido*

WHEELCHAIR-ACCESSIBLE? No, due to steep and rocky areas

FACILITIES Public restrooms near park-ing lot, and chemical toilets along the trail

INFO 858-668-4770, **powaytrails.com**

SPECIAL COMMENTS Choose a day in late fall, winter, or early spring to avoid extreme heat on this trail, shared by equestrian and bicycle riders. Weekday traffic is low.

The downhill slope changes to a gradual incline at about 0.2 mile, and you soon pass the marked Sumac viewpoint and trail, on your right. A little farther, the route turns right and levels as it heads away from the lake for a few hundred yards, then bears left again.

At about 0.75 mile, you'll turn right uphill towards the signed Mount Woodson Peak Trail. Continuing, stay left, ignoring side trails. On the left, you'll pass a dry pond bed—a victim of low precipitation in recent years. The depressed terrain is ready to teem with life again once Mother Nature delivers adequate rainfall. The trail levels a bit, approach-ing another marker at 1.5 miles, where you'll again stay left. You'll note lots of charred brush here, evidence of the 2007 fire whipping heat through this area. At 1.7 miles, you'll take the left-hand path and begin climbing steadily to Mount Woodson Peak. The right path goes into Warren Canyon.

The sounds of the lake are whipped away by the breezes that offer an updraft to the ravens coasting through the sky. Since the fires, engine noise from vehicles on nearby Highway 67 is more easily heard, perhaps only temporary while sound-absorbing vegeta-tion regenerates.

The boulders become more and more prominent, encroaching on the narrowing trail. After zigzagging about 0.5 mile up the hill, you'll reach a northerly stretch, allowing a view of CA 67 to the east with what look like toy cars from several miles away.

At this point, the trail is steep and rocky. At 2.2 miles, a beautiful spreading oak tree provides a shady spot if you decide to rest. We've seen bobcat tracks in this area but never spotted the elusive cats that make their home here.

At about 2.3 miles, stay to the right. The Fry-Koegel Trail intersects on your left. You could take this short loop if you wish; it curves back and intersects the Mount Woodson Peak Trail again.

The route levels briefly, then begins to climb gradually but steadily. Continue toward a pair of bookend-shaped boulders in the distance. After an additional 0.3 mile, the trail flattens, then slants downhill briefly. You'll spot the antennas atop Mount Woodson in the distance, reach an open ridge with a view to the north, and then cut back into very thick chaparral and begin to climb again. Manzanita grows densely here, its elevation-loving nature testament to the fact that you're almost there.

At 3.2 miles, you'll come to an odd wavelike boulder formation nicknamed Potato Chip Rock for its thin jutting section. The rock has become a bit of cliché for San Diegans who use online dating sites. A single friend recently mentioned how common it is to see photos of prospective beaux standing on the thin rock. Maybe it's time to get more creative? Anyway, you'll hit asphalt road and the peak just a few steps ahead. Find yourself in an antenna forest. Many flattish boulders are perfect spots to picnic or perch.

The downhill return goes much more quickly. Try to take your time and step with care. Gravity's pull as you head down the mountain on rocky and sometimes slippery terrain could produce a tumble.

Nearby Activities

While you're in the area, don't miss a chance to eat at **The Incredible Cafe,** at 11828 Rancho Bernardo Rd. Indoors or on the patio, savor the tastiest of breakfast entrees (served all day) plus more scrumptious meals. Open daily until 3 p.m.; 858-592-7731, **theincredible cafe.com.**

GPS INFORMATION AND DIRECTIONS
N33° 0.389' W117° 0.806'

From I-15, take Rancho Bernardo Road and head east. Rancho Bernardo Road becomes Espola Road after about 2 miles. Travel slightly less than 5 miles and turn left on Lake Poway Road. Proceed to the entrance booth and park in the lot.

---

44 Lake Wohlford North:

KUMEYAAY TRAIL

Rustic wilderness overlooks peaceful Lake Wohlford.

In Brief

The sparkling blue-green water remains in sight for most of this simple hike along a sometimes unkempt trail on the lake's north side.

Description

Past the restrooms, spot a sign for the Kumeyaay Trail, which moves east near Lake Wohlford Road for a stretch. Spotty oak shade and the sparkling lake on your right make for a pleasant beginning. The trail crosses some low-lying boulders after a short distance. Look for the telltale indentations in the rock, evidence of days gone by when the area's Kumeyaay Indians gathered to pound acorns into flour.

Just past these boulders, the shade becomes thicker, nurturing poison oak that you'll want to avoid. Tread quietly so as not to frighten the birds; you'll reach large oak trees where herons roost at about 0.25 mile. A bench placed beneath the trees overlooks the water; rocks rise from the lake, giving pelicans a place to rest. Cormorants join them, standing with their wings held out to dry in the breeze. Because the Kumeyaay Trail is not

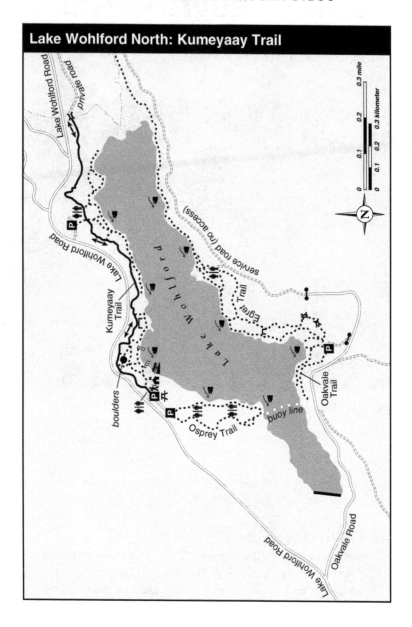

Lake Wohlford North: Kumeyaay Trail

well-maintained, this might be a good place to turn around and head back. The trail is usually unkempt from here on out, requiring you to push aside bushes and step over rocks.

Ready for a little adventure? Then watch your head for low-growing branches as you continue east, quickly reaching a rocky slope. A few feet ahead, the earthen path resumes, heading uphill toward the right, then back down toward the lake. The scent of sage hangs heavily in the air. Plenty of smooth rock perches make good spots to sit and watch the water lap lazily at the shore.

LENGTH & CONFIGURATION 2-mile out-and-back	MAPS Google map at the website below; USGS *Rodriguez Mountain*
DIFFICULTY Easy	**WHEELCHAIR-ACCESSIBLE?** No, due to rocky sections
SCENERY Native plants, birds	
EXPOSURE Sunny and shady	**FACILITIES** Restrooms in the parking area
TRAFFIC Light	
TRAIL SURFACE Earthen path, leaf litter, sand	**INFO** 760-839-4346, **escondido.org/lake -wohlford.aspx**
HIKING TIME 1 hour	**SPECIAL COMMENTS** The area teems with anglers on weekends, but the hiking trails are usually peaceful.
ACCESS Free; open daily, mid-December– weekend after Labor Day	

At close to 0.5 mile, shade envelops the trail. Gnarled, fallen trees are clumped with tangled vines beneath the living trees that grow densely here.

At 0.75 mile, you'll see a dirt access road heading down from Lake Wohlford Road. A side path heads toward the lake on the right; depending on the water level, you can meander along the shore for another 0.25 mile or so, watching the birds dive for food, before heading back.

Nearby Activities

Odds are good that you'll find the food tasty at **Valley View Casino**'s buffet or other restaurants. From the lake, turn right on Lake Wohlford Road and travel east, then north for about 3 miles to 16300 Nyemi Pass Rd., in Valley Center. Call 866-VIEW-WIN or visit **valleyviewcasino.com** for more information.

GPS INFORMATION AND DIRECTIONS

N33° 10.459' W116° 59.996'

Take I-15 to the Valley Parkway exit. Head east about 5 miles—Valley Parkway becomes Valley Center Road at Washington Avenue. Turn right on Lake Wohlford Road and drive 2.6 miles, then turn right into the parking area by the ranger office and dock.

45 Lake Wohlford:

SOUTH TRAILS

In Brief

Walking these short, easy trails in the dewy morning hours is a feast for the senses.

Description

Find the sign for Oakvale Trail to the left of the parking area and take the narrow, grassy path that heads west for 0.2 mile through oak shade. You'll quickly come to a plank bridge placed over a natural rainfall runoff ditch. Be careful of poison oak: The abundant plant is distinguished by its three-leaf pattern, with two leaves anchored opposite one another and the third having a small stem of its own. It grows in small, bushy clumps in a bigger, almost treelike form or as a spindly vine cascading from tree branches. Nonirritating plants such as caterpillar phacelia also grow in lush abundance here. Its dusky-white or pale-lavender flowers on hairy, coiled stems earned the plant its name.

Over the bridge, the trail narrows, heading through what feels like a mountain-ridge trail. The lake laps gently against the shore about 100 feet away, downhill on the right. Keep your eyes open for cormorants drying their wings on rocks, and blue herons near the shoreline. Look up into the trees above the path, too. We saw a pair of herons roosting just a few feet away on our last visit.

It isn't just the treetops that hold interesting sights. This area is a favorite of the funnel web spider. The spiders have woven their nests all around—small sheets of spider silk lie across the grassy ground. A funnel-like hole extends down into the bush or grass, providing an escape route for this shy resident you're unlikely to spot. On cool mornings, dewdrops gather on the silken sheets, creating a uniquely beautiful, almost eerie sight.

At about 0.1 mile, the path narrows even more, heading through lichen-speckled boulders up to a small clearing with a bench that overlooks the water. The trail goes just a little farther, ending abruptly at a clearing before coming to boulders and masses of poison oak.

From here, head back to the parking area, cross the entry road, and access Egret Trail on the right. This northwestward path is wider than the last and has more oak forest. About 100 yards from the entry point, cross a railed plank bridge over a shallow gulch where water flows after rains. Hooker's evening primrose grows here, in its typical showy yellow form, on tall, upright stalks. Another bridge lies just a short distance ahead; across it, the trail bends due north.

Wild cucumber grows here, as it does almost everywhere in the county. The inedible plant's bright-green fruit is covered in soft, fleshy spikes that dry in the summer, becoming sharp and prickly. This thistly skin peels back to release attractive black seeds that

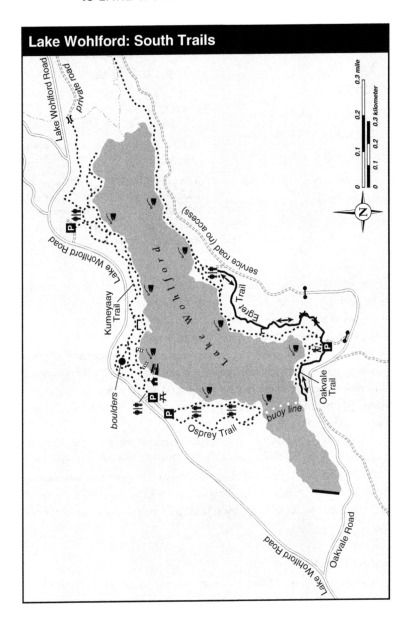

Lake Wohlford: South Trails

area Native Americans used to gather and polish for necklaces. The vine's dry, inner pod shells lie along the trail. The lacy, oblong, inner pod structure, dropped after the seeds, looks a little like a sea sponge.

A bench overlooks the lake at 0.2 mile, where the trail heads through forest. The bushy undergrowth serves as a perfect habitat for the California towhee, a perky, light-brown bird seen foraging in the bushes, using its feet to stir up leaves and food.

LENGTH & CONFIGURATION 1.5 miles combined on 2 short trails; out-and-back	MAPS Google map at the website below; USGS *Rodriguez Mountain*
DIFFICULTY Easy	WHEELCHAIR-ACCESSIBLE? No, due to uneven terrain
SCENERY Native plants, birds	FACILITIES Portable toilets in parking area and at the end of Egret Trail
EXPOSURE Mostly shady	
TRAFFIC Light on weekdays	INFO 760-839-4346, **escondido.org/lake -wohlford.aspx**
TRAIL SURFACE Earthen path, leaf litter	SPECIAL COMMENTS The area teems with anglers on weekends. In the early morning on weekdays, the trails are a peaceful delight—especially in late spring and early summer.
HIKING TIME 30 minutes	
ACCESS Free; open daily, mid-December– weekend after Labor Day	

Near the end of the hike, many of the trees are bare at the top, providing a good perch for bigger birds. On our last visit, we saw five turkey vultures in one tree. Wondering if the carcass of an animal might be in the bushes below the tree, we watched the big black-brown birds awhile. But they were apparently only roosting. They held their red, featherless heads in a tucked position, occasionally spreading impressive wings with silver-gray undermarkings to their 6-foot span, as if attempting to dry them in the morning air. Wildflowers grow in rainbow tangles along the last few steps, leading to a portable toilet that marks the turnaround spot. A path leads down to the shore for those wanting to get closer to the water.

Lake Wohlford's trails may be short, but the abundant wildlife makes them a delight. The easy trails are perfect for less-agile hikers. We once brought a family member who was recovering from surgery. He was happy to get back into nature without too much strain.

As you retrace your steps to the parking lot, let the soft lapping of water, the flutter of wings, and the constant *twrp, twrp* call of the California towhee cast nature's relaxing spell on you.

Nearby Activities

Back on Valley Parkway, you'll find lots of fast-food and café-type restaurants.

GPS INFORMATION AND DIRECTIONS
N33° 10.036' W116° 59.867'

Take I-15 to the Valley Parkway exit. Head east for about 5 miles—Valley Parkway becomes Valley Center Road at Washington Avenue. Turn right on Lake Wohlford Road and drive 1.9 miles to Oakvale Road. Turn right and travel 0.7 mile to a gated dirt road that leads to the lake. Park in the dirt area on the right.

46 Los Jilgueros Preserve Trail

Walking the plank

In Brief

A pleasant 1-mile loop frames two ponds in this well-managed site that is popular with bikers, dog walkers, and those out for an invigorating walk through nature.

Description

Notice kiosks to the left of the parking lot and head into the preserve just past those. A bench placed at the start of the trail sets the tone for this adventure—easy-paced with lots of places to reflect.

After the short northwestern stretch that passes sycamore trees and scented sage, a wood-plank bridge appears on the left. Head across the bridge, where yerba mansa grows all around. The flowers' conical centers stretch up above white petals that form the crowning bloom for bright-green leaves on red stems. In winter, the plants die back to an ugly matte brown. This westward walk of a few hundred yards takes you closer to Mission Road, which runs along the outside of the preserve. The wood-plank bridge will cross

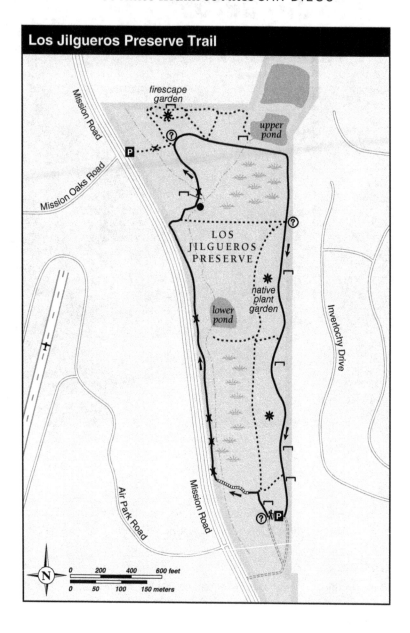

Los Jilgueros Preserve Trail

water at some point; how much water depends on the season and rainfall amounts. On our last visit in early June, there was no visible water here at all.

Where the plank bridge ends, turn right onto the dirt path. The route heads north alongside Mission Road for close to 0.5 mile, passing a series of short wood-plank bridges along the way. This stretch is considered the nature trail. Dragonflies buzz, birds sing exuberantly, and cottontails hop in and out of the bushes. Thistles reach up, their purple blooms turning to tufts of fuzz as spring becomes summer. At two-thirds of the way in on

LENGTH & CONFIGURATION 1-mile loop	**WHEELCHAIR-ACCESSIBLE?** Partially, although muddy and soft, silty areas could cause difficulty. For the best condi-
DIFFICULTY Easy	tions for wheelchairs, take the east trail,
SCENERY Birds, stream, ponds, frogs, waterfowl, trees, and native plants	to the right from the parking lot.
EXPOSURE Some sunny and some shady	**FACILITIES** None
TRAFFIC Moderately heavy	**INFO** 760-728-0889, **fallbrookland**
TRAIL SURFACE Dirt and boardwalk	**conservancy.org/los-jilgueros**
HIKING TIME 45 minutes	**SPECIAL COMMENTS** Even with busy Mis-
ACCESS Free	sion Road to the west and a housing tract to the east, this space teems with animal
MAPS Google map at website below; USGS *Bonsall*	and plant life and offers a natural respite. Leashed dogs are allowed—and common!

the nature trail, notice the lower pond to your right. Vegetation makes the pond inaccessible. Stay on the path, respecting the area's designation as a preserve.

The trail bends to the right and continues. Look for another path on the left, heading northeast down into the trees. Take this route, where you'll see a concrete silt dam and a bench overlooking the creek. Here in the shade of the trees, you'll spot frogs lazing in the shallow creek water. Bright-orange nasturtiums thrive in this cool, shady environment where spotty sunlight filters down. Butterflies flit about and birdsong fills the air.

After spending time reflecting, cross the small bridge and head left into the open for a moment before reaching the shade of trees again. You'll notice another kiosk with information about the preserve up ahead. Two trails run off to the left of the kiosk. One crosses a wood-plank bridge toward the north entrance. The other, a single-track trail, delivers visitors up to the "firescape" garden, which is worth a look for those interested in native California plants that retard fire. If you choose to stroll through the garden, you can still access the main loop from that path later.

Sticking to the main loop trail, walk to the right up the hill (northeast). After a short distance, you will see the upper pond on the left. A short trail on the left leads to a bench near the shore that is shaded by lush pecan trees—a nice place to sit awhile and enjoy the birds. Continuing east on the path leads you along the right side of the pond. In past years, this pond has been very full. On our recent visit though, the water level had receded. Still, ducks were enjoying themselves, floating along.

The route turns abruptly southward for a long trek. Notice the rusty frame of an old truck and some old farm equipment partially hidden in the weeds on either side, remnants of Fallbrook's history.

You'll come to a kiosk, and to the right of the path, see a native plant garden that blooms in a variety of colors in spring. The showy Matilija poppy—which blooms in spring and summer—grows in the garden. The large, yellow-centered flowers with crinkly white petals have a uniquely pungent scent. A trail leads down around the garden (which may look bedraggled by summer) to a shaded bench near the lower pond.

The main loop trail continues south all the way back to the parking area. Benches along the way allow visitors to stop and reflect while enjoying birdsong and the sound of gentle winds.

Nearby Activities

The **Fallbrook Gem & Mineral Society Museum** is nearby at 123 W. Alvarado St., Suite B, across the street from Fallbrook's Art & Cultural Center. Free admission; open Thursday–Saturday, 11 a.m.–3 p.m.; for more information, call 760-728-1130 or go to **fgms.org.** Air Park Road (almost directly across Mission from the preserve entrance) will take you to picnic benches that overlook Fallbrook Air Park, affording views of the afternoon's takeoffs and landings.

GPS INFORMATION AND DIRECTIONS

N33° 21.227' W117° 14.728'

Take I-15 north to the Pala/CA 76 exit and go left (west) 4.9 miles and turn right onto Mission Road. After 4.4 miles, you'll see signs for Los Jilgueros Preserve. Turn right and head down the dirt road, then park in the dirt- and bark-surfaced lot on the left.

---

47 Monserate Mountain Trail

Offshoot trail at Monserate Mountain

In Brief

Serenaded by birdsong, hikers traverse a trail lined with wildflowers, chaparral, and rock formations within 340-acre Monserate Mountain Preserve. A steep mile-and-a-half climb is rewarded with panoramic views of mountains in the east and the Pacific Ocean to the west.

Description

From Pankey Road, take the easterly path, lined with wild mustard and some laurel sumac that grew more densely prior to the 2007 Rice Fire that ravaged the area. A gate at 0.2 mile is open dawn–dusk, and in warmer seasons you'll want to arrive early. The trail turns south, then east again, in a repeating pattern that begins this steep climb up a rocky, sometimes rutted path.

After about 0.5 mile, the path points steadily east in a more gradual climb lasting about 0.3 mile. You'll begin to see some yucca here, a variety of wildflowers in the spring, and thatches of creeping rattlesnake weed hugging the gritty ground. A round-leafed

Monserate Mountain Trail

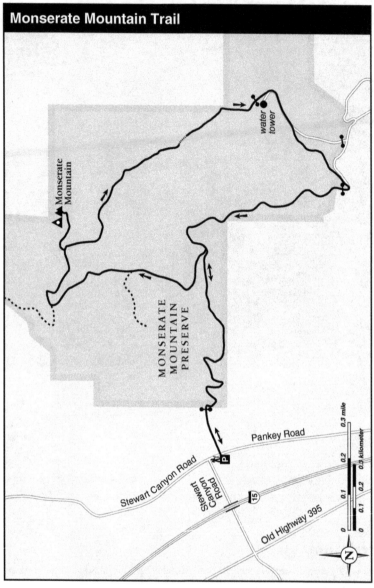

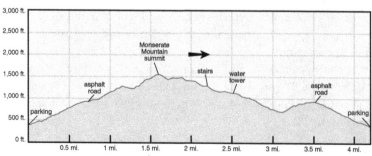

LENGTH & CONFIGURATION 3.6-mile balloon-and-string	**MAPS** Google map at website below; USGS *Bonsall*
DIFFICULTY Strenuous	**WHEELCHAIR-ACCESSIBLE?** No, due to steep, rutted path
SCENERY Sweeping views, chaparral, possible wildlife	
EXPOSURE Open to sunlight	**FACILITIES** None
TRAFFIC Heavy	**INFO** 760-728-0889, **fallbrookland conservancy.org/monserate-mountain**
TRAIL SURFACE Silty soil, some rutted and rocky areas	**SPECIAL COMMENTS** This steep trail is unsuitable for young children. Bring lots of water, and hike at cooler times of the day and year.
HIKING TIME 1.5–2 hours	
ACCESS Free; open daily, sunrise–sunset	

perennial, rattlesnake weed blooms spring–fall and is common on dry Southern California slopes. Spanish settlers used the weed to treat rattlesnake bites by pounding its leaves into a wet mass they bound over the wound.

You'll spot lots of coyote dung as you forge ahead, but are more likely to see leashed pets than any wild canines on this popular trail for dog lovers. Many people come here, so don't expect solitude. On my last visit here, one hiker said he keeps trim by making the climb a few days a week. Another happily shared his age: 83. He didn't look a day over 60, proving once again that hiking in nature can be a fountain of youth. You'll see runners here as well, the dirt making tiny dust clouds as their feet pound past and away.

At a little more than a mile, you'll come to an old asphalt road. Turn left and head northwest up the hill. Here, Fallbrook's groves appear like fancy patchwork across I-15. The pavement ends after a short distance as the road curves more to the north, becoming hard-packed dirt. The trail remains defined, leveling off for a bit of breath-catching. The trail will head abruptly east toward the summit, and at 1.55 miles, you'll come to a fork. Head to the left to reach the summit just ahead, marked by a pile of rocks—one includes an USGS marker. Sign the guestbook that's in an old metal box, and enjoy a break while enjoying the panoramic view. Once you're done, head back down below the summit. For a 3.2-mile round-trip hike, you could head back the way you came. But since you've already hiked this far, you might as well make a left below the summit and explore the other trail that makes up the fork? The only drawback is a short 225-foot climb near the end (when you're tired!).

Heading southeast on this new section of trail, you'll soon come to a set of stairs leading steeply down the hill. At the bottom, the steps end at a level southeasterly path. To your left (east), you'll see some planted fields on neighboring farmland, while the water tower looms ever closer ahead. Keep your eyes open on this more hidden side of the mountain. On a recent spring visit, a young coachwhip snake slithered by, its head held high on the lookout for prey. Unfortunately, it was moving at the characteristic breakneck speed. By the time I raised my camera for a shot, the snake was gone, its drab brown color indiscernible from the native brush.

You'll pass through a gate with a step-over bar close to the water tower, and then another as you again head out beyond the tower area. You'll pick up the paved road heading downhill more to the west. Rather than stick to the pavement, there's a short offshoot trail that soon comes in on the right. Take this singletrack trail over and down the other side of the hill where you'll again meet the pavement. Continue around to the right where you'll head north for a stretch, uphill. Eventually, you'll come to the junction point with the string part of this balloon-and-string trail. Make a left and head back down the rutted path toward Pankey Road as the sounds of I-15 traffic and civilization reach your nature-rested ears.

Nearby Activities

People drive for miles to eat at **Nessy Burgers,** on the right side of Highway 395, just before you reach the Highway 76 intersection. Enjoy the secret blend of premium chuck and sirloin and special seasonings that Nessy Burger fans have been savoring since 1989. Open 7 a.m.–7 p.m. most days; for directions and more information, visit **nessyburgers.com.**

GPS INFORMATION AND DIRECTIONS

N33° 21.957' W117° 9.543'

Take I-15 North to the Pala/CA 76 exit. Head west 0.25 mile to Old Highway 395 and turn right. Travel 2.6 miles and turn right on Stewart Canyon Road. Pass under the freeway and turn right on Pankey Road. You'll immediately spot the trailhead on the left. Park on the right side of Pankey, where there's room for cars to pull in head-first toward I-15.

48 Mount Gower Open Space Preserve Trail

Dinosaur-bone boulders mark the trail.   PHOTO: RORY McGREGOR

In Brief

This hike's strenuous climb rewards your efforts with remote upper meadows and rock shelves where, depending on recent weather, a seasonal stream may run. The remote quiet of the upper areas envelops you in peace and tranquility—but you'll have to work to get there!

Description

Mount Gower offers a strenuous workout trail that's especially good for those training for long hiking trips with uncertain or rugged conditions. Steep, exposed trails are composed of grainy soil that becomes extremely slippery in dry weather. Even experienced hikers with the best boots and gear can easily slip on the abrupt ups and downs of this trail. The moderate weather of late fall or early spring is the best time to hike this demanding trail. Give yourself plenty of time. Bring a walking stick and lots of water, wear a sun-protective hat, and be prepared for extreme heat or even chilly winds near the top.

From the kiosk at the trailhead, start up the well-defined northerly trail. At about 0.1 mile, you'll come to a fork in the path. The left fork leads about 1.8 miles to a 2,300-foot

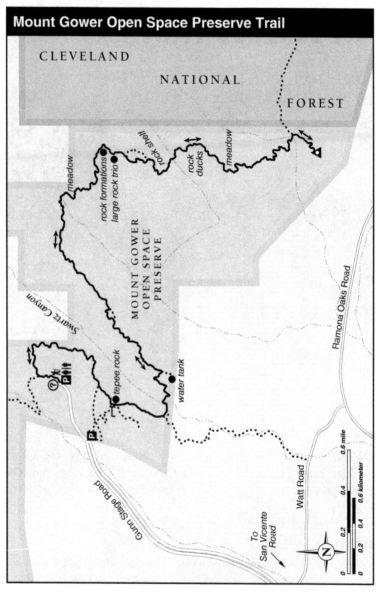

Mount Gower Open Space Preserve Trail

CLEVELAND

NATIONAL

FOREST

MOUNT GOWER OPEN SPACE PRESERVE

meadow

rock formations

large rock trio

rock shelf

rock ducks

meadow

Swartz Canyon

tepee rock

water tank

Ramona Oaks Road

Watt Road

Gunn Stage Road

To San Vicente Road

0.6 mile

0.6 kilometer

0.4

0.4

0.2

0.2

0

0

N

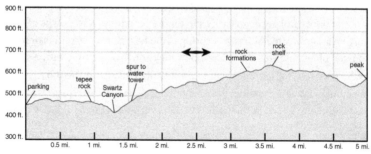

900 ft.
800 ft.
700 ft.
600 ft.
500 ft.
400 ft.
300 ft.

parking

tepee rock

Swartz Canyon

spur to water tower

rock formations

rock shelf

peak

0.5 mi.   1 mi.   1.5 mi.   2 mi.   2.5 mi.   3 mi.   3.5 mi.   4 mi.   4.5 mi.   5 mi.

LENGTH & CONFIGURATION 10-mile out-and-back	HIKING TIME 5–6 hours
DIFFICULTY Strenuous	**ACCESS** Free; open daily, 8 a.m.– sunset. Entire preserve closed the month of August due to extreme heat.
SCENERY Chaparral, rock formations, views of wide-open space, distant mountains, and horizon	**MAPS** Online at **tinyurl.com/mtgower map;** USGS *Ramona*
EXPOSURE Mostly exposed to sun; a few short stretches with shade	**WHEELCHAIR-ACCESSIBLE?** No, due to soft sand and steep, rocky sections
TRAFFIC Moderate during first mile; very light on remaining trail	**FACILITIES** Rustic restrooms near trailhead
TRAIL SURFACE Grainy, sediment-rich soil and some rocky areas; slippery where steep, especially in dry weather where topsoil is loose over hard underpack	**INFO** 760-788-3326, **tinyurl.com/mtgower preserve**
	SPECIAL COMMENTS See longer note at beginning of Description.

viewpoint—perhaps trek it another day. Go right instead, heading southeast on gradually descending and ascending hills and dales for about 0.9 mile. An unmarked trail split appears. Ignore the right-hand route and continue forward, where you'll quickly come to a large, angular boulder to the left of the trail. A bench faces the boulder, which leans on a second boulder to form a tent. Locals have nicknamed this formation "tepee rock," and people like to pose for pictures in the shady triangle of open space formed by the rocks. You'll have come 1 mile from the trailhead.

Just beyond the tepee rock, you'll notice another trail split. The path on the right leads 0.2 mile uphill to a viewpoint that overlooks Ramona's suburbia, San Diego Country Estates. Most of the preserve's foot traffic ends at this viewpoint, and it's a logical turnaround for those wanting a pleasant, fairly easy stroll. For a more strenuous adventure, continue along the left route, which descends at a dusty, semisteep clip for a little more than a third of a mile down into Swartz Canyon.

At the bottom, find a seasonal creek and the welcome shade of oaks and sycamores. Be careful of poison oak growing under the trees. This shady section ends after a few short yards. Climbing out of the canyon, the trail steepens, giving hikers a glimpse of how strenuous this hike will be. In the spring, watch for golden California poppies brightening the rutted path. You'll pass a 1.5-mile marker pole, head past a water tower on the right, and continue climbing as the route curves in a northeasterly direction.

For the next mile or so, very steep inclines alternate with equal downhill sections. The up-and-down pattern repeats itself through the chaparral on the gritty, slippery path. Lush views to the northeast are a focal point along this stretch. From here, the green land of a local ranch that neighbors the preserve looks inviting.

Continuing, the route bends south again, still following the up-and-down pattern, sometimes framed by scrub oak. Stop for a moment or two and absorb the serenity of nature. The quiet is so thick you'll hear one another's breath. Not much life seems evident along this stretch, but upon close inspection, you'll notice an array of insects thrives here.

Silverfish hide, camouflaged against sand-colored rocks, and beetles cluster around coyote dung on the path. At 2.9 miles, reach a meadow where the wind rushes refreshingly through the open space. If you're lucky, you might surprise a pearly, blue-green centipede resting in the shade. Witness how fast its multiple bright-orange legs can carry it away. Don't get too close, though: These creatures can bite. After a look at this odd insect, it's common to squirm, imagining one you didn't see has somehow crawled up your pants leg!

Continuing, the path moves upward for another 0.5 mile before reaching an area full of interesting rock formations. After rainfall, water trickles in cascading rivulets down the sides of the hills, which consist of exposed rock face. Fleshy and succulent ladyfingers grow here, sprouting like pale-green sea urchins from cracks in the stone.

Continue west, watching for three large, pointy boulders standing in a row to the right of the trail at 3.4 miles. When you spot this trio, which appear like sentry guards standing watch to guide hikers who've gone astray, turn left. The trail may appear to continue forward and lead to a nice view, but go left, scurrying up the immediately steep section of exposed rock, then continuing upward as the trail meanders alongside Mount Gower Peak, which is to your left. You'll reach a plateau where a huge rock shelf opens. Notice the small rock towers called "rock ducks" left by previous visitors at around 4 miles.

The trail continues, moving gradually downhill to the west. You'll come to another small meadow where water sometimes trickles melodically down a series of tiny falls on a flattish section of rock. The trail continues at a gradual downhill clip on easy footing with views of distant mountains. On clear days, you may even see the ocean, which appears as a bright band along the western horizon.

At about 4.7 miles, enter the final steep segment of trail, which delivers you to the peak at 4.9 miles.

Retrace your steps along the trail, which seems even longer on the way back. The steep sections you earlier sweated up now become a major workout for the tips of your toes, which grip the inside of your boots as you carefully tread back down. You'll be glad you brought a walking stick on the slippery paths.

Back at your car, kick off your shoes and give your hardworking feet a well-deserved rest.

Nearby Activities

Drive back to Tenth Street and, instead of turning left and following CA 67 back to I-8, make a right. Here, you'll find a stretch of road with antiques stores and coffee shops.

GPS INFORMATION AND DIRECTIONS

N33° 1.614' W116° 47.544'

Take I-8 East to CA 67 North and turn right on 10th Street, which becomes San Vicente Road after about 0.5 mile. Continue on this road for almost 2 miles. Turn left on Gunn Stage Road, which leads into the entrance of Mount Gower Open Space Preserve. Continue about 0.3 mile to the graveled parking lot near the trailhead.

49 **Mount Woodson:** EAST TRAIL

Watch for the "turtle rock" and other creature-feature boulders on Mount Woodson.

In Brief

This is a popular area for rock climbers, runners, and hikers who enjoy an uphill workout; be sure to bring water any time of year, and on hot summer days, hike in the early morning or late afternoon.

Description

The trail begins moving south through oak forest parallel to CA 67, where the car sounds quickly begin dissolving, filtered away behind joyful birdsong and the gentle rustle of wind in the leaves. At about 0.1 mile, you'll come to the asphalt route, which bears left, then back to the right, then left again. You'll notice a home, fenced off on the left. Pass by as the road gradually grows steeper. The road is framed with smooth, pale-sided boulders—a sunning lizard's paradise.

About halfway up the road (0.9 mile), the view opens to the south but curves back to afford the northeastern views. All along the road, boulders pile upon boulders. The pale granodiorite surfaces are smoothed by exposure to weather, forming curved shapes

Mount Woodson: East Trail

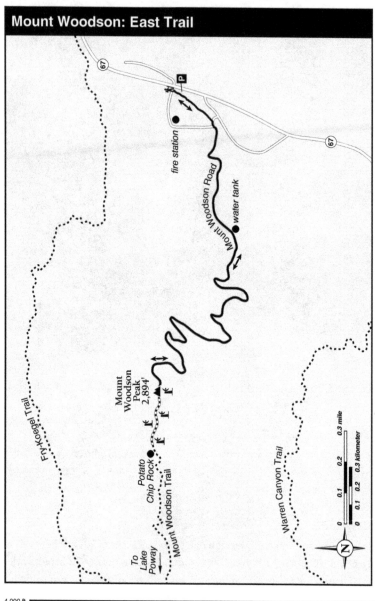

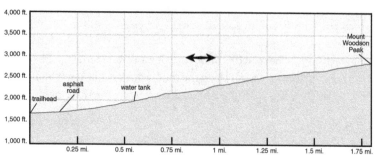

LENGTH & CONFIGURATION 3.6-mile out-and-back	WHEELCHAIR-ACCESSIBLE? No, due to uneven terrain at outset
DIFFICULTY Moderate (uphill)	**FACILITIES** None
SCENERY Huge boulders and odd rock formations	**INFO** 858-668-4770, **powaytrails.com**
EXPOSURE Mostly sunny	**SPECIAL COMMENTS** The continuous uphill cadence with a gain of close to 1,200 feet in elevation makes this hike difficult for some, but physically less-fit hikers can turn back anytime. The asphalt route makes for a safe, quick descent. Leashed dogs allowed.
TRAFFIC Moderately heavy	
TRAIL SURFACE Earthen path, asphalt	
HIKING TIME 2.5 hours	
ACCESS Free	
MAPS Online at **poway.org/502/trails -hiking** and **tinyurl.com/mtwoodsontrail**; USGS *San Pasqual*	

within which a good imagination can see a primitive cityscape or animals, such as the tortoise rock that appears to sleep in the sun near the top. Manzanita finds life within the great rocks, rising from cracks where the boulders have split apart. Sometimes, the boulders split several times, so they lie alongside one another like a stack of giant chips.

Nearing the top of the mountain, the boulders rise vertically, towering two and three stories high and shading the road in spots. Watch for climbers' metal pitons and chalk marks on the rock faces. You'll likely see climbers carrying their ropes and equipment on the hike. Families with children and people walking their dogs are common on this hike, too. Runners are also familiar here, their breath a steady puffing rhythm as they run, sweating, up the steep path.

As you huff and puff up the asphalt road, open your mind to the patterns of nature—the Mount Woodson experience, like any other, is what you make of it. Notice the vibrant blue light of sky breaking through repeating green frames formed by the bristly pine branches. Gathered sap glistens like honey on spiky pine needles. The trees cast a mosaic shadow on the wide, pale faces of the boulders that serve as canvas for nature's ever-changing montage of art.

When you reach the crest of the mountain, you can continue forward to a small eastern lookout point amid the shade of pines. Or take the asphalt road as it begins to descend through a maze of towering communication antennas. Just past the last antenna tower, some big, flat boulders provide the perfect picnic spot, with views of Poway to the southwest. At nearly 2,900 feet, it's a bird's-eye view, illustrated by the many ravens that hang out here at the top of the mountain.

You'll notice that the road continues southwest. After a short distance, it changes to dirt. If you'd like, you can take the trail all the way to Lake Poway (3.6 miles away). That's a hike in and of itself, most often done from the west end.

Nearby Activities

Travel north on CA 67 for 5 minutes into the town of Ramona. The highway becomes the city's Main Street and hosts a variety of businesses.

GPS INFORMATION AND DIRECTIONS

N33° 0.497' W116° 57.326'

Take I-15 to the Poway Road exit and drive east until Poway Road runs into CA 67. Turn left and drive on CA 67 for about 3 miles. Watch for the fire station on the left. You'll also see a marker sign for Mount Woodson. When safe, make a U-turn (turn into a side road and then make a left back onto CA 67 going the opposite direction) and drive back to park on the southbound shoulder of CA 67, near the marker sign.

50 Santa Margarita River Trail

Bring your imagination—and ride a stony Santa Margarita River trail turtle!

In Brief

Mother Nature opens her welcoming arms here, filling visitors' senses with a bountiful harvest of sights, scents, and sounds along the Santa Margarita River.

Description

From the parking lot, head east (away from the road) and enter the trail, which meanders upstream as the water rushes past. After a short stretch, oaks shade the path in a suddenly lush landscape. In spring, milk thistle with large, rosy-purple blooms towers as high as seven feet. A white pattern that looks like spattered milk adorns the spiny, variegated green leaves, giving rise to an Old World belief that the drips of "milk" came from the Virgin Mary as she nursed her infant son Jesus. The plant's species, *marianum*, means "of Mary."

The Santa Margarita River soon comes into view, flowing steadily in all but the driest of years. About 200 yards from the trailhead, the path narrows and climbs 20–50 feet

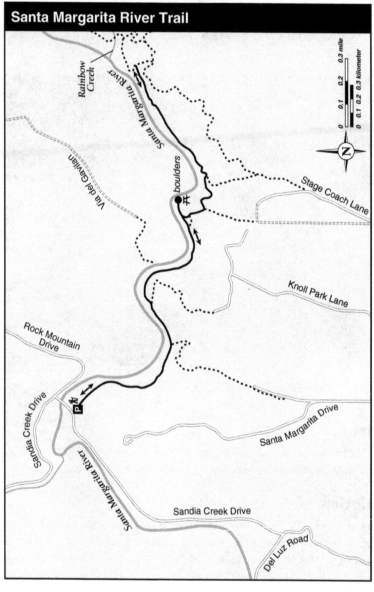

Santa Margarita River Trail

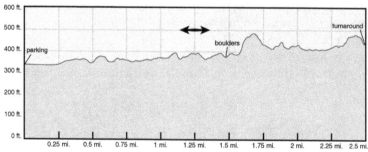

LENGTH & CONFIGURATION 5-mile out-and-back	**WHEELCHAIR-ACCESSIBLE?** No, due to creek flow/possible crossing, silty sand, and narrow path
DIFFICULTY Easy	
SCENERY Lush riparian landscape and dense forest	**FACILITIES** None
	INFO 760-728-2303, **tinyurl.com/santamargaritapreserve**
EXPOSURE Mostly shady	
TRAFFIC Moderate	**SPECIAL COMMENTS** Except for a short, slippery section near the trailhead, this is an easy route that is good for families. Smaller children will need lots of help in the slippery area. As always, watch children around water.
TRAIL SURFACE Packed silt	
HIKING TIME 3.5 hours	
ACCESS Free; open daily, sunrise–sunset	
MAPS Online at **tinyurl.com/santa margaritamap;** USGS *Temecula*	

above the river while hugging a steep rock slope. Stepping carefully makes it easy to cross this 600-foot section, but be careful of a few slippery spots.

On weekends, it's common to spot unwary hikers trying easier-looking offshoot paths that run level with the river. My family has learned that these sandy-shore paths dead-end into thick stands of willow. Some hikers will double back to where they originally went off-track; others, like us, will climb through the bramble and up rocks back to the main path above. Some ford the river upstream till it converges with another offshoot path and rejoins the main trail. Save yourself some trouble and stick with the official trail. Doing so protects the habitat. Besides, now you know those trails dead-end anyway.

The trail evens into a flat silt path through a forest rich in oak and sycamore. Poison oak grows in masses, and wild grapevines twine up through the trees. A variety of colorful butterflies flit through the air, and birdsong echoes all around. The sound of the water gurgles up from the river on the left, which can sometimes be seen from the trail.

At about 1 mile, the trail bends to the right. For a few moments, you'll lose sight of the river behind rising rocks and hills. But the rushing Santa Margarita also curves right, heading slightly more south than east for a short distance. Here, the forest grows thicker, and the path veers closer to the water. Short trails lead down to huge, flat granite boulders that rise from the water. The level expanses of sun-warmed rock provide the perfect place to sit and let the whooshing of the current lull you. Children—and perhaps some adults—will want to venture out to play on a rock that looks like a giant stone eel. The "eel" pops its head from the water, its mouth poised in a sinister smile beneath a glossy "eye."

The eel rock fuels the imagination, and back on the path, other large rocks seem to take on human or animal form. As the trail climbs slightly, moss grows heavily on the rocks at whose bases feathery ferns grow, adding to the mystique.

At 1.4 miles, the trail splits. As you continue on the left trail for several hundred yards, clusters of boulders block passage. This is a pleasant place to picnic if you're careful to avoid poison oak. Watch for snakes, too, but mostly you'll see lizards. In spring, they scurry about in pairs. The male will bob up and down, doing push-ups to attract his mate.

Back at the trail split, take the right-hand trail uphill out of the forest into a more barren landscape. You're likely to hear the roar of many honeybees along this route, which crests, then descends, bearing left back down toward the water. Ignore the offshoot trails on the right and continue to the left along the Santa Margarita River, which disappears, then reappears beyond an area of luxuriant foliage. The rushing gurgle can be heard whether its source is visible or not. Also nice is that you'll find fewer people on this leg of the trail. Many hikers turn around back at the split, so you're likely to have the route to yourself.

While walking, watch for wild gourds growing in sunny meadows along the trail. At 2.5 miles, the trail splits again. A sign identifies Willow Glen on the left and Rainbow Creek on the right. This is the turnaround point for the 5-mile out-and-back hike.

If you want a little more adventure, continue along the route on the right that leads to Willow Glen Road about 1 mile away. The left-hand trail ends a short distance ahead. Regardless of your choice, pause awhile in the cool shade near the water before you head back.

Nearby Activities

Just 20 minutes from Fallbrook, the **Antique Gas & Steam Engine Museum** is located at 2040 N. Santa Fe Ave., in Vista. Open daily; call 760-941-1791 or visit **agsem.com** for hours and more information.

GPS INFORMATION AND DIRECTIONS
N33° 24.798' W117° 14.479'

Take I-15 to the Mission Road/Fallbrook exit. Head west on Mission Road for 5.1 miles to Pico Avenue, then turn right. Pico becomes De Luz Road after just a few feet. At 1.1 miles, turn right again, onto Sandia Creek Road. A large dirt parking area is 1.2 miles ahead on the right.

51 Sycamore Canyon:
GOODAN RANCH OPEN SPACE PRESERVE LOOP

In Brief

This peaceful hike leads you through both Sycamore Canyon, a 1,700-acre wilderness area nestled between Poway and Santee and bordering the 325-acre Goodan Ranch. The diverse landscape is especially beautiful in mild spring or fall weather, when wildflowers or autumn leaves add color. Devastated by the 2003 wildfires, this area is a wonderful example of how the earth regenerates after fire.

Description

From the staging area, don't pass through the main gate at the southern end of the parking lot. Instead, head up a southeastbound narrow trail on the left to reach a ridge path overlooking Sycamore Canyon. In the spring, notice the bright yellow-orange splotches made by California poppies, and the drifts of white created by masses of popcorn flowers.

As the trail continues southeast, it goes first uphill and then down, then northeast, then down and around to the southeast again, helping you understand why hikers, bikers, and horse riders are allowed to go only one way on the opening 1.7-mile stretch. It's safer when all traffic moves in one direction on this narrow, rutted trail where areas of loose dirt mean slow going and slippery footing. Cyclists even get off and walk their bikes in some spots along the first 0.5 mile.

Despite short uphill stretches, the trail generally descends for 0.75 mile or so to Martha's Grove, then levels. Dense shade from the massive old oaks embraced the level trail before the fire, and the tree canopy is increasing again. Coast live oaks regenerate quite well. Take a few moments to rest on a bench planted here among the greenery.

Heading southwest, continue through the wooded section. Before the fires, the words "enchanted forest" were good descriptors for this 0.25-mile wooded section. That description is getting closer to fitting once again . . . see what you think. Monkeyflower and wild California fuchsia add fiery spring and summer color, inviting yellow-and-black swallowtail butterflies to flit from bloom to bloom. In the fall, the oak trees change color and drop their orange-brown leaves to carpet the ground. The autumn tones eventually change to drab gray litter in winter. Oak forest continues near the trail, providing some shady areas interspersed with sunny ones.

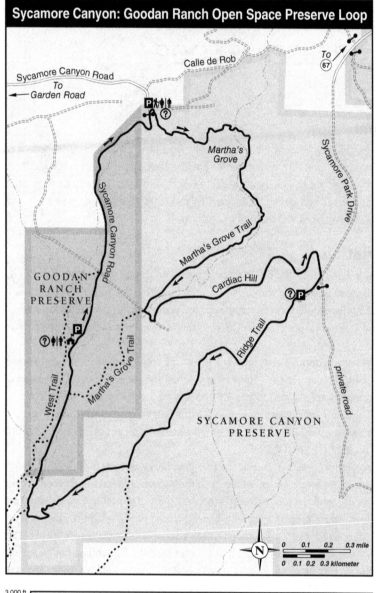

Sycamore Canyon: Goodan Ranch Open Space Preserve Loop

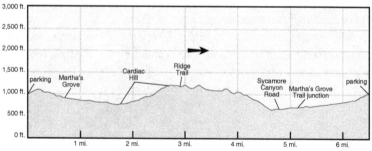

LENGTH & CONFIGURATION
6.5-mile loop

DIFFICULTY Moderate–semi-strenuous

SCENERY Oak forest, canyon views, chaparral, wildflowers in spring

EXPOSURE More sunny than shady

TRAFFIC Moderate

TRAIL SURFACE Packed dirt, leaf litter, river rock, and some rutted areas

HIKING TIME 4.5 hours

ACCESS Free; open daily, 8 a.m.–5 p.m. October–March, until 7 p.m. April–September

MAPS Available from the park ranger and online at **tinyurl.com/goodansycamore map;** USGS *San Vicente Reservoir*

WHEELCHAIR-ACCESSIBLE? No, due to steep, rocky areas

FACILITIES Portable toilet at Goodan Ranch trailhead

INFO 858-513-4737, **tinyurl.com/goodan sycamore**

SPECIAL COMMENTS A walking stick is helpful; be conscious of ticks in spring and summer. The trail is shared with horseback riders and bicyclists, so follow the posted right-of-way rules. Leashed dogs allowed.

Listen for the repetitive, bouncing-ball sound of the wrentit, the call of raucous crows, the buzzing of bees, and the gentle rushing of a breeze—nature's lullaby. The trail opens to a meadow. Continue past a narrow offshoot that you'll spot on the left at 1.3 miles from the trailhead.

At 1.5 miles, the trail intersects with another. Turn left here, heading southeast for a short uphill stretch on a truck-wide trail, and then bear left again and ascend a mile-long stretch of trail framed by scrub oak and grassy meadows. Watch for tiny tricolor flowers shaped like badminton birdies in the meadows. Colored white, lilac, and yellow, these flowers, named shooting stars, hang upside down, their tiny petals stretching back. The climb grows steeper near the top of this route nicknamed "Cardiac Hill" for its sustained climb.

At the top of the hill, turn right onto the service road and head toward the staging area. This particular parking and staging lot is open only on weekends. Pass through it and pick up the trail from the southern edge of the lot. Lined with river rocks and framed by chaparral, the path stretches upward, then down, for several short sections heading southwest. The trail bends almost due west, then descends another 0.5 mile into the canyon. Smooth-sided river rocks through here vary in size from walnut to watermelon. The smaller, loose, round rocks can roll as you step, so be careful not to slip and fall on this slow-going downhill stretch.

At the bottom, pass through an area where oak trees grow and turn right onto the wider, flat trail. Head to the right (north) about 200 yards, then turn left, move past the stream (often a trickle), and make another left, where you'll enter Goodan Ranch Preserve property. The trail moves through stands of oak, serenaded by crickets in the morning and late afternoon, for about 0.75 mile. A turnoff point used to lead to a water tower and other historic buildings prior to the 2003 fire. The newly constructed visitor center opened in

2007. Continuing on the narrow uphill trail, you may see cottontails hopping about. The route gradually bends to the east, reaching a trail junction after another 0.25 mile.

Don't turn right or left—just continue straight and keep heading north through open, rolling meadows dotted with sage, sumac, and chamise bushes. This green, fertile land was once a working ranch and is now jointly managed by the cities of Poway and Santee, the California Department of Fish and Game, and the County of San Diego Parks and Recreation Department.

The last 0.6 mile moves gradually uphill on a wide trail where beetles scuttle about, hawks fly overhead, and mourning doves coo in the late afternoon. The chorus of nature caps off a rewarding hike as you approach the staging area where you began.

Nearby Activities

After hiking on hot days, nothing beats an ice-cold Slurpee, which you can get at the **7-11** at the intersection of Garden and Poway Roads. One mile west, at 13538 Poway Rd., is **Smoothie King,** another source of refreshment.

GPS INFORMATION AND DIRECTIONS

N32° 56.445' W116° 58.830'

Take I-15 to Poway Road and travel northeast 5.2 miles to Garden Road. Turn right on Garden Road and drive east for 1 mile, then turn right onto Sycamore Canyon Road and drive southeast 2.3 miles to the staging area and park.

---

52 Wilderness Gardens Preserve:

COMBINED TRAILS LOOP

Mistletoe hangs in clumps high in the trees along this peaceful trail in the wilderness.

In Brief

The pond, quiet forest, meadows, and hillside scenery make this preserve a relaxing retreat that doesn't require a long drive. Even on weekends, you may be the only hiker on these trails.

Description

What's great about Wilderness Gardens Preserve is that there are several individual trails for hikers wanting to make a number of short visits. This description covers three trails that make a loop, giving you a 3-mile trek that enables you to see nearly everything the preserve has to offer.

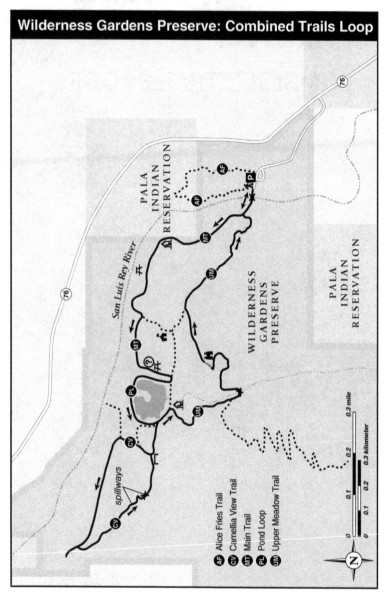

Wilderness Gardens Preserve: Combined Trails Loop

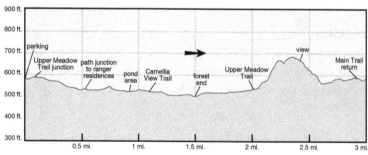

LENGTH & CONFIGURATION
3 miles; 2 connected loops with short out-and-back at end

DIFFICULTY Easy

SCENERY Trees, pond, animal tracks, flowers, views of lower meadow and San Luis Rey River when the water is running

EXPOSURE Mostly shady

TRAFFIC Light

TRAIL SURFACE Packed dirt

HIKING TIME 2.5 hours

ACCESS $2 self-pay parking fee. Open Friday–Monday, 8 a.m.–4 p.m.; closed Tuesday–Thursday and December 25; closed during the entire month of August due to heat.

MAPS Available at trailhead kiosk or online at **tinyurl.com/wilderness gardensmap**

WHEELCHAIR-ACCESSIBLE? No, due to creek crossing

FACILITIES Chemical toilets at parking lot and on the trail

INFO 760-742-1631, **tinyurl.com /wildernessgardenspreserve**

SPECIAL COMMENTS No drinking water available. Pets are prohibited in the preserve, as are horses, bicycles, and motor vehicles. Visitors under the age of 18 must be accompanied by an adult.

Peaceful and *tranquil* best describe the 700-acre Wilderness Gardens Preserve in Pala. For thousands of years, this area was used only by Native Americans. The Upper Meadow Trail seems untouched by modern civilization. And when walking along the narrow path, one can almost imagine going back in time.

To begin, head west from the parking area across the San Luis Rey River bed, which, in California's drought conditions, is usually dry. A wooden footbridge was put here five years ago when heavy rains washed away the concrete. Hop on or walk alongside it to enter Pond Trail, which is where the loop begins.

Continue northwest through the shady oaks, cottonwood, and sycamores. You'll pass the exit marker for Upper Meadow Trail on the left. Keep going. About 0.25 mile in, you'll see a portable chemical toilet. A picnic table nearby, on the north side of the trail in a small outlet, overlooks the riverbed to the north. Stop and listen to the birds in this enchanted place, which was the first preserve owned by San Diego County. Saved from condominium builders in the 1970s, the land represents the county's first attempt to preserve natural habitat and wilderness. Park rangers, along with the statewide organization Small Wilderness Area Preserves (SWAP), have worked hard to maintain the atmosphere that one park ranger calls "magical." Continue west toward the pond on this quiet, woodsy trail where poison ivy grows beneath the trees. Posted regulations encourage speaking softly and forbid pets, loud music, and cookouts to protect the preserve's natural serenity.

A short distance ahead, a southward bend passes the ranger residence. The trail then heads west again, passing a kiosk with maps and information about ticks, which are common here. There is another chemical toilet to the south of the trail. A picnic table overlooks the artificial pond. The water level is kept low. In the 1950s, this property was owned by Manchester Boddy, who intended to cultivate a botanical garden. He built the pond as part of a recirculating system to irrigate the camellias he planted. Take the short offshoot that leads around to the north edge of the pond for a closer look at the water. Here, the breeze causes the cattails to rustle softly and stirs up ripples in the sun-glinted water. The rapid music of the elusive wrentit and the low, vibrating sound of frogs fill the air. In summer, the cattails bloom in long, compact clusters that later open, releasing fluffy seeds that the wind blows around like cottony snow. Enjoy the peace before heading back to the main trail.

Head northwest where the trees grow thicker, then pass the Camellia View Trail exit marker and, a little farther, that same trail's entrance. You're likely to see signs of wildlife here along the last 0.25 mile of the main trail. Raccoon and bobcat tracks, perhaps enlarged by gentle rains or nighttime moisture to look like bear or cougar tracks, mark the same trail you tread. Coyotes, deer, possums, and foxes also live here, but their natural shyness makes spotting them a rare occurrence. You're likely to see their droppings, though, and perhaps even get a whiff of skunk scent lingering somewhere along the path.

The trail halts at the end of the forest. Turn around and head southwest back to the Camellia View Trail entrance, now on your right. Enter the trail and head south. My family calls this area the "Tarzan trail." Old-growth grapevines twist up through the trees. The deciduous vines turn to weathered, knotty ropes stretching up through oak branches in the winter, so no matter what the season, this section looks like a jungle. A rustic bench where the trail curves east provides a resting spot. Just be careful of poison oak amid the tangled foliage. In spring, the camellias bloom. In summer, grape clusters hang from the vines. The fruit is especially abundant in wetter years. Continuing along the trail, you'll cross a 2-foot concrete spillway and then a wooden footbridge over a larger spillway; they were part of the irrigation system designed by Boddy but are now dry. Exit the 0.75-mile Camellia View Trail back near the pond and take the main trail south several yards to the entrance for the Upper Meadow Trail.

The Upper Meadow Trail heads southeast, gradually ascending through the trees along a river rock–lined path. You'll see holly-leaf cherry, toyon, and large boulders covered with seafoam-green lichen. The trail narrows, crosses a split-log bridge over a ravine, and then becomes steeper as it briefly heads north. Curving east again, the trail opens up to meadows on the south side, then begins to descend. A set of steps made from railroad ties aids you in the steepest section. The ridge path overlooks the pond and the forested area below. Ferns cascade from the steep hillside wall like waterfalls, and moss covers sections of trail, tree trunks, and boulders. You'll hear wrentits and woodpeckers and see birds flitting among the trees. The route descends to level ground, meanders through a rocky section, and makes its way back to the main trail. From the upper meadow view exit sign, go right and head back across the wooden footbridge to the parking lot.

Nearby Activities

After experiencing the peace and tranquility of nature, perhaps some excitement is in order. At nearby **Pala Casino,** 5 miles west on CA 76, the shrill sounds of slot machines advertising jackpot winnings provide a sharp contrast. Even if you don't gamble, Pala has six restaurants that serve everything from Asian food to steaks. The Terrace Room features an exhibition kitchen with 12 chefs preparing more than 60 dishes. For more information, see **palacasino.com.**

GPS INFORMATION AND DIRECTIONS

N33° 20.916' W117° 1.642'

Take I-15 North past Escondido. Turn right on CA 76 East and drive about 10 miles, then turn right into the preserve.

INLAND SOUTH

Tranquil glimpses await you at Santee Lakes (see Hike 59)

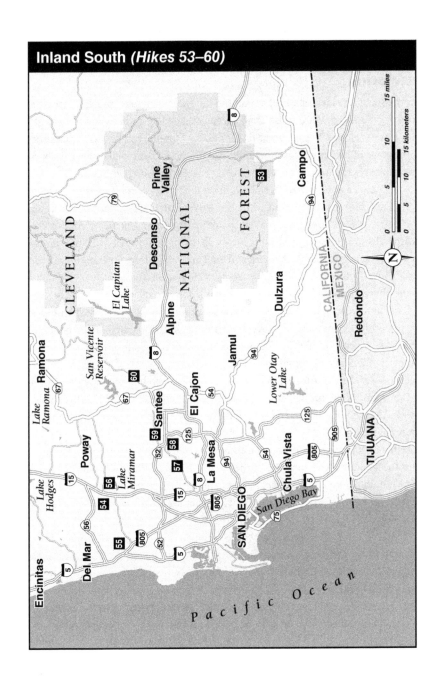

Inland South *(Hikes 53–60)*

53 Lake Morena Trail

In Brief

This pleasant hike through varying landscapes offers view after view of postcard-perfect scenery that makes the 60-mile drive from San Diego worth the time.

Description

From the small dirt lot, walk back around to the gate you passed to park. Access a southwest-bound dirt road, Ward's Flat Trail, partially shaded by cottonwood trees on the right. The route curves, traveling around a finger of Lake Morena, and begins to head northwest. Outcroppings of lichen-encrusted granite rise on the left, some like sheer walls with oak trees seemingly growing right from their craggy faces. Birdsong fills the air.

At 0.7 mile, a granite step stretches out on the right, creating a natural balcony overlooking Lake Morena that is framed by the gnarled branches of an old knotty oak. The trail climbs very gradually past Indian paintbrush growing in fiery, coral-red clumps; boulder walls soon give way to flat meadows. In spring, yellow daisylike flowers no bigger than your fingertip carpet the ground and emit a nearly suffocating tangy-sweet scent.

At about 1 mile, you'll notice the connecting trail on the right. Pass it for now; also pass the short, dead-end road on the left that leads to a dilapidated metal storage barn. The trail curves south, heading away from the lake, and moves slightly downhill onto the Morena Butte section of the hike. As you continue, look for a dilapidated concrete chimney and a few steps—all that's left of a recreation building built some 80 years ago. In the distance to the right, a red-brown rock butte, reminiscent of those in New Mexico, reaches toward the sky. Atop it, freestanding boulders perch precariously along the ridge.

Continue hiking through an area of mature pine and oak that opens into wide, grassy prairies. Although the landscape is varied, the towering pines lend an alpine feel to this segment of the hike.

Half a mile past the chimney, you'll come to side trails heading southeast and west— ignore these and instead turn the corner to reach the northwest section of the Morena Butte Trail, making your way back toward the lake. You'll pass through more towering pines and spot a connecting trail on your right that leads back to Ward's Flat Trail. Stay to the left here, heading northwest onto Hidden Cove Trail.

Continue down through a shady, oak-dominated forest. After 0.2 mile from the end of Morena Butte Trail, the lake comes into view again and another 0.4 mile takes you to the gated end of the trail, where you can enjoy views of Lake Morena.

Heading back up Hidden Cove Trail, watch for a singletrack path on your right. You might not have noticed it as you passed by the first time, but after backtracking about 0.4 mile, you'll discover the path in a washed-out area in a narrow meadow break in the trees.

This narrow path, the Hauser Overlook Trail, heads uphill but is not strenuous. Giving you a bird's-eye view of the surrounding area, the trail invites you to pause and look

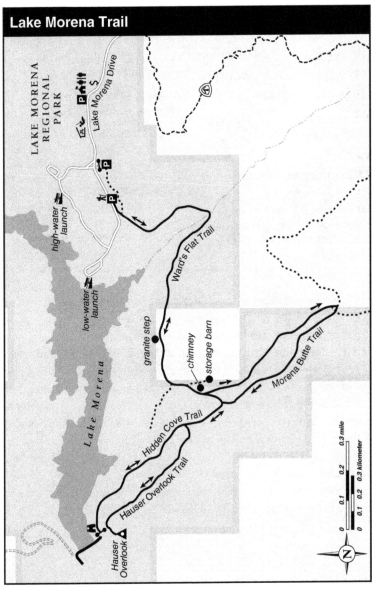

Lake Morena Trail

LAKE MORENA REGIONAL PARK

Lake Morena Drive

high-water launch

low-water launch

Lake Morena

Ward's Flat Trail

granite step

chimney

storage barn

Morena Butte Trail

Hidden Cove Trail

Hauser Overlook Trail

Hauser Overlook

0.3 mile
0.3 kilometer
0 0.1 0.2
0 0.1 0.2

N

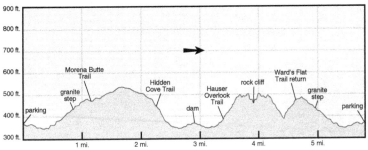

900 ft.
800 ft.
700 ft.
600 ft.
500 ft.
400 ft.
300 ft.

Morena Butte Trail

granite step

parking

Hidden Cove Trail

dam

Hauser Overlook Trail

rock cliff

Ward's Flat Trail return

granite step

parking

1 mi.   2 mi.   3 mi.   4 mi.   5 mi.

LENGTH & CONFIGURATION 5.8-mile out-and-back	**WHEELCHAIR-ACCESSIBLE?** No, due to silty and rocky areas
DIFFICULTY Easy	**FACILITIES** Restrooms in the campground area
SCENERY View of lake; pine-and-oak forest	
EXPOSURE Partially shaded	**INFO** 619-579-4101, **tinyurl.com /lakemorenapark**
TRAFFIC Light	
TRAIL SURFACE Packed soil	**SPECIAL COMMENTS** Watch for snakes, including rattlesnakes; the wide-open space of the trail makes for good observation. If you have small children, stay safe and skip the high, narrow Hauser Overlook Trail section; remain on the wide main trail, where even pushing a stroller is possible. Leashed dogs allowed.
HIKING TIME 3.5 hours	
ACCESS $3 parking fee; open daily, sunrise–sunset	
MAPS Distributed with parking fee at ranger booth; online at **tinyurl.com/lake morenabrochure** and **tinyurl.com/lake morenamap**	

out over the lake, which reflects the sky—changing from blue to gray according to the weather. Watch, and listen, for rattlesnakes, especially in spring.

The trail continues up, bending to the west, where it ends on a rock cliff looking out to the west and down over the dam. Standing on the edge of the cliff, ponder the history of Lake Morena, which includes a 1916 contract between a drought-riddled City of San Diego and Charles Hatfield, a man known as "The Rainmaker." Shortly after Hatfield set up his towers near the dam and concocted his secret rain recipe that caused smoke to billow into the air . . . the rain began. It poured for days, deluging San Diego with so much rain that bridges washed away and homes slid off their foundations. Citizens then sued the city for damage to their property! The city never paid Hatfield, reasoning that the rain was an act of God rather than a result of Hatfield's magic.

Retrace your steps downhill. When you reach the connection, turn right and follow it back to Ward's Flat Trail (to the left), which will deliver you back to your car.

Beautiful Lake Morena with its rocky shore

Nearby Activities

The **Campo Stone Store and Museum,** at 31130 CA 94, is an interesting historical diversion about 20 minutes from Lake Morena; call 619-663-1885 or visit **cssmus.org** for more information.

GPS INFORMATION AND DIRECTIONS

N32° 41.063' W116° 31.696'

From Interstate 8 East, exit and turn right onto Buckman Springs Road, continuing west for about 6 miles. Turn right on Oak Drive and travel another 1.5 miles to Lake Morena Drive. Turn right and drive straight into Lake Morena Regional Park. Pay for parking at the ranger booth, then continue just past a gate on the left (the trailhead), where you'll turn into a small dirt parking area.

54 Los Peñasquitos Canyon Preserve: EAST END

TO WATERFALL LOOP

Beauty blooms among the sharp spines of the prickly pear, or "paddle," cactus.

In Brief

Popular for mountain biking and equestrian use, and featuring a year-round creek and waterfall, 3,720-acre Los Peñasquitos Canyon Preserve is a favorite of San Diego urbanites looking for an extended backyard in which to exercise. The "no bicycle" offshoot paths looping out from the main trail offer a wilderness feel in this wide-open preserve in the heart of San Diego.

Description

From the parking lot, head west toward the kiosk and continue on the wide, westward trail edged with the narrow-leafed mulefat and its cottony pink-tinged blooms in spring. You'll likely encounter bikers and horseback riders on this first stretch of flat trail. On the wide main trail, pedestrians yield to both bikers and horse riders. Horses have the right-of-way, so it's best to stop and give them a wide berth.

At about 0.1 mile, go right onto the first of several singletrack trails marked with yellow signs barring bicyclists. On the narrow path, you'll pass through thick stands of

Los Peñasquitos Canyon Preserve: East End to Waterfall Loop

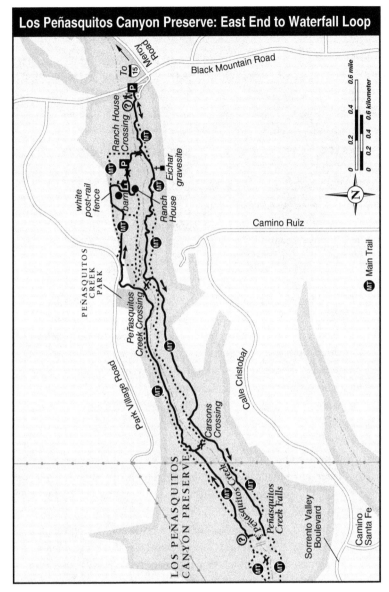

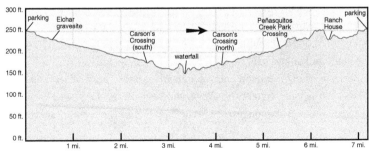

LENGTH & CONFIGURATION
7.2-mile loop

DIFFICULTY Easy

SCENERY Oak forest, wildflowers, birds, creek, and waterfall

EXPOSURE Half-shady

TRAFFIC Heavy on weekends

TRAIL SURFACE Packed river rock, silt, and leaf litter

HIKING TIME 3.5 hours

ACCESS $3 parking fee at self-pay station; open daily, 8 a.m.–sunset

MAPS Online at **tinyurl.com /lospenaquitosmap;** USGS *Del Mar*

WHEELCHAIR-ACCESSIBLE? No, due to creek crossing, muddy areas

FACILITIES Portable toilets at East End parking lot and public restrooms at ranch house

INFO 858-484-7504, **tinyurl.com /lospenasquitospreserve**

SPECIAL COMMENTS If you're looking for a private, relaxing hike, don't come here on weekends, when the preserve is overrun with bikers, runners, and horseback riders. Leashed dogs allowed. Also open to horses.

lemonadeberry and buckwheat. At nearly 0.2 mile, prickly pear cactus grows in clusters alongside the trail. As early as February, the pink blooms, curled like onions, begin to unfurl, displaying vibrant, sunny-yellow insides. Birds flit about in the brush and, if you're quiet, a coyote might appear on this portion of trail. We witnessed one carrying a bird in its mouth one winter afternoon—despite the heavy weekend-visitor population. The startled animal immediately fled, as is usual for these cunning but shy animals. A few yards past the pale-green cactus clumps, you'll come to a wide clearing. A sign indicates the Ranch House creek crossing to the right. Go left onto the cleared path instead to rejoin the main trail.

Back on the main route, turn right. After a few yards, you'll notice a small gravesite memorial for Eichar, an individual whose connection to the ranch house isn't completely understood. He died of consumption in 1882. Several yards farther up the main trail is another marked side trail. Go right and follow the single track through oak forest. Poison ivy grows thickly here, so remember the "three-leaf" rule and stay on the trail. Through the trees, you'll hear the creek rushing. Queen palms grow in a tangled mass up through Western sycamore trees, their arching, orange-spined, green fronds contrasting with the sycamore's creamy white bark. This short section of trail loops south again, joining the main trail for a few feet, then another sign directs you to the third singletrack section. Take this trail for a shadier hike through oak forest and continue for about 1 mile (passing the northerly offshoot trail leading to Peñasquitos Creek Park Crossing). It will loop back out to the main trail once again.

Continue west on the main route for nearly 1 mile, passing the offshoot for yet another creek crossing (Carson's Crossing), and head under the power lines. This sunny section of trail will feel the longest, but relief appears in the form of another side trail, marked with a yellow sign. This takes you off the main path for a short distance before looping south to rejoin the main trail. Horses aren't as common this far into the preserve, but you may see some, and their droppings are everywhere. Watch your step—leashed dogs are also allowed in the preserve—and some visitors don't clean up as they should.

Counting the singletrack side trails, you'll have hiked about 4 miles when you see a sign marked waterfall. Head uphill. Several years of drought have decreased the water flow, but especially after rains, you'll begin to hear laughter and splashing. A large lava-rock formation to the right of the trail marks the spot where stone steps lead down to the water. People often amble along the narrow shoreline for a few yards and picnic here. Watch out for rattlesnakes. We've spotted rattlers swimming across the creek just east of the waterfall—and they slither along the same shore that visitors use.

Using the protruding rocks, agile adults and older children can cross the creek here at the waterfall in a couple of jumps. Be careful! Stone steps lead up from the water on the other side. Others prefer to head back to Carson's Crossing, where there is a footbridge, as there are at all of the officially marked crossings. You may prefer to simply turn back here and retrace your steps out of the preserve.

Assuming you've crossed at the waterfall, proceed up the stone steps on the north side of the creek and turn right (east). A marked singletrack trail opens several yards east. A slower-running area of the creek comes into view amid a chorus of frogs. The trail is in the open here, but after 0.5 mile, mulefat bushes and willows growing on either side of the trail afford some afternoon shade. At 0.75 mile, heading east, one encounters an area where young oaks, planted as part of a revegetation project, grow on either side of the trail.

At the marker, consider taking the short southward trail about 100 yards to Carson's Crossing. Stop on the north side of the babbling creek in the cool shade of the oaks. Picnicking is peaceful amid the soft whistles of hummingbirds and the cackle of inquisitive crows.

After a restful stop, continue east on the singletrack trail that meanders through the oak forest briefly before the trail opens to the sky again. A mosaic of hoofprints is pressed into the path. Layer upon layer, weekend after weekend, this evidence proves that Los Peñasquitos Canyon Preserve is popular with riders. Horse traffic becomes heavier closer to the east end of the preserve. Be alert for horses and riders making their way like a clip-clopping train along the path.

About 2.5 miles from the waterfall, the narrow trail connects with the wider main one. Pass the side trail for Peñasquitos Crossing. The trail bends northeast, heading past Peñasquitos Creek Park, which is outside the preserve. When you spot a white post-rail fence to the right, head south on the side trail and continue past the ranger's storage barn. South, beyond the barn, is the ranch house that George Alonzo Johnson, the second land-grant owner, built in 1862. Francisco Ruíz got the tract as part of the first Mexican land grant in San Diego County in 1823 and built a small adobe house here. Its walls still stand within those of the larger ranch house, which was restored by the county. It's a popular wedding and special event site now.

Watch for rattlesnakes that also cross the creek.

Having seen the ranch house, head east again and cross a small footbridge. The trail will lead through a parking area and pick up where the asphalt ends. Go south toward the marked Ranch House creek crossing, and head across the wooden bridge. From here, you'll retrace your steps on the south side of the creek, heading east out of the preserve and to your car.

GPS INFORMATION AND DIRECTIONS
N32° 56.310' W117 7.788'
Take I-15 to the Mercy Road exit and head west. Black Mountain Road intersects Mercy Road and runs straight into the East End parking lot and equestrian center.

55 Los Peñasquitos Canyon Preserve: WEST END

TO WATERFALL LOOP

In Brief

The creek provides a relaxing riparian backdrop in this popular preserve. The 3,720-acre oasis of nature amid the traffic and city excitement offers a home to wildlife such as coyotes, birds, and rabbits.

Description

Access the trail from the east end of the large parking lot, and head through the dense, cool shade provided by sycamore trees. At the kiosk about 100 yards from the trailhead, go left beneath the Sorrento Valley Boulevard bridge. Begin heading northeast, up the hill. The trail soon levels off.

In the spring, you'll spot fuzzy caterpillars also hiking this route. As if racing against the clock, the tiny creatures move quickly, leaving behind smooth channels in the dirt. On a recent visit, we counted 92. Look carefully and perhaps you'll count even more.

The route descends into the canyon and joins another trail at about 0.6 mile. You'll head right (east) here and soon spot a sign marked wagon wheel crossing on the left. Continue past this for now, taking note of the water level. Decide whether you will feel comfortable crossing from the other side or will need to find another route across the creek (other options are described later).

The route surface changes to coarse gravel and small, smooth river rocks as you continue east. Watch for bright red splashes of California fuchsia and perhaps see coyote scat full of fur—evidence of a thriving canyon population sustained by rabbits and other rodents. In the spring, you may hear pups practicing their yelps from within the off-trail brush, even during the day.

At 1.5 miles, a rocky viewpoint where the trail bends south offers a look up the creek toward the waterfall. The route straightens again, heading into oak forest with lots of shade. Wood roses are among the flowers here. You might also spot the feathery herb chamomile growing in clumps midtrail. Where there are flowers there are butterflies, and you'll likely see a variety flitting about here. Bigger river rocks make it easier to carefully cross this stretch.

At about 2 miles, you'll pass the Sycamore Crossing path on the left. Check the water level here to help you decide where to cross the creek. To reach the waterfall, continue another 1 mile east on mostly level ground that is open to the sunlight. Rocky in areas, the

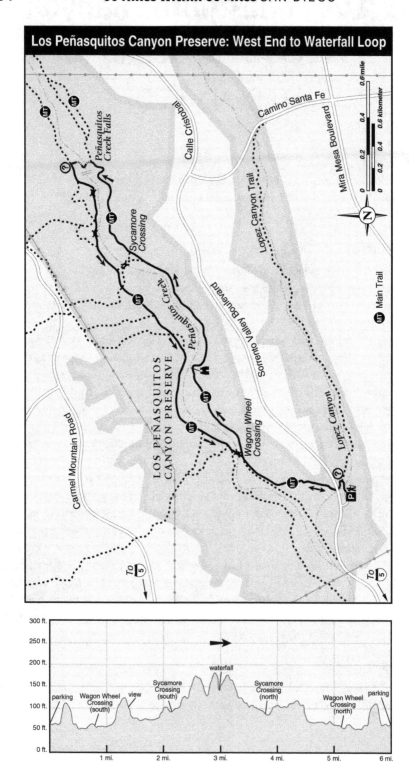

Los Peñasquitos Canyon Preserve: West End to Waterfall Loop

LENGTH & CONFIGURATION 6-mile loop	**MAPS** Online at **tinyurl.com /lospenaquitosmap;** USGS *Del Mar*
DIFFICULTY Easy	**WHEELCHAIR-ACCESSIBLE?** No, due to soft sand in some areas
SCENERY Oak forest, birds, creek, and waterfall	
EXPOSURE Mostly sunny	**FACILITIES** Portable toilet at the West End parking lot
TRAFFIC Heavy on weekends	**INFO** 858-484-7504, **tinyurl.com/lospenasquitospreserve**
TRAIL SURFACE Packed dirt, river rock, silt, and leaf litter	
HIKING TIME 3 hours	**SPECIAL COMMENTS** A favorite of many, the preserve sees many bicyclists, runners, and walkers on weekends. If you want a quiet hike, come on a weekday.
ACCESS Free; open daily, 8 a.m.–sunset	

trail has a variety of sage and mint plants growing alongside it, pleasantly scenting the air. Although California's drought has decreased the flow so that people sometimes balk at calling it a "waterfall," you'll find the splash of water on the left, where rock steps lead the way. On weekends, especially after recent rains, you'll find bustling activity up and down the creek banks all around the waterfall. Some hikers choose to cross here, scampering across the rocks like agile mountain goats. Others meander upstream and then remove their shoes to trek across the shallow waters. You could also continue on the main trail for about another 0.5 mile to Carson's Crossing, where there is a bridge, or stop here and return on the same route by which you came. Be wary of snakes that also visit this area. Rattlesnakes are not uncommon anywhere in the canyon, but they're as attracted to the water as human visitors.

Assuming you've crossed near the waterfall, watch for poison oak as you head right and up the trail along the split-rail fencing. Head slightly east above the creek, then north back to a wide main trail, where you'll go left (west) to begin the return loop. After several yards, the trail splits right and left. Head left down toward the creek, where you get good views of the babbling water as it moves west.

Cross two cement bridges and continue on a path above the creek. The narrow path gradually loses altitude, descending almost to creek level for a time. Sycamores dot the meadow as the trail heads into open space and continues west. The canyon is quieter on this side of the creek. Watch and listen for signs of life: lizards, birds, and perhaps a cottontail rabbit hopping along in early morning or late afternoon looking for a snack. Be respectful of any wildlife and plants in the canyon. You'll notice multiple bicycle tire and foot tracks layered along the trail, where visitors do the least damage to this natural habitat. But having planned paths doesn't protect all the wildlife. Occasionally, a creature as fascinating as the seldom-seen millipede lies dead in the middle of the path—the victim of a fast-moving bicyclist.

Trail time is thinking time.

If you decided on the way out that Sycamore Crossing is your best way across, watch for the sign about 1 mile from the waterfall. Cross, then take the trail on the south side of the creek back to the beginning. If you decided on Wagon Wheel Crossing, head left at the sign and wade through the water, or find a nearby shallower spot to get to the other side.

Once across, head west for a short distance, then south up over the hill. Under the bridge, the mulefat bushes release cottony fuzz in the spring, spilling white bits of fluff into the air where they drift on the breeze. At the kiosk, head right and back to the parking lot and civilization.

GPS INFORMATION AND DIRECTIONS

N32° 54.389' W117° 12.367'

Take I-5 to Carmel Valley Road and drive east for 0.2 mile. At El Camino Real, turn right and continue another mile to Carmel Mountain Road. Turn right, travel 0.6 mile to Sorrento Valley Road, and turn left. Another 0.3 mile brings you to Sorrento Valley Boulevard; turn left again, this time at the traffic signal, and go 1 mile to the staging area on the right.

56 Miramar Reservoir Loop

In Brief

This easy paved loop, framed by a verdant setting, is an excellent example of natural-resources management that makes a positive impact on the community. The tranquil eastern end fosters reflection and serenity, and then slowly delivers visitors to the more urban western edges and a slow return to everyday life.

Description

In your car, bear right past the boat-launching area into the large south parking area. Begin at the kiosk, which features Project Wildlife information, near the public restrooms. With the reservoir on your left, head east. The paved road is quickly framed by native plants. Bushy lemonadeberry and chamise contrast with the more delicate leaves of twining wild-cucumber vines and the bright-red and coral blooms of monkeyflower. You'll also spot some nonnative vegetation. Eucalyptus trees, though common to and thriving in San Diego's climate, aren't indigenous. A few pines also mix into the landscape, as does cottony-plumed pampas grass.

As you head away from the bustle of the parking lot, the paved road dips slightly and a more peaceful setting surrounds you. The lake stretches out in fingerlike folds to your left, tall reeds lining the shore in some spots and the water's edge wide open in others. Narrow side trails reach down to the lake. Couples picnic on colorful spread blankets, and fishers patiently wait for a catch. The reservoir is stocked December–March with largemouth bass, bluegill, catfish, sunfish, and trout. You may also spot people fishing from boats. Canoes, motorboats, and rowboats are available for rent on weekends.

At about 0.75 mile, you'll round the lake's southeastern finger and spot the dam to the west, across the length of shimmering water. When full, Miramar Reservoir has a surface that spans more than 162 surface acres—dramatically reflecting sunrises, sunsets, and San Diego's beautiful skies.

The loop continues along this rural, quiet end of the lake, where hikers are occasionally interrupted by skate, bike, and foot traffic. Greet others with a smile or nod, allowing the lake's peaceful ambience to infuse you with goodwill returned by fellow visitors. Perhaps they're happy that the complete loop is open these days: Crossing the dam was prohibited for about six years after 9-11.

In keeping with the anatomy of this body of water and its fingerlike points, at 2.5 miles you'll come to marked Peñasquitos Arm, with side trails leading up into the hillsides. Just 0.1 mile ahead is signed Woodson Point, with a fishing pier and picnic area. Poway Arm is the next signed area, with an entry to Natalie Trail within a few steps. The optional narrow (but easy) side trail delivers you to Natalie Park, 3 miles from the trailhead, which is a lovely spot to picnic or simply rest in tree shade.

Miramar Reservoir Loop

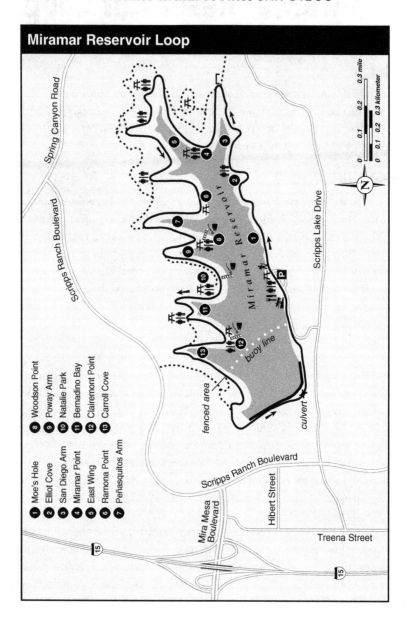

1 Moe's Hole
2 Elliot Cove
3 San Diego Arm
4 Miramar Point
5 East Wing
6 Ramona Point
7 Peñasquitos Arm
8 Woodson Point
9 Poway Arm
10 Natalie Park
11 Bernadino Bay
12 Clairemont Point
13 Carroll Cove

At 4 miles, you'll enter the chainlink fence–secured portion of the loop, which delivers you across the dam itself. Here, you'll begin to encounter slower foot traffic. Many people park in the small west lot at the lake and enjoy a stroll only along the dam. Others walk from neighboring communities, making views of the water the high point of their exercise routines without adding the entire loop. In any event, exit the fence-framed dam and head left, making the loop back toward the kiosk and your beginning point. You'll have walked 4.85 miles.

LENGTH & CONFIGURATION
4.85-mile loop

DIFFICULTY Easy

SCENERY Native plants, shimmering water

EXPOSURE Open to sunlight

TRAFFIC Heavy

TRAIL SURFACE Asphalt paving

HIKING TIME 1.5–2 hours

ACCESS Free; open daily, sunrise–sunset

MAPS Locator map online at the website at right

WHEELCHAIR-ACCESSIBLE? Yes

FACILITIES Public restrooms near parking area; portable toilets at frequent intervals around the lake

INFO 619-465-3474, **tinyurl.com/miramarreservoir**

SPECIAL COMMENTS The best days to hike are Wednesday–Friday, when the loop is closed to automobiles. Picnic benches, barbecues, boating, and fishing make this a popular place, especially on weekends. Be prepared for company at any time; exercisers love the reservoir loop for jogging, inline skating, and biking. Obey the posted stay to the right, pass on the left signs for your safety. Leashed dogs allowed, but not within 50 feet of the water.

Nearby Activities

Finish off your urban getaway with a taste of fine French cuisine. Escargot, shrimp, and vegetarian entrees await you at **La Bastide Bistro** (10006 Scripps Ranch Blvd., #104), just half a mile from Miramar Reservoir; 858-577-0033, **labastidebistro.com.**

GPS INFORMATION AND DIRECTIONS

N32° 54.858' W117° 5.889'

From I-15, exit east on Mira Mesa Boulevard and travel 0.3 mile, then turn right on Scripps Ranch Boulevard. Travel 0.3 mile, then turn left on Scripps Lake Drive. The reservoir entrance is on the left, at 0.4 mile.

57 Mission Trails Regional Park: COMBINED TRAILS LOOP

The San Diego River provides a rushing backdrop in Mission Hills Regional Park.

In Brief

This nature lovers' mecca in the middle of suburbia is a favorite of hikers, cyclists, and dog walkers.

Description

From the visitor center parking lot, head east down the sidewalk back to the road, which is Father Junipero Serra Trail, the street you entered on. Go left at the gate, which is where the road divides. A yellow-striped curb stretches the distance like a long, lazy snake, keeping cyclists and foot traffic safe on the left-hand side while allowing cars to travel the one-way road on the right.

After walking on the level road for about 0.25 mile, listen for the San Diego River meandering through the trees below on the left. At almost the 0.5-mile point, stone steps lead down to the river. Large, flat stones show signs of the ancient Kumeyaay Indians' habitation of this area, in the form of indentations in the rocks. Acorns were ground into flour with a pestle.

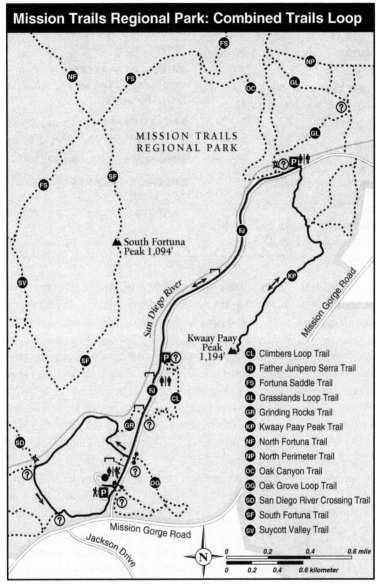

Mission Trails Regional Park: Combined Trails Loop

MISSION TRAILS
REGIONAL PARK

▲ South Fortuna
Peak 1,094'

San Diego River

Kwaay Paay
Peak ▲
1,194'

Mission Gorge Road

Jackson Drive

- **CL** Climbers Loop Trail
- **FJ** Father Junipero Serra Trail
- **FS** Fortuna Saddle Trail
- **GL** Grasslands Loop Trail
- **GR** Grinding Rocks Trail
- **KP** Kwaay Paay Peak Trail
- **NF** North Fortuna Trail
- **NP** North Perimeter Trail
- **OC** Oak Canyon Trail
- **OG** Oak Grove Loop Trail
- **SD** San Diego River Crossing Trail
- **SF** South Fortuna Trail
- **SV** Suycott Valley Trail

N

0   0.2   0.4   0.6 mile
0   0.2   0.4   0.6 kilometer

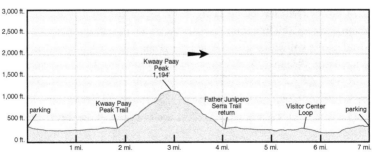

LENGTH & CONFIGURATION
7-mile balloon with long string

DIFFICULTY Easy, with a more strenuous 1.3-mile climb to peak

SCENERY Old Mission Dam, waterfowl, San Diego River, views from peak

EXPOSURE Mostly sunny

TRAFFIC Heavy

TRAIL SURFACE Asphalt, sandy soil, packed soil, rocky areas on peak

HIKING TIME 3 hours

ACCESS Free; open daily, sunrise–sunset, except for major holidays

MAPS Available at the visitor center or online at **tinyurl.com/mtrptrailmap** and **tinyurl.com/mtrpmap2**

WHEELCHAIR-ACCESSIBLE? No, due to rocky areas. See website below for accessible areas.

FACILITIES Public restrooms at visitor center, portable toilets near dam

INFO 619-668-3281, **mtrp.org**

SPECIAL COMMENTS To keep this hike easy, skip the 1.3-mile trek to the Kwaay Paay summit.

Back on the Father Junipero Serra Trail, a portable toilet sits to the right of the road, just a bit farther down. Look up at the vertical rock areas on the left. These rocks are among San Diego rock climbers' favorite climbing spots, and you can often see climbers high above.

At 0.7 mile, a huge rock formation stretches out from the road, extending to the San Diego River. Step onto the warm, stone surface and have a rest or read the old and new initials carved into a mature oak tree that stretches up to the rock.

As you continue northwest on the trail, a wooden bench waits at just more than a mile. Beyond this, you'll notice a short metal bridge that crosses the river below, and trails leading into the northwest sections of Mission Trails Regional Park. When you reach the stop sign on Father Junipero Serra Trail, look to the right. A narrow trail heads up the mountain to the Kwaay Paay Summit. Head southeast on this uphill stretch for about 0.25 mile, when you'll come to a trail split. Go to the right and continue uphill, heading southwest now. The eroded trail makes its way up through the chaparral. The bushes grow taller as the route climbs: white and black sage, lemonadeberry, coast mountain mahogany, warty-stem lilac, and mission manzanita—blooming with light-pink flowers in the typical urn shape characteristic of this species—all grow here.

At about 0.8 mile on the Kwaay Paay Summit Trail, the route opens into a mesa clearing. You'll spot the trail starting up again on the other side of the mesa, rising at a suddenly severe grade. Children may use all fours on this steepest section, and even experienced hikers will move slowly when the ground is dry. On one visit, a group was heading down the hill with a dog that moved too fast, tumbling head over tail. (He jumped up and took off again uninjured.) The loose, gritty soil makes the trail surface slippery. The steep section is about 0.2 mile long, and then the route levels again, leading to the 1,194-foot summit, where a group of flat rocks offers a view all the way to the ocean.

Retrace your steps down the mountain to the stop sign on Father Junipero Serra Trail. The historic Old Mission Dam is down the road on the opposite side and is worth a quick look if you have time.

Back on Father Junipero Serra Trail, head southwest toward the visitor center. Before you reach the modern building, watch for a side trail leading off into the chaparral. This is your entry to the Visitor Center Loop. The trail bears northwest with some views of the San Diego River, eventually curving to the southwest, where the water runs over multilevel stones. The sight makes you realize that those popular backyard ponds and falls are modeled after Mother Nature's works. Head uphill, where the trail curves southeast, then northeast, leading back to the parking lot.

Nearby Activities

While you're here, the visitor center itself is a worthwhile diversion. On the walkway leading to the entrance, audio panels and information boards offer insight into the sights and sounds of the area's wildlife. Inside the center, video presentations and state-of-the-art exhibits tell the history of the region. A gift shop offers Kumeyaay Indian baskets, pottery, and jewelry, along with books, posters, and other items.

GPS INFORMATION AND DIRECTIONS

N32° 49.176' W117° 3.401'

Take I-15 to CA 52 East and drive to the Mast Boulevard exit. Turn left on Mast and drive 0.2 mile to West Hills Parkway. Turn right on West Hills Parkway, drive 0.5 mile to Mission Gorge Road, and then turn right. Drive 2.4 miles to Father Junipero Serra Trail and turn right, then almost immediately turn left into the visitor-center parking area.

58 Mission Trails Regional Park:
COWLES MOUNTAIN LOOP

Hazy view of Lake Murray from Cowles Mountain

In Brief

A pleasant trek through chaparral and along a stream, punctuated by a final climb to a peak. Cowles Mountain is a favorite of locals seeking an aerobic workout with a view.

Description

From the trailhead kiosk, head up the wide trail running southwest past houses on the right, and crossing a narrow section of Big Rock Creek. The trail bears left through chaparral. A rainbow of wildflowers blooms in spring. Even the wild grasses seem to bloom, their dusky mauve broom-heads swaying in the wind.

The route switchbacks to climb, and the sounds from nearby homes and the park begin to fade. But evidence of people still lingers. An aluminum can cast haphazardly into the bush makes a shady home for beetles; the shiny shell of a deflated Mylar balloon hangs from a tree that snagged it.

At about 0.8 mile, the chaparral becomes denser, and partially buried boulders jaggedly line the trail. You may see quail running in the brush or hear the fluttering hum of their wings as they fly off, spooked by your presence. A short distance farther, Mother Nature offers you a seat on a stone.

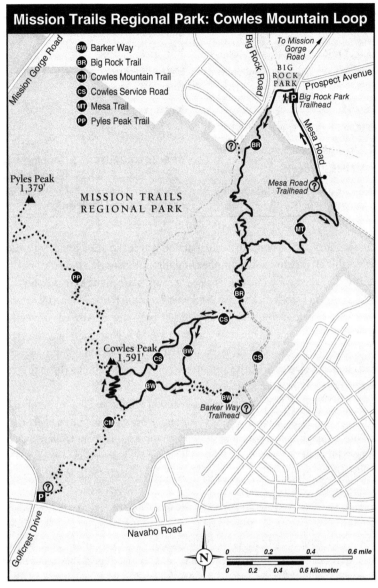

Mission Trails Regional Park: Cowles Mountain Loop

- **BW** Barker Way
- **BR** Big Rock Trail
- **CM** Cowles Mountain Trail
- **CS** Cowles Service Road
- **MT** Mesa Trail
- **PP** Pyles Peak Trail

To Mission Gorge Road

Big Rock Road

BIG ROCK PARK

Prospect Avenue

Big Rock Park Trailhead

Mesa Road

Mesa Road Trailhead

Pyles Peak 1,379'

MISSION TRAILS REGIONAL PARK

Cowles Peak 1,591'

Barker Way Trailhead

Navaho Road

Golfcrest Drive

Mission Gorge Road

0   0.2   0.4   0.6 mile
0   0.2   0.4   0.6 kilometer

N

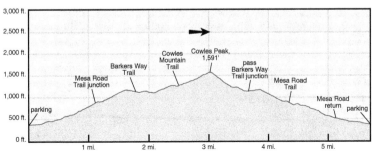

LENGTH & CONFIGURATION 5.7-mile loop	**MAPS** Available at the visitor center or online at **tinyurl.com/mtrptrailmap** and **tinyurl.com/mtrpmap2**
DIFFICULTY Strenuous	
SCENERY Birds, chaparral, views of the city	**WHEELCHAIR-ACCESSIBLE?** No, due to steep, rocky areas
EXPOSURE Mostly sunny	**FACILITIES** None
TRAFFIC Moderate–heavy	**INFO** 619-668-3281, **mtrp.org**
TRAIL SURFACE Soft soil, rocky areas	
HIKING TIME 3.5 hours	**SPECIAL COMMENTS** Climbing to the summit requires a high fitness level and lots of water. Overall, the route gains nearly 1,200 feet in elevation.
ACCESS Free; open daily, sunrise–sunset, except for major holidays	

At about 1 mile, you'll come to a trail junction where the Mesa Road Trail leads off to the left. Pass this by for now, and continue climbing. After another 0.5 mile, you'll reach a T where the trail meets a wide, gravel service road. Turn right here. On hot days, the breeze will cool you as you make the 0.2-mile walk up the road. When you see a sign for the Barker Way Cowles Mountain Trail, veer left onto this narrow, downward-sloping path. After gently descending the trail bordered by thick chaparral, take the right-hand trail that begins climbing toward the west. Lake Murray comes into view in the southwest while a sea of roofs stretches out to the southeast. The path climbs through a few very steep sections alternating with long, level sections.

Another 0.3 mile brings you to an intersection where you'll turn right and climb steep switchbacks to the peak of Cowles Mountain. Here's where you're likely to encounter lots of other hikers accessing a shorter route to the summit from Golfcrest Drive.

At the 1,591-foot summit, there are lovely views in all directions—clear to the Santa Rosa Mountains in the northeast and Catalina and Coronado Islands in the west. Information panels provide details.

When you're ready, either go back the way you came or take the service road on the northeast side of the summit. Watch for cyclists pushing their mountain bikes up the steep ascent—then be wary of them coasting back down. It's about 0.8 mile back to the T where you originally turned onto the service road. Make a left here, back into the chaparral. Retrace your steps 0.5 mile to the marked mesa road route that you passed on the way up. Hang a right here, traveling through the thickets of tall chaparral that shade the path. Cross the stream and turn left onto Mesa Road. Follow the road, with the stream to your right, for about 0.7 mile back to the trailhead kiosk where you parked your car.

GPS INFORMATION AND DIRECTIONS
N32° 49.793' W117° 1.075'

Take CA 52 east to the Mission Gorge exit and turn right, heading west about 0.3 mile to Mesa Road. Turn left (south) and travel 0.4 mile to a point just past Big Rock Park. Find a space on the right, along the street.

59 Santee Lakes Loop

A fowl trio at Santee Lakes

In Brief

Maybe it's the way people while away the time at the end of a fishing pole here, or the contented waterfowl that rest in lazy clusters near the shore—but time seems to move more slowly in this city-close recreational oasis. The easy 2-mile stroll described here lets you absorb the park's afternoon siesta atmosphere, while giving your legs a decent stretch.

Description

After parking in the day-use area, head west along the patchy grass. Number 2 of the 7 lakes here will be on your right. To your left, across the day parking area, you'll see Lake 1, a large shelter, and the park's "spraygrounds," where kids can play. The park gets busy on weekends and in the summer. But in other seasons, particularly on the weekdays, you're likely to see only people walking and fishing, and perhaps a pensive thinker or two, pondering the rippling water or the sky.

On our last visit, in early May, we saw cliff swallows as we started the hike. They dipped low to the water surface, soared into the air, and then circled back. Their soft, buzzy calls filled the air with a pleasant hum. Meanwhile, a chunky white duck nestled in

Santee Lakes Loop

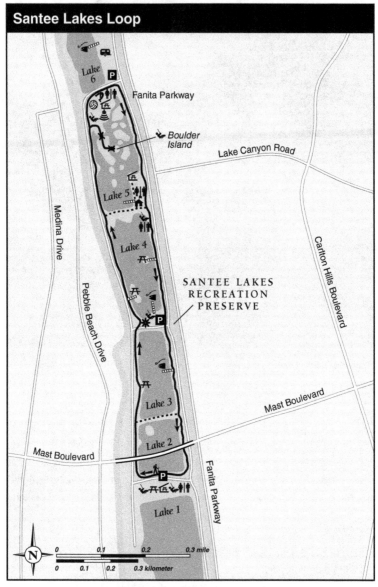

Lake 6

Fanita Parkway

Boulder Island

Lake Canyon Road

Lake 5

Lake 4

SANTEE LAKES
RECREATION
PRESERVE

Medina Drive

Pebble Beach Drive

Carlton Hills Boulevard

Lake 3

Mast Boulevard

Lake 2

Mast Boulevard

Fanita Parkway

Lake 1

| 0 | 0.1 | 0.2 | 0.3 mile |
| 0 | 0.1 | 0.2 | 0.3 kilometer |

N

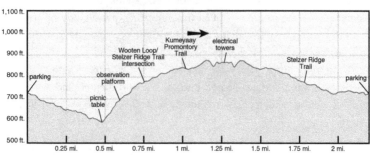

LENGTH & CONFIGURATION 2-mile loop	change, so visit **santeelakes.com/things-to-do** for the latest information.
DIFFICULTY Easy	**MAPS** Online at **santeelakes.com/maps/dayusemap.html**
SCENERY Birds, flowers, lake	
EXPOSURE Sunny	**WHEELCHAIR-ACCESSIBLE?** Yes
TRAFFIC Moderate–heavy	**FACILITIES** Plentiful restrooms
TRAIL SURFACE Mostly paved, some grassy areas, and earthen paths	**INFO** 619-596-3141, **santeelakes.com**
HIKING TIME 45 minutes	**SPECIAL COMMENTS** Mostly paved, this is a good place to take the family. Dogs are prohibited in the day-use area described here.
ACCESS $3 weekdays, $5 weekends. Hours vary seasonally and are subject to	

the grass and cocked his head, his beady eyes hopeful. People do feed the ducks, so some birds expect a handout. On that morning, our snowy-feathered friend didn't budge. We'd disturbed his nap. After we passed him, I looked back to catch a glimpse of his profile. The eye that faced us was closed. Birds can sleep with one eye open, with half the brain staying awake to watch for predators. Scientists call this ability unihemispheric slow-wave sleep. In this park, where the birds are used to people, I couldn't help but speculate that this lazy fellow had closed his other eye, too.

At the end of the water, make a right turn and walk north, keeping the lake on your right. Move toward the wide swath of shade from the Mast Road overpass. It can be surprisingly peaceful beneath the concrete structure with its curving pillars. Escape the sun's heat, or rain, like we did on our early-May visit.

In just a few more northerly steps, you'll leave Lake 2 behind, and join Lake 3, which stretches out on your right. More birds huddle in packs, or meander toward you from the water. This is one of the few places around San Diego County where you may see the ashen-colored American coot with its darker head and white bill moving about on land. Get a look at their interesting feet—floppy, like clumsy swim flippers out of water. But imagine how those yellow-green feet look from beneath the surface. The long, vaguely striped toes have fleshy fringe. To unsuspecting fish on the coot's menu, those feet look like aquatic vegetation.

A short path leads out to picnic spots that overlook the water. From the path, the picnic areas are obscured by reeds, as are parts of the shore along this section. The vegetation makes shyer birds feel more secure, so you may find yourself in a game of peek-a-boo with a cautious Blue Heron. Maybe you'll spot a mother wood duck paddling along with her yellow-cheeked babies trailing.

At the north end of Lake 3, be sure to take the short walkway to the right that leads to the park's sensory garden. In the small space next to a playground, sniff the tangy herbs and fragrant spices growing in raised beds along the path. Be sure to stop and smell the roses that spill out in masses of peach, white, and red blooms. If you have children with you, they'll want to use the swings and other play structures. Much of the equipment is large and sturdy enough for adults, so be a big kid if you're in the mood. Adjacent to the playground is a fishing pier that hangs out over Lake 4.

Back on the west side, with Lake 4 now on your right, continue along where people park and fish. Take in the restful feeling these sportsmen and women exude. Some keep watch over several poles at once, positioned in stands so they bend toward the lake. You may spot clutches of caught fish, tethered in the water close to the shore—nature's refrigeration while the fishing continues.

Leave Lake 4 behind, and travel along the west edge of Lake 5, which ends in a northerly finger lined with reeds. On our last visit, swallows swarmed here—dipping close to the reedy edge, soaring high, and then twirling back again, in an aeronautics show complete with song. From here, turn right and cut across the grassy picnic area. Linger on benches beneath the shady oaks, or walk the bridge to Boulder Island, a kids' rock-climbing playground.

Once finished delighting in the serenity of the trek's peaceful halfway point, make your way back north through the picnic area, then head right, past the restrooms. Bear right again to start the loop south, on the other side of the lakes you've seen. North of here are Lakes 6 and 7, RV and tent campgrounds, and lakefront and floating cabins—worth reserving for a few days' stay. The cabins and campsites fill quickly, so plan ahead.

As you approach the south end of Lake 5, you'll see the park offices, boat and bike rental facilities, and a store. There are restrooms in the complex, and others straight ahead, just as you reach Lakes 4 and 3. Pause at any of several benches, or stretch out on the grass someplace along the shore. The pavement path continues south. You'll walk under the overpass again and make your way back to your car—likely talking with your group about returning to ride bikes, visit the playgrounds, or even camp at this award-winning recreational park.

GPS INFORMATION AND DIRECTIONS
N32° 50.960' W117° 0.350'

Take CA 52 East and exit at Mast Boulevard. Turn left, drive east 1.4 miles to Fanita Parkway, and then turn right. The main entrance to Santee Lakes and the day-use area is 0.2 mile ahead on the right.

60 Stelzer Park Loop

Gracefully arching oak branches form a shady canopy at the trail's outset.

In Brief

This serene family park in the trees provides a starting point toward the dry, upper trails where lizards reign and hawks keep eyes peeled for a meal.

Description

The ranger station adjacent to the parking lot hosts a small museum room with animal and plant specimens as well as historical information. It's worth a quick peek if you have time, and may help you identify vegetation or animals from your hike. Educators may want to contact the park ahead for a teaching kit and take a field trip with students.

To the right of the ranger station, enter the park through a small gate and turn immediately right onto a shady path. The route leads down through oak forest alongside Wildcat Canyon Creek—which may surprise you by having water present clear into summer. The trail crosses a couple of footbridges as it meanders west. Wild grapevines twist up through the trees that allow the sunlight through the dense canopy only in patches. At 0.3 mile, the trail grows rocky, and large, flat boulders pave the path. Watch your step here. Some stick up at awkward angles.

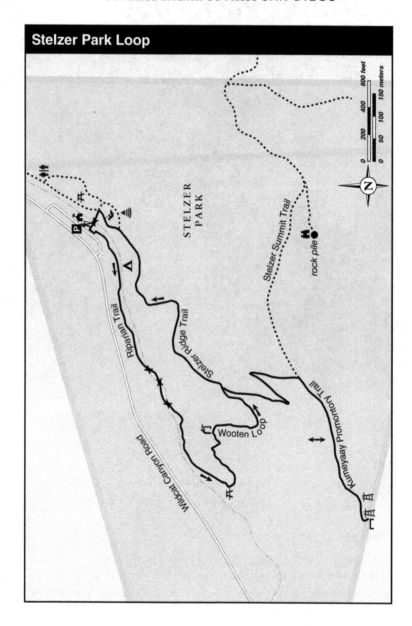

Stelzer Park Loop

At 0.5 mile, the trail halts its westward route, ending at a picnic table in the shade. The trail turns left and begins heading uphill. After you've climbed 0.1 mile, a wooden observation deck with benches allows another opportunity for rest, this time in full sun. From this vantage point, the cars zipping by on Wildcat Canyon Road look tiny. Watch overhead for hawks taking advantage of the canyon's wind currents to soar above the landscape with little effort.

Past the observation deck, the trail levels a short distance, then becomes semisteep again. Footing is fairly easy, though, since the ground is packed. You'll come to a trail

LENGTH & CONFIGURATION 2.2-mile loop (with some backtrack)	**MAPS** Available at ranger station or online at **tinyurl.com/stelzerparkmap**
DIFFICULTY Moderately easy	**WHEELCHAIR-ACCESSIBLE?** No, due to steep, rocky areas and uneven terrain. See website for accessible areas of Stelzer Park.
SCENERY Chaparral, wildflowers, birds	
EXPOSURE Mostly sunny	**FACILITIES** Restrooms near ranger station
TRAFFIC Light	
TRAIL SURFACE Packed dirt	**INFO** 619-561-0580, **tinyurl.com /stelzerpark**
HIKING TIME 2.5 hours	
ACCESS $2 day-use fee (self-pay); open daily, sunrise–sunset	**SPECIAL COMMENTS** Best visited in fall and spring, when lakeside temperatures are moderate

intersection at 0.9 mile from the entrance—go right here to head west and uphill. You'll catch the easterly Stelzer Ridge route on your downhill return. The trail bends west and east again, then comes to a T. Choose the right-hand route, which leads gradually uphill through pleasant terrain filled with honeybees, spring flowers, and interesting rock formations, to two electrical towers where a resting bench awaits.

The left-hand choice isn't recommended for casual hikers. It heads 0.5 mile up to a rock pile with a decent vantage point, but the route is so steep and slippery that all but the most agile, experienced, and daring will be on hands and knees to get there. Coming down is also very difficult and requires crab-walking, which still results in dangerous sliding—unless you're one of the many lizards accustomed to the dry, slippery terrain here.

After sitting awhile under the power towers, retrace your steps to the intersection you passed earlier. This northeastward Stelzer Ridge Trail leads back down to the shady oasis of the park, where you'll likely want to slow your pace. Finally, make your way past the playground and a quiet birdbath area to the gate.

GPS INFORMATION AND DIRECTIONS

N32° 52.993' W116° 53.822'

Take I-8 East to CA 67 North. Turn right on Willow Road and travel about 1 mile east to Wildcat Canyon Road. Turn left (north), drive about 1 mile into the entrance, and park in the lot.

Appendix A:
Outdoor Shops

ADVENTURE 16

adventure16.com
4620 Alvarado Canyon Rd.
San Diego, CA 92120
619-283-2374

143 S. Cedros Ave.
Solana Beach, CA 92075
858-755-7662

BARGAIN CENTER SURPLUS

bargaincentersd.com
3015 North Park Way
San Diego, CA 92104
619-295-1181

BIG 5 SPORTING GOODS

big5sportinggoods.com
364 E. H St.
Chula Vista, CA 91910
619-427-6900

1253 E. Valley Pkwy.
Escondido, CA 92027
760-480-6860

2301 Vista Way
Oceanside, CA 92054
760-757-4154

16773-B Bernardo Center Dr.
Rancho Bernardo, CA 92128
858-673-9219

4348 Convoy St.
San Diego, CA 92111
858-560-0311

6061-A El Cajon Blvd.
San Diego, CA 92115
619-583-7930

666 Fletcher Pkwy.
San Diego, CA 92120
619-444-8139

8145 Mira Mesa Blvd.
San Diego, CA 92126
858-693-4941

3729 Rosecrans St.
San Diego, CA 92110
619-298-3350

949 Lomas Santa Fe Dr.
Solana Beach CA 92075
858-755-5953

9805 Campo Rd., Ste. 195
Spring Valley, CA 91977
619-644-5733

33321 Highway 79 S.
Temecula, CA 91977
951-302-9458

760 Sycamore Ave.
Vista, CA 92083
760-727-2859

DICK'S SPORTING GOODS

dickssportinggoods.com
565 Fletcher Pkwy.
El Cajon, CA 92020
619-447-0191

1200 Auto Pkwy.
Escondido, CA 92029
760-233-2700

3514 College Blvd.
Oceanside, CA 92056
760-945-5444

3265 Sports Arena Blvd.
San Diego, CA 92110
619-523-0975

GI JOE'S MILITARY GEAR

gijoesmilitarygear.com
799 El Cajon Blvd.
El Cajon, CA 92020
619-401-7589

GI JOE'S MILITARY GEAR *(continued)*
404 Pier View Way
Oceanside, CA 92054
760-757-2484

NOMAD VENTURES
nomadventures.com
405 W. Grand Ave.
Escondido, CA 92025
760-747-8223

REI
rei.com
2015 Birch Rd., Ste. 150
Chula Vista, CA 91915
619-591-4924

1590 Leucadia Blvd.
Encinitas, CA 92024
760-944-9020

5556 Copley Dr.
San Diego, CA 92111
858-279-4400

ROSEBUD ARMY & NAVY SURPLUS
642 Hollister St.
San Diego, CA 92154
619-424-9034

STARS & STRIPES SURPLUS STORE
starsnstripessurplusstore.com
1198 E. Main St., Ste. A
El Cajon, CA 92021
619-442-3800

ONLINE SHOPS

ALTREC
altrec.com

BACKCOUNTRY
backcountry.com

CC OUTDOOR STORE
ccoutdoorstore.com

EASTERN MOUNTAIN SPORTS
ems.com

GOSSAMER GEAR
gossamergear.com

HIKINGANDBACKPACKING.COM
hikingandbackpacking.com

JAX MERCANTILE
jaxoutdoor.com

OUTDOOR GEAR EXCHANGE
gearx.com

OUTDOOR OUTLET
outdooroutlet.com

NAU
nau.com

REI
rei.com

SIERRA TRADING POST
sierratradingpost.com

Appendix B:
Sources for Trail Maps

ADVENTURE 16

    adventure16.com
    4620 Alvarado Canyon Rd.
    San Diego, CA 92120
    619-283-2374

    143 S. Cedros Ave.
    Solana Beach, CA 92075
    858-755-7662

CC OUTDOOR STORE

    ccoutdoorstore.com

MAP CENTRE

    3191 Sports Arena Blvd.
    San Diego, CA 92110
    619-291-3830

REI

    rei.com
    2015 Birch Rd., Ste. 150
    Chula Vista, CA 91915
    619-591-4924

    1590 Leucadia Blvd.
    Encinitas, CA 92024
    760-944-9020

    5556 Copley Dr.
    San Diego, CA 92111
    858-279-4400

Appendix C: Hiking Clubs and Public-Land Organizations

BACK COUNTRY LAND TRUST OF SAN DIEGO COUNTY
bclt.org, facebook.com/backcountrylandtrust
PO Box 1148
Alpine, CA 91903
619-504-8181

ENCINITAS TRAILS COALITION
trails4encinitas.org
330 Rosemary Lane
Olivenhain, CA 92024

FALLBROOK LAND CONSERVANCY
fallbrooklandconservancy.org, tinyurl.com/fblc-facebook
1815 S. Stagecoach Lane
Fallbrook, CA 92028
760-728-0889

HIKING MEETUPS IN SAN DIEGO
hiking.meetup.com/cities/us/ca/san_diego

SAN DIEGO HIKING CLUB
sandiegohikingclub.org

SAN DIEGO SIERRA CLUB
sandiegosierraclub.org, facebook.com/sierraclubsandiego,
twitter.com/sdsierraclub
8304 Clairemont Mesa Blvd., Ste. 101
San Diego, CA 92111
858-569-6005

Index

DEAR CUSTOMERS AND FRIENDS,

SUPPORTING YOUR INTEREST IN OUTDOOR ADVENTURE, travel, and an active lifestyle is central to our operations, from the authors we choose to the locations we detail to the way we design our books. Menasha Ridge Press was incorporated in 1982 by a group of veteran outdoorsmen and professional outfitters. For many years now, we've specialized in creating books that benefit the outdoors enthusiast.

Almost immediately, Menasha Ridge Press earned a reputation for revolutionizing outdoors- and travel-guidebook publishing. For such activities as canoeing, kayaking, hiking, backpacking, and mountain biking, we established new standards of quality that transformed the whole genre, resulting in outdoor-recreation guides of great sophistication and solid content. Menasha Ridge continues to be outdoor publishing's greatest innovator.

The folks at Menasha Ridge Press are as at home on a whitewater river or mountain trail as they are editing a manuscript. The books we build for you are the best they can be, because we're responding to your needs. Plus, we use and depend on them ourselves.

We look forward to seeing you on the river or the trail. If you'd like to contact us directly, join in at trekalong.com or visit us at menasharidge.com. We thank you for your interest in our books and the natural world around us all.

SAFE TRAVELS,

Bob Sehlinger

BOB SEHLINGER
PUBLISHER

Printed in the USA
CPSIA information can be obtained
at www.ICGtesting.com
JSHW011217080224
R13319200001B/R133192PG49575JSX00001B/1